Nottingh... Within Living Memory

Compiled by the Nottinghamshire Federation of Women's Institutes from notes sent by Institutes in the County

Published jointly by
Countryside Books, Newbury
and the Notts. FWI, Newark

First Published 1995
© Nottinghamshire Federation of Women's Institutes 1995

COUNTRYSIDE BOOKS
3 Catherine Road
Newbury, Berkshire

ISBN 1 85306 356 8

The cover photograph shows a charabanc outing
near Edwinstowe

Designed by Mon Mohan
Produced through MRM Associates Ltd, Reading
Typeset by Acorn Bookwork, Salisbury
Printed by Woolnough Bookbinding Ltd., Irthlingborough

Contents

Acknowledgements

Many thanks to the members and friends of the Nottingham-shire Federation of Women's Institutes who have submitted items for this publication. Sadly it was impossible to include every item, for reasons both of length and of duplication, but each and every one was of use in forming the finished book.

A special thank you to Elaine Baker (Abbey Gates WI) for the delightful drawings and to Penny Veys (Upton WI) for her map of Nottinghamshire. My personal thanks also to Iris Mar-shall (Abbey Gates WI) and Jean Varnam (Gunthorpe WI) who gave help with the typing.

Jenny Holmes
Co-ordinator

N

WORKSOP

FOREST

EAST
RETFORD

R. TRENT

SHERWOOD

MANSFIELD

SOUTHWELL

NEWARK ON TRENT

R. TRENT

FOSSE WAY

NOTTINGHAM

Nottinghamshire

Foreword

Without memories, where would we be? The past, before our own memories start, is normally hidden from us, unless we can somehow find a way back.

One of the best ways of learning about the past is to listen to someone older reminiscing. It brings it all to life and puts more meaning into events that we might have read about. It is often the only way of really getting the feel of what it was like to be young all those years ago, how life functioned and what was expected of people.

Reading the *Within Living Memory* series is like listening to someone remember. If their memories were not recorded in print they would soon be lost. I am delighted that Nottinghamshire has been able to produce this book. I am sure it will bring forth more memories from the people reading it. To the ones too young to remember, it will give a very good picture of what life was really like in the not too distant past.

Ann-Marie Morley
County Chairman

TOWN & COUNTRY LIFE

SOME TOWNS AND VILLAGES REMEMBERED

Life in our towns and villages has changed so much within living memory. It is not really so long since the sound of the blacksmith's hammer was a part of everyday life, lamps were lit at dusk by the local lamplighter, and the only traffic was horse-drawn. Here are just a few memories of life as it was, including a reminder of that terrible winter of 1947 when flood followed snow.

KIRKBY IN ASHFIELD

'I was a little girl, the apple of my father's eye. I was happy, I was loved, I wanted for nothing. My father was a miner.

I would sometimes wake in the deep dark that comes before the dawn, to the sound of the metal on miners' boots as they went down the hill at Kirkby in Ashfield to catch the train to the mine. My stone hot-water bottle would be cold but I would feel warm and safe, and sleep would quickly come again.

I was growing up and I could read. My father would often send me down to the local chip shop at night, not for food but to see which pits would be working the next day.

During school holidays I would often go down the road to the station to meet my Dad home. The gates of the station would close across the road, stopping all traffic. I would climb the steps on to the bridge over the line and await the train. In the distance I would hear the hoot as it warned of its approach then it would chug in, covering everything with a thick white smelly steam. I liked the smell and my eyelashes would be wet. It was exciting when the men poured from the train, feet dragging, their faces black but around their eyes would be a ring of white.

On reaching home my Dad would take off his boots and jacket and, with hands that trembled with fatigue, eat his dinner. The Yorkshire pudding with jam and cold milk would be first, then a mountain of potatoes with a little meat. Later he curled up on the settee and slept, still in his dirt. He washed later and I thought it a treat to soap the flannel to wash his back and pick out the small "slack" pieces embedded in his skin. I still remember the bruised and cut hands. It was cruel work in those days.

We had a stair-hole, a cavity under the stairs, and my Dad's coat would hang inside. We children often played in there with a bottle of water and an empty snap tin. When the door was shut it was very dark and we pretended to be down the pit – the smell was there.

Although we were poor by today's standards, we were happy. In summer we had fruit and vegetables from Dad's allotment garden but times were often very hard for our parents. On Saturday nights we would often have to go to bed early to allow Mother to wash our underclothes and get them dry and ironed ready for Sunday school next day. I would awake on summer mornings to a special peace on Sunday. There were no tramping feet and no sounds of traffic, the silence to be broken only by the sweet trilling of the larks. Later the sound of distant bells called the faithful to prayer. We wore all our clean best clothes and went to Sunday school. Sunday dinner was special, then we would only play in the garden and made little noise as it was God's day.

Sunday was also the day for visiting the churchyard with flowers. It was a ritual, I would tiptoe so as not to awaken anyone and was very careful not to step on any grave. After chapel it would be a walk round the "Forest". The whole family would go and, of course, we met our friends and neighbours as well. Later on Sundays we would have callers. Friends and relations would sit in the front room behind our lace curtains and drink tea, never stopping for very long.

Chapel played a big part. There was the Whitsun Walk. We children would walk around the streets following the minister and the banner of our church. It was a great honour when I was older to be allowed to hold one of the cords of the banner. All the churches walked and the colliery bands and the Salvation Army played their hearts out. The roads would be lined with onlookers and it was a great day in a child's life. Later we had a simple tea in the schoolrooms to be followed by a visit to the recreation ground, a green field where everyone congregated. The adults sat on the grass whilst the youngsters went wild and a good time was had by all.

Chapel played a part for Mum too. Dad would be asleep on the sofa, face covered with a newspaper, and Mother would make sure all our faces were clean. Coats on and down to the chapel we would go.

In a small room at the side of the main hall we would gather, women of all ages, shapes and sizes, and we three children. We didn't mind. It was warm and friendly, and the old pedal organ would wheeze out *Shall we gather at the river* (I learnt most of the chapel hymns listening and joining in). At the end we all said a prayer, and I am afraid I often peeped through my fingers in curiosity. There was then a rattle of tea cups, and biscuits were passed around. I loved the small ones with pink and white icing sugar. The big moment then came, one of the ladies opened the suitcase she had brought, and the ladies gathered around. Aprons, knickers etc. All the names of customers carefully entered into a book, while a little money passed over.

We didn't seem to go shopping for clothes then. A very stately old man used to come to our house on Friday nights, and sit on a chair in the kitchen. For years I thought he was an uncle, but later learned he came from a store in Mansfield that supplied men's clothes, and of course Mother paid him the weekly amount. That is if she was able.

Miners as I remember them were a cheerful band of men, fond of their children, and often with a dog. No tinned food in those days, but anything left over. The difference in a man working and one with no work was devastating. Chins sunk into chests, shoulders hunched, and feet dragged as they gathered in groups on street corners waiting to hear of work. I well remember my mother crying and my grandmother trying to comfort her. We had run out of the coal allowance, and we had no heat, or means of cooking. My father with cap in hand nervously approached the colliery manager to ask if he could possibly have his allowance brought forward. He had only two more shifts to work (but it might have taken a week to get that much work). The manager listened, then brutally said, "No, you might get killed on the next shift." Those same miners during the war worked their fingers to the bone for their country, and many suffered early ill health.

A sound which has gone forever – our town crier. He would stand on street corners, ring his bell, then his raucous voice would shout the message. We once had to use him when my little sister got lost.

The *Post* boys would shout *"Post, Post"*, around the streets as it grew dusk and if something awful happened the cry would be "Special! Special!".

Mother baked all our bread and the barm-man would call several times a week. He carried a large wicker basket with portions of barm [yeast] screwed up in paper packets, covered over by a large white cloth. It had a warm rich smell.

In the mornings the clatter of the milk cart as the horse slowly plodded up the hill. The milkman would ladle milk from an urn into a pail and come down the entry shouting "Milko!". He would pour the milk into a jug which was left on the window ledge.

Except for the butchers and the market we shopped mainly at the Co-operative. As little children we all remembered Mother's "divi" number for her checks. It was a large shop with a tiled floor which was scattered with sawdust. I would pass Mother's order book over the counter, wait and watch. I loved to watch the butter being patted into shape with wooden "paddles". There was a lovely smell in that shop that has gone today, the smell of bacon hanging from the hooks, of tea and soap – great, green, chunky bars. There were bundles of fire-wood on the floor, candles on the shelf and boxes of fruit and biscuits would stand open on the floor.

I would walk for miles with my father. We would leave the town and go over the Annesley Hills (we called it "The Warren") to the pit. It would be pay day; not much pay when a man only worked two days. Men would gather into groups in the pit yard, then squat upon the floor – I squatted too. The butty would come with a tin with money to pay his men. Sometimes there would be a penny for me or, better, some chocolate. We stood in the dole queues, we paid into the National Deposit Club to cover us for sickness expenses. The old Scottish doctor was a real friend to us and loved all the "bairns". We lived simply but were happy in our way.

I loved Fridays because after tea we would go with Mother to the market. It was held in the Market Hall and outside stood several fruit stalls. On winter nights they were lit by naphtha flares and the men would shout their wares. Inside the hall was a milling, chattering throng; just to go in was excitement in itself. We would never ask for anything because we knew our mother would buy a big bag of boiled sweets, which she would keep in her drawer and ration out during the week.

Now the towering dirt tips that scattered their dust over the town have gone along with my childhood. Landscaped into gentle hills. The headstocks may have gone but the bloodstock remains, along with memories.'

CAUNTON

'Caunton is a pretty, friendly village that once boasted two windmills, a brickmaker, two shops, a post office and two pubs, as well as a chapel. Sadly, they have all gone now apart from one pub and one windmill.

The remaining mill, which was built in the 19th century, was run by two brothers, Leonard and Bert Sharp. Len made the bread and Bert took it round the village on a cart, giving the children a hot cob as he went.

Mr Smith was the brickie on Mill Lane. Bricks were made from the clay from surrounding fields. Kiln Cottage now stands where the kilns were and Brick Pillar Lane still runs opposite.

The Hole Arms, built in about 1853, is now closed. It was called the Manor Arms when Mrs Williams kept it. The taproom had a huge grand piano and Windsor chairs but spittoons under the seats. Mrs Williams had to walk through three rooms to the cellar to fill up the white enamel jugs with beer. The farmers would get off the bus from Newark cattle market at one o'clock, go into the pub, then when the pub closed they would play in the skittle alley eating barm cake and cheese until the pub reopened at tea-time. Mr Williams was a carpenter and amongst other things made babies' high chairs and dressing tables. Mrs Williams kept the pub for 40 years. When she left in 1933 the name was changed to the Hole Arms.

During the Second World War, two land mines were dropped on a farm just outside the village – one exploded making a huge crater, while the other came to rest by the barn door. Most of the local boys were called up for active service. One boy was killed in the Ransome & Marles factory blitz. Most of the girls from the village worked at the factory making ball bearings, and this place took a direct hit. It was rumoured that the pilot had known exactly where to drop the bomb because he was once a resident in Newark.'

WATNALL VILLAGE LIFE

'Watnall is a village composed of the very old Watnall Chaworth and the new Watnall Cantelupe. It was dominated by a beautiful Elizabethan mansion, the home of Lady Maud and Sir Lancelot Rolleston, around which a great deal of village life was built. We were all dressed in our best straw hats with rosebuds round to greet the arrival of King George V and Queen Mary at Watnall station.

Lady Maud was our Sunday school teacher and we enjoyed lots of parties at the Hall, especially in the summer on the lawns, and also Christmas parties indoors and presents for all of us. We always came home with a currant bun and an orange.

We loved walking in the woods and gathering wild flowers. We were never nervous and used to chat to the tramps on the wayside. All our pleasures were very simple, playing in the fields surrounding our homes. The muffin man came round once a week which was a treat for us. Haymaking was a marvellous time too, riding to the field in the empty cart. We used to be out quite late and see the lamplighter come round on his bicycle.

Most of the houses had paraffin lamps, which seemed to make the room look warm and cosy. There was no church, the nearest being at Greasley about two miles away. The village children loved the blacksmith's shop and to watch the blacksmith shoe the horses. One old man in the thatched cottage used to brew his own beer from the hops in the hedgerow near his house. The postman used to come on foot and tell us *when* our visitors were arriving.

One of the local customs was the annual rent dinner on Lady

Day, when all the tenants of the estate paid their rent at the Queen's Head. Other customs were the annual ploughing match and Moorgreen Show, which still continues today, at which the greasy pig hunt created a lot of fun. The hounds used to meet at Watnall Hall; it was spectacular to see the riders in their bright red coats. Children gathered round to watch them start off.

Many children were Girl Guides; the meetings were held at the Hall, where the Guides sometimes camped out in the grounds.

We all walked to Kimberley for school and took our lunch with us – some children walked from Watnall Pit three to four miles; all their shoes had studs in to make them last – parents always mended their children's shoes.'

SYERSTON – PLACES AND PEOPLE

'In 1927 there were 26 houses, a church and a chapel. The Hall with its range of Georgian buildings was the largest and most ostentatious dwelling: not many villagers went there unless they worked there. It seemed a world of its own.

At the foot of its long drive stood the lodge. Once it was the lodgekeeper's duty to man the big gates, open and close them and lock them securely at night. The Lodge was said to be haunted by a little girl, in a pinafore with frills on the shoulders.

At the top of the lane leading down to the village stood a Mockbeggar – the local name for a ruined house. There were still two downstairs rooms and one upstairs, but only from the front did it look habitable; in the rear missing doors, windows and pieces of wall took over.

Of course Greengate was still a meadow then; a beautiful meadow, rich in flowers and grasses we never see now. The hay from it had the rich intoxicating smell of very expensive tobacco, and when the grass was shorter, mushrooms abounded. The way a meadow should be.

The first house in the village was Meadow Farm. At one time it had been the pub but no one could recall a polite name for it; the Glory Hole was the cleanest appellation. Here lived Mr and Mrs Bagguley: Meg and George William. They were both quite old (or seemed old). Meg was small and square built, Welsh, she was as swarthy as a gypsy, and her hair was coal-black. Her house was fascinating to a little girl, the dairy with its brick floor, the three-sided churn, the butter-bowl carved out of solid wood, the separator and syles and pails, the coats and harness and all kinds of saucepans; but the milk was good and so was the butter.

A cream coloured rose grew by the dairy door, its long brambles climbed right over the house. Near the road, a Dorothy Perkins and a moss rose wreathed the parlour window; and along the back of the house ran a long narrow garden, with irises, phlox, hollyhocks and monkshood.

The parlour itself was something to write about. Its lace curtains were never drawn aside; its aspidistras sat in corners like silent brooding observers. A tall old grandfather clock stood against the wall, and a stuffed peacock, tail outspread, stood in the fireplace. Meg's crochet covers and antimacassars were on the chairs and on the sofa was a particularly handsome patchwork cushion, lovely silks and velvets, all faggot-stitched together with yellow silk, a real work of art. I thought about those pretty materials, but could *not* imagine Meg wearing them. One day I asked, "Were those pieces of the dresses you used to wear?". The answer was surprising. "No my dear, them was neckties from young men I walked out with before I met George William!". I had nervous imaginings of throttled boyfriends – or did she snip the ends off when they weren't looking? I dared not ask.

Their horse was called Ginger, a tall bony, aged Shire who took Mr Bagguley to see to the cattle, fetch home hay and fruit, and help out other farmers in exchange for the loan of their horses. The old people loved their fields to be pretty, and showed me many wild flowers. The stable near the road was covered with ivy, and every year there was what the boys called a "bum-barrel's" nest in it, a tennis-ball sized construction of moss, feathers horse-hairs and human hairs, containing up to six little longtailed tits, plus mother and father. On the wall facing the road was a big round yellow tin sign with SYERSTON across the middle and the distances to Newark, Lincoln, Nottingham and Leicester painted above, thanks to the AA. Kind of them thus to adorn the notable city of Syerston!

15

The little orchard next to our place belonged to the Bagguleys. It was surrounded with hazel bushes: every year the yellow lambs'-tails dangled in the wind, and later fat rounded clusters of cobnuts hung there instead.

In the middle of the orchard was a great patch of snowdrops in the spring, with daffodils and bluebells later. Meg told me this was where their first dog, Nell, had been buried. The Bagguleys and Nell are long gone, but the flowers are still there year by year.

Mr Kirkland's orchard was neat and well-tended, with fowl houses under the trees; he would mow the grass by scythe, nearly as short as a mower. He had land as well, "The Meadow". He scythed that too, making a very tidy stack to feed the two bullocks he "finished" each year – buying calves and selling as "beasts". His pigs always seemed happy and his garden was always full, adorned by his pride and joy, a row of yuccas along the roadside. The little holding took all the time he could spare from being cowman at the Hall. His hard working wife was kept busy with the house and four children, but her spare time was spent in sewing and embroidery. She did beautiful patchwork, winning the All England Prize offered by the *Farmer and Stockbreeder* twice; a fine patchwork spread for each of her daughters.

She also had a famous "little tin trunk" which came to every garden fete or church fundraising effort, and into that little tin trunk, all the year round, went articles made or given to be sold. Relations added things like dusters and d'oyleys and potholders and teacosies and all sorts of things; and every time "Mrs Kirkland's Fancy Stall" headed the list of takings.

In the other cottage of the pair lived a Mr and Mrs Misson. When we came, in 1927, it was the post office and very rigorously kept. In the back kitchen was a bureau. To buy a stamp, you asked, very politely. Mrs Misson always wore a white apron over her ankle length black dress, and a wide black leather belt: from this a thin chain vanished somewhere, to be hauled up and reveal a bunch of keys. One unlocked the bureau lid, another unlocked a drawer inside. Another unlocked a cash box in the drawer. Your stamp having been dispensed and paid for, the locking up was reversed, all secure, and the keys returned to their hidden depths. The pillar box was in the wall of her little front hall, and after a lot of coaxing she let me look into its dark, iron-smelling interior.

Mrs Misson sold sweets as well. The most expensive item was a sixpenny bar of chocolate, a truly prodigal luxury only to be bought after a present of money from some opulent visitor. There were lollipops and bullseyes and satin cushions and rosebuds and kali and liquorice and hundreds and thousands – all weighed out in a twisted paper cone – and pop, in strong glass bottles with marbles in the neck.

Like everyone else in pre-WC days, they had a "drop it and run" earth closet down the yard. Hurrying in one day I sat down to see, on the door, a beautifully painted text – "Thou, God, seest me". Well, I knew God watched everything I did, but it was not very nice of Him to watch *there*. . . .

One day Mrs Misson had another lady with her and they were discussing some particularly spicy bit of gossip, not intended for seven year old ears. They looked at me, and then I was invited to sit in the big armchair, earphones were put over my head, and I was told to listen. A man's voice suddenly said, "Hallo, children, everywhere!". It was such a shock, I tore off the headphones and screamed, "There's a MAN in there!". It was Uncle Mac, Derek McCullough – and not many people can remember so distinctly the first time they heard radio!

The chapel was at the other end of the village. It had been inaugurated in 1858 with a great concourse of 500 people, who brought food and shared, rather like the feeding of the Five Thousand. That was 70 years previous; but the little chapel kept going, people walked over from Flintham to swell the congregation. There was a tall American organ there and a cast iron stove gave out tremendous heat, chiefly on wood. We used to go there to have a warm, meet friends, and sing much more fervently than in church, the atmosphere was homelier. Along the walls were indispensable items of chapel furniture – did you ever hear of someone so astonished that his eyes were sticking out like chapel hat-pegs!

Over the road stood the Croft. Built as a dower house for William Fillingham's widow, Sarah, after her death it had become a farmhouse: and here lived Mr and Mrs Gash and their married daughter and her husband. They farmed the land which went with the Croft, and one of their three sons, married and living at Elston, began the famous bus service.

Mr and Mrs Gash were kind, hard working, friendly people, always ready to help a neighbour or do good for the village. It was in the Croft field that the caravan mission set up its tent for gospel services, it was in their big barn that we celebrated George V's Silver Jubilee in 1935: a merry occasion, we had a meeting to plan it. One farmer gave a shoulder of bacon, to be boiled: another a joint of beef, another a pair of fowls. Stepfather didn't like the man who was collecting money, so, being a market gardener, sent me with this message: "I'll give them salad goods enough for everyone" – quite a handsome donation, though the "collector" would have preferred cash. I made this promise and a lady said, "Well if Mr Asher's giving salad goods, I'll make half a gallon of my prize winning salad cream instead of a donation". (She didn't like the "collector" either.)

When we all sat down for the feast, the big barn looked really good, swept out and whitewashed, with Union Jacks and patriotic pictures of George and Mary, long tables (of planks on boxes) spread with bedsheets and crockery from everyone (you took your own cutlery to make sure of getting it back). Each plate had its ration of beef, "ham" or chicken, bowls of salad were here and there, little bowls of relish, and jugs of prize winning salad cream; bowls of sugar, jugs of milk, bread and butter (none of your margarine, it was home-made butter) and very good it looked. Three stalwart ladies came round with large pots of scalding tea to fill the cups; and we set to.

Before the feast we had had a fancy dress parade for the children: Mrs Gash had promised two prizes, and the children were very keen. One family had two little girls and not much money, but two ninepenny rolls of crepe paper, over their petticoats, turned out a Golden Sunflower and a Dear Little Shamrock. Just too bad there was a little shower on the way to the barn. Sunflower only looked slightly tanned, but poor little Shamrock had a green neck and arms for several days.

After the feast we all went up the Croft, for races and fun. Mr Gash had given a little pig, to be "run for" by the men. The idea was to line up the contestants, release the pig, and who could catch it, kept it. The piglet had other ideas – one glance, it turned round and ran into a well-grown cornfield and it was never seen again. By us, at any rate. But we youngsters each had a Jubilee mug, and as it was Lilley & Stone School's Silver Jubilee as well, that was quite a busy year.

The church is still there of course. In those days the heating was an under-floor heater, glowing red and ominous. Stepfather would poke me if I fidgeted and say, "That's Hell, that is, that's where you'll go if you don't behave." But the church was very cosy, thanks to Mr Masson, the sexton. The lighting was by candles, two on a T-shaped stand at the end of every other pew, except for a paraffin lamp on the harmonium. The curtains flanking the altar were a rich bulrush brown. They did *not* match the dark crimson velvet frontal, which had an appliqued Lamb and Flag in the middle. When the church was refurbished 30 years ago the Lamb and Flag disappeared (none knows where), the bulrush brown velvet curtains were so frail and threadbare they nearly disintegrated – but ended up as pairs of bloomers for two little girls in striped tee-shirts, posing as bumble bees at a fancy dress party.

The first vicar I remember was Mr Cotton, a square-built man with a beard. He was a good preacher, and when Stepfather became "People's Warden" he would often come to our house for a cup of coffee. There were quite a few rules about church, outside the ones ordained by the lectuary. *All* females wore hats, grown up ones wore gloves; in those days church was often the outing of the week, and had special clothes and behaviour. The ladies took turns at doing the flowers, but there was an official church cleaner, paid a small salary; the sexton was paid, too. When a feast time came there were rules for that, too; different ladies decorated special parts, jealously guarded, woe betide the newcomer who "did" someone else's window!

The church was always full for Harvest, we even had forms in the aisles, and there was always an interesting display of extra special Sunday clothes and hats, with a powerful blend of mothballs, boot polish, perfume, fruit, flowers – yes, and *people.* That was the era of a Saturday night bath and that was that.

The churchyard grass with its many flowers was left to grow until hay-time, threaded with butterflies, hovered over by birds, until it was scythed, then left, turned, ripened, cocked and carried off in footcloths, usually to feed Mr Kirkland's bul-

19

locks. The mowers were paid for their work until machinery took over; at least one ex-mower complained: "That money used to pay for my winter working boots."

Mrs Fillingham, as long as she was able, used to come down to tend her husband's grave, inside the black chain-surround under the chestnut tree. It was unlucky that Stepfather's dog, Bruce, fancied that enclosure for his den, he would carry over bones, sticks, balls, scrubbing brushes etc. When the old lady came, she would always call at our house for some water. Mother would hiss at me, "Go and fetch Bruce's bones", and say in her sweetest tones, "Do come in Mrs Fillingham. Mother does so look forward to your visits." Granny was a lady of similar vintage and culture; they would easily embark on a discussion of Tennyson or Marie Corelli. Tea would be served and by that time the enclosure would be immaculate, all Bruce's bones were hanging up in a bucket, and a thwarted dog was skulking under the kitchen sofa. Eventually both old ladies went to their graves in the churchyard and Bruce died too.

A footpath ran over to Candle Lane beside Mrs Ewin's garden at Montague House. It was such a secluded place, I used to crawl through the hedge and dance on the lawn, none of the other children did. Beside the house was an odd little piece of land, Mrs Ewin called it the Emplin. In those days there were three oaks where now there is only one, and next to the road were three tall elms. Some branches hung over the road, and when Willy Whiteman's garage set up on the village green, he put up two lengths of wire hawser and made a huge swing – originally for Willy junior and Maurice, his boys, but of course, everyone else swung. The only drawback was, it was so heavy you really needed someone to push. The risks we ran were terrible – three or four children at once linked by arms round waists on a swing about 20 feet high!

Up one of the oaks we made a tree house with pieces of board and lots of binder twine. It was a marvellous den and look-out post. Once we were being Robin Hood and Co, and having kidnapped a "fat Abbot" (really he was a skinny six year old) we hauled him up to the tree house, tied him up with more binder twine, and promised to come back, as the Sheriff of Nottingham & Co to rescue him. Unluckily, we got distracted, and a very frightened, tearful little boy was rescued by his brothers who waited Father's homecoming with well-founded apprehension. Fleeing a scolding from their mother, I ran home to a worse one from mine, a dose of slipper, and a Kept At Home.

In a row of cottages past Montague House lived Miss Fanny Wade; she was quite old when we came. We heard she had been a lady's maid up the Hall. Her little house was very spick and span, but rather dark; older people then seemed to keep their curtains half drawn, perhaps to keep the sun from fading things.

She told me her grandfather had been the village blacksmith, and that he had lived in my house, and set the japonica bush on his wedding day. If that were true, it must be 200 years old by now. Miss Wade was a famous wine maker. She knew Stepfather had a market stall at Mansfield, and used to ask him to bring her the oranges and lemons she sometimes needed. At Christmas he would get a bottle or two of her wine; some of it was so powerful, he said you could fuel an aeroplane on it.

She had beautiful lace-edged covers on her sideboard and chest of drawers, with embroidered antimacassars on the chairs and a valance on the mantelshelf. She was hardly every seen outside her house and garden, but in those days the baker, butcher, fishman, milkman, and travelling shop came regularly every week, selling nearly everything.

In the cottage next door was a very different person. We were told that he had been gamekeeper, but got the sack for poaching. He certainly looked the part, unshaven, woolly-haired, and far from clean, he seemed to go out only at night. From time to time he would be away for a day or two: then someone's cat would go missing, and it was widely believed he caught them and put them in the cottage to provide his ferrets with exercise and fresh food. Certainly, in the pub of the next village, he would put a ferret and a live rat down the neck of his shirt and take bets on which would win.

The blacksmith's shop was the last building along the road: the blacksmith I knew only came sometimes, on a noisy motor bike, presumably "by appointment" and did all the horses in the village that needed shoeing; also mending things like harrows and hayrakes and reapers and ploughs. The children seemed to sense his coming by instinct and turned up to watch fascinated as he made "shoes to measure" – none of your ready to wear blanks then. The boys pleaded to work the bellows, or pass the tools when he pared hooves or cleaned out frogs, tried on the red-hot shoes with a lovely sizzling unforgettable smell, and finally nailed it on. We picked up the discarded nails and treasured them, and took offcuts of hoof to put on the fire at home before retreating hastily. The blacksmith was kind as long as we were good but pranksters were chased with his long hot tongs; shades of St Dunstan!

In the end house of Cedar Terrace lived Mr and Mrs Wade, no relation at all to Fanny over the wall. I don't remember where Mr Wade worked but Mrs Wade was a very useful person; she brought babies, laid people out when they died, helped with housework if a mum was ill, and among other accomplishments did miles of crochet lace and iced special cakes – wedding, christening, Christmas, etc. She was hardly ever seen without a blue cotton overall and very substantial handknitted brown woollen stockings. When Mother had rheumatic fever, Mrs Wade came to keep house for us. Not used to "new-fangled" inventions, she left the electric iron switched on till it charred its way through the wooden ironing board and fell to the floor.

Along Doghill Lane were the remains of a farmstead, two ruined rooms downstairs and one upstairs: there was a well, a crewyard, some sheds, all abandoned to decay, but for us children it was our den. What happy times we had there, we would light a fire in the old grate and roast potatoes and "mash" tea and cook anything we could pinch or scrounge from home or anywhere else – lovely smoky toast and mysterious gypsy stew, the less you knew about the ingredients the better, but none of us seemed any the worse.

Proceeding along Doghill Lane you came to a huge mound of hedge which had once been the boundary between the two meadows. It was covered with the biggest, juiciest blackberries in the parish; until somebody who didn't like blackberry pickers grubbed it out. Just past this was a very, very old oak tree, almost but not quite dead: it was called Crookle Tom, and many years did Crookle Tom stand, till one day he just quietly fell down and disintegrated. Next along was a magnificent elm, but that has now succumbed to Dutch elm disease. The last tree in this field was, and still is, the Old Hollow Oak – all our gang, seven or eight, could get inside it. Robin Hood's cave, an outlaw's lair, a dragon's den – the possibilities were enormous.

In those days there were always mats of primroses along the banks of the well trimmed ditches: pussy willows gleamed golden round the Glebe Field; and in a marshy patch in the right-hand field grew kingcups. Gone, all gone. On the other side was the Old House Field, in those days full of little bushes which sheltered young animals and harboured early grass, bugle flowers grew there, little orchids, and totty-grasses; also sparse but sweet little round mushrooms, and even in some seasons "Bluebutton" mushrooms. You either loved or loathed them. Many older people would gladly buy any we children took home.

Dog violets grew by the hedge of Low Farm's garden, and at one point wild hops shot up their bines and later hung long tresses of hops from the height of the tall hedge, for us to carry home and dry and make sleepy-pillows for anyone who was not very well. A little further along was the Pound, and we all knew what it was there for, also that if *we* strayed too far we would be shut in there for the night to "larn us". We were careful. Although no one bothered much about where we were, so long as we turned up for meal times.

Over the road stood the Laundry, a real gem. It had been erected by the people who lived at Elston Hall, who were in some way connected with Huntley and Palmers, the biscuit manufacturers. It had its own rainwater store, besides its own well, and in it were washing tubs and rinsing tubs, and a great copper to heat the water and boil the "whites". There were pulley-racks to dry on, in case it rained too much to use the little drying green beside the building. In the second room was a coal-fired stove, to heat the flat irons and Italian irons and gophering tongs, and a table to iron on, and more pulley airers to air the washing afterwards. This was a well known laundry: well off people from quite a distance would bring laundry to be done here.

Opposite stood the house that had once been the village school: it is recorded that when the Squire's daughter married, in Victorian days, the schoolmistress and her dressmaker

23

Bulwell Market Place in the early 1900s and two ways of travelling. We still look back on the trams with nostalgia.

daughter made clothes for the village children to wear at the wedding, from material given by the ladies at the Hall.

When I first knew it, a family called Haslam lived there: then, they used the erstwhile schoolroom as a working men's club. For sixpence a week the men could meet there, play dominoes, draughts, darts, cards, chess and read a selection of donated books, quite good books, including Dickens, Edgar Wallace, Rider Haggard, etc. Later on a Library Box was brought once a month, to be enthusiastically patronised. Stepfather was elected secretary of this club; but with a better bus service the club dwindled and died.'

BECKINGHAM

'These are some of the happenings in Beckingham when my father was a lad. When he was three he remembers falling into a dyke that ran past his house on its way through the marshes into the river Trent. There were many floods, one in 1910 and 1940, then the one in 1947 which was the longest. The marshes between Bole and West Stockwith were under three or four feet of water and during the 1947 floods the banks on the Lincolnshire side burst, flooding Gainsborough streets and houses.

It was in 1888 that a Mr Joseph Watson established his shipyard at Beckingham bringing some of his workmen and equipment from London (the shipyard has now closed down). The yard turned out flat-bottomed boats and some were exported to Africa. Some were launched into the river Trent.

In 1908 Mr Watson had several houses built for his workmen, and a village institute where the men could play billiards or table tennis and read the daily papers. The four dwellings adjoining and a bungalow are left to provide for the upkeep of the institute. Mr Watson was also connected to the village school as he gave the land on which it stands. The new school was built in 1901. He also offered to build some old people's cottages on the green but the parish council refused.

The first telephone installed in Beckingham was in 1915; it was in the post office and the only one for some years. In 1903 a chiming clock was erected in the church tower which chimes every quarter hour. My father, who was a joiner, made the case for the clock and helped to fix it.

My father could remember that for one evening every summer donkeys used to stand on the village green and take children for rides round the village for one penny. This was varied by a boat pulled by a horse which also went round the village, rocking by means of a crank, carrying children. Other summer visitors were a German band of four men playing stringed instruments outside the houses begging for coppers; occasionally a foreign man came with a bear, going round the houses doing a dance also begging for coppers. Sometimes a man came with a hurdy gurdy; he had a small monkey fastened by a small chain. Another musical instrument which visited the green was a piano on two wheels which was played by a handle.

On each Whitsun Monday Beckingham Feast was held and the day was marked by the local branch of The Ancient Order of Foresters' demonstration which began with a service in the church after which a colourful procession was formed, the members wearing bright green sashes and carrying green staves and headed by Gainsborough Britannia Brass Band. The procession went round the village calling at the principal houses collecting for the club funds and on return dinner was served in the schoolroom. Sports were held after it. Someone set up a stall in the school yard and sold sweets, nuts and ginger beer and a man set up a hand-operated roundabout for the children.

A custom called "mumping" was carried on years ago when old women went calling on the big houses in the village on St Thomas's Day (21st December), collecting money. On Bar Road there was a cottage kept by a widow which was a dame school; my mother used to go paying one penny per day.

Concerts were held in the schoolroom in wintertime and the villagers provided their own entertainment.

My father used to tell me of men walking to Gainsborough every day to work. Work started at 6 am and finished at 5 pm. Mr Watson who owned the shipyard was driven there in a horse and trap and sometimes in a four-wheeled carriage.

When I was a young girl carrier carts used to go to Gainsborough and would take anything for the villagers as there were no buses and not many people had cars. I remember our milk was brought round the village in a trailer carrying a churn, pulled behind a bike and we brought out a milk jug for the milk to be poured in.

My mother had her groceries brought from Gainsborough by a van pulled by a horse. Every Saturday morning she would give the van driver her order for the next week (no charge was made for this).

Before the local water was laid on in the village we had to fetch some of our drinking water from my Granddad's who lived a few yards up the village. We had a pump in the yard, which needed priming before the water would come up.'

WIDMERPOOL

'I was born at Manor Farm, Widmerpool. My parents rented the farm from the Widmerpool estate and in the 1920s there were several small farms in the village which have now all gone. The estate was sold off, farm by farm, from 1957 onwards.

My father was born at the New Inn, which in those days was a farm. I remember him saying how, before the First World War, he used to rent out keys for a lock-up shed in a field near the station, so that people from the surrounding villages could leave their bicycles there when travelling by train to Nottingham or Melton.

The village had no shop, except that Mrs Gamm, the blacksmith's wife, sold sweets and cigarettes from boxes in her front room. Everything was delivered to the door – bread by Mr Watson of Willoughby, meat by Mr Trafford of Wysall, vegetables by Mr Warden of Keyworth and groceries by Mr Potter of Aslockton. Mr Potter came twice a week, Monday to take your order and Wednesday to deliver it. Our shoes were taken to Mr Whitaker of Willoughby for mending.

There was a small copse opposite the station road that used to be covered in snowdrops and aconites in the spring. We would go in and pick them, then try to hide the flowers behind our backs if Mr Rimmer the estate gamekeeper caught us, as the woodland was out of bounds.

Bonfire night was always held in the hole in the paddock, with Mrs Rimmer making the home-made treacle toffee to be handed round. In the cricket field we used to keep ten large hen huts, and in the corner was quite a large pond which has now been filled in, but in sharp winters villagers used to skate on it.

When Mrs Forman Hardy lived at Widmerpool Hall we used to have a whist drive and dance in the Hall on Boxing Night. Two rooms for whist and the main hall for dancing. I wore my first long evening gown at one of these dances. It was like a fairy story, driving up between the trees with the frost glittering in the lights as we arrived. Village fetes and garden parties were held at the Hall or in the garden of the old rectory. This was a typically large country garden, with a big spread of lawn and flower beds with a huge cedar tree. The usual stalls would be there, and there would be a fancy dress competition, and almost everyone in the village would take part in some way or another to make it a success.

In the summer when the men were busy making hay or scything the corn, meals were always taken to them in the fields. We would tack the horse up, get her in the cart, load dinner or tins of sandwiches up and lots of flasks of tea. There would be a lot of men to be fed, when everything was done without automation.

The young people in my era used to sit on the bridge wall, or under the two lovely beech trees which were on the green opposite the village school, or on the pond wall at New Inn, to have a weekly chat.'

GOTHAM

'There was very little transport from Gotham before the 1920s. The link with Nottingham was the railway, the nearest station over a mile away. The most popular form of transport was the carrier's cart taking the people to town on market days, would-be passengers having to book their seats about two weeks in advance. Passengers often had to get out and walk up the hills as the horses were unable to pull the load.

Children of the village were usually taken to town three times a year: to the Goose Fair held in those days in the old market square, to see the shops at Christmas, and to get new clothes for the Sunday school Anniversaries.

Village life at that time was centred around the parish church and the two Methodist chapels, most people attending every Sunday. Only work of bare necessity was done on Sundays.

Sunday school Anniversaries were a red letter day, the platforms being full of children and the chapels filled to capacity, people coming from far and wide for this great day. The singing was most inspiring. The parish church had their Sunday school festival in the form of a flower service.

The highlight of the summer was the annual united Sunday school treat held on Whit Monday when all the Sunday school scholars, teachers and most of the villagers assembled on the rectory lawn for a service, then paraded the village headed by the Gotham Brass Band, who always turned out on such occasions and of whom we were very proud in their smart uniforms. After the parade the children went to their respective Sunday schools for tea, then on to the field at the Manor for sports. Almost the whole population turned out for this occasion, a real treat in those days.

People made their amusement and enjoyment in their own homes. A lot of people had American organs in those days, some had a piano, and one could come through the village, especially on a Sunday evening and hear hearty singing, knowing the family were gathered together for this form of entertainment which they made themselves and thoroughly enjoyed.

Gotham has always been noted for its singing and at Christmas time wherever people were gathered together the "Three Harks" would be sung, this being Gotham's own tune to *Hark the Herald Angels Sing*. After writing this tune on manuscript from memory I was asked by the City Librarian to send a copy for the Historical Music Unit in the City Library, Shakespeare Street.

Choral societies have been formed over the years, giving oratorios etc, and with people's love for singing this gave them a great deal of pleasure. We had been fortunate in having two schoolmasters and a schoolmistress who were musical. Both Mr and Mrs Laws, headmaster and mistress of the senior school were musicians and contributed quite a lot to the life of the village. Mr Naylor followed Mr Laws as schoolmaster. He formed the school choir and the school song which he composed was sung on many occasions, the theme of the song being the school motto "Play the Game". It was during the 1920s that cookery was introduced at school and the senior girls from Gotham school had to go to Ruddington for these lessons, walking to Rushcliffe Halt to catch the 8.20 am train.

The social centre for men was what is now the church hall, this being used each evening for billiards, dominoes etc. Concerts, dances and whist drives were held in the school on Kegworth Road. It was in 1921 that the new Memorial Hall and recreation ground was opened where all social life took place, activities of one kind or another going on every night. In 1920 the Women's Institute was formed, the first meetings taking place at the Old Rectory, in what was originally the nursery but owing to the kindness of the rectors was used for many village meetings.

It was between the two world wars that the infants' schoolmistress had an idea to take the village schoolchildren to the sea for the day. Money was raised during the winter months and a train was booked. This was an event that was looked forward to with great excitement and one day of the year that left the village deserted.

Feast Days were recognised, known commonly to us as Gotham Wakes. This was marked during the fourth week in October and for a few days roundabouts etc were set up in the orchard where the post office now stands. The post office in those days was a small addition to one of the cottages on Nottingham Road. The postmaster was what one would class as a "cantankerous character". There were no private telephones in those days so villagers had to go to the post office to send messages, or enquire about hospital patients and he would do this for you just as he thought fit. Our postal address in those days was Derby and the mail came to Kegworth and the regular postman delivered it from there. During the holiday season he would hand the householder a postcard (no letter boxes in those days) and say "It rained all day at Cleethorpes yesterday", the recipient knowing full well the postcard had been read. Along the main street was the local wheelwright and to watch the process of putting new rims on cart wheels was interesting. Further along the road was the village black-

30

smith's and on our way home from school we were fascinated to call and watch horses being shod. Most of the work then was done with horses and carts.

Friday night was Band of Hope night when most of the village children and teenagers went to the hall on Moor Lane. As there was little else to do in those days this was counted as a night out. The hymns were sung to a very old harmonium with a lot of "wheezes", one had to pedal very hard to keep enough wind in it to produce music and it was once said in jest that "the wind that escaped from the harmonium helped to keep the stove going". The Friday before Christmas we were all given a bar of chocolate and an orange which we looked on as a treat.

"Mod cons" were unthought of. We had no drinking water in the houses. There were six drinking water taps in the streets and householders had to take a bucket and a tap key to fetch it. Most people had an earthenware vessel in the pantry called a "pippin" in which they kept the water to keep it cool. People sometimes had to queue and one old character was known to get up halfway through the night to avoid the queue.

The only industry in the village for men was the plaster mines now called "British Gypsum", men starting at 6.30 for 7 am and working until 5 pm. Those working underground only saw daylight at weekends during the winter months as it was dark in the mornings when they went down the mines and dark again in the evenings when they came up, working in poor conditions.

Some of the men had an allotment and from the spring until the autumn this was where they spent their evenings, digging, sowing, reaping, and it was the usual thing in the autumn to see them coming home with barrow-loads of produce, potatoes, onions, carrots etc, enough to store and feed the household through the winter. Apples were bought by the peck from the people with orchards, these were stored for cooking during the winter. No deep freezers in those days, all preserves had to be stored on the pantry shelves.

Milk wasn't delivered in bottles as it is today, we had to take a can or a jug to fetch it from the farmhouse. Everyone had a coal fire, but coal wasn't delivered in bags, it was ordered from the coal merchants by the ton. They brought it in carts and

31

tipped it outside the house and the householder then had to wheel it in a barrow to the coal place. This was usually an evening's work. No electricity, consequently no electric cookers! Practically every household had a black range, with an oven on one side and a boiler for hot water on the other, and it took housewives most of Friday morning to clean the flues and blacklead the grate.

There have been occasions when we have had power cuts when our minds have gone back to the times when we had only candles and paraffin lamps. Lamps were trimmed during the day and on long winter evenings the paraffin was often used up by 9.30 pm and we had to toddle off to bed because the lamp had gone out. If one turned up the wick to get a better light the lamp glass would get overheated and smash to pieces, glass flying all over the room. In spite of inadequate lighting it seems remarkable that not more than a third of the population wore spectacles. We had a few street lights and one of the villagers could be seen going round to light them at approximately 6 pm and to put them out at 10 pm.

There are many tales of the "Wise Men of Gotham" centred round the days of King John, but even in this era we had what one would call "characters". One of these, when the wind was in the west, would push his bicycle up Kegworth Road just to have the pleasure of freewheeling back. Another one, very fond of poaching, who would often have to go to court for doing so, a day or two later would have a line of pheasants hanging up in his outhouse having what he called "his own back" on Lord Belper or Lord Byron.

And so the seasons come and go, the years roll on and changes keep taking place, even the harvest time is far advanced owing to mechanisation. We remember the time when farmers had to wait for fine weather but now with combine harvesters and dryers it can all be done in much less time. The majority of the population own a car, and we have the East Midlands airport on our doorstep, so we have moved on from carrier's cart, to buses, cars and aeroplanes.'

OLLERTON

'I came to Ollerton with my parents in 1922. My father had rented the village blacksmith's shop. He had worked in the mines in County Durham as a shoeing smith, shoeing the pit ponies. The blacksmith's shop was at the junction of Bescar Lane and Wellow Road.

I remember Ollerton as a busy place, eight farms in and around it. Most had cows, some having only two or three, others large herds, which from April to October we saw taken from the fields to the farm for milking. One farmer had threshing tackle, and we would see this being pulled by a very large steam engine from farm to farm.

In the village was a saddler who made and repaired harness and other leather goods. We used to watch him at work using a large needle with a bent point and a type of twine which he rubbed with beeswax. In the village there was also a rope-maker; he made all kinds of things, snares to catch rabbits, net bags, washing lines and ropes of different thickness. At the top of his garden he had what he called his "rope-walk", this was a long straight path and it was here he made and twisted the ropes.

The river Maun ran through the village where many years ago a mill was built. The water used to drive a bucketed wheel which drove the millstones that ground corn for flour and for feed for the animals.

At the other end of the village was the blacksmith's shop where my father worked. He had a hearth on which he used to light a fire to heat the iron. At the side stood some bellows, between three and four feet high, made of very thick leather and worked by a strong wooden handle, moved up and down at a regular pace. This directed air to the base of the hearth and soon the fire was glowing white hot. He worked long days, starting at six in the morning, and he always went back to the shop after tea. It was at this time that he did some of his heaviest work. Young men used to gather there in the evening, it was warm and lit by a paraffin lamp and they used to help my father by striking with a large hammer.

In the village at this time were two grocers, three butchers, two drapers, a milliner, two newsagents, a post office and chemist, and two or three small shops selling sweets, fruit and vegetables, as well as a baker, a milkman and a cobbler. There were also in the village a joiner, an undertaker and a garage with a taxi, a painter and decorator.

Ollerton at this time had a doctor living in the village and a district nurse. There were three public houses, the White Hart, the Hop Pole and the Royal Oak. The Hop Pole, the largest, stands facing the river and it had been a coaching inn in times past. It was used by people visiting the Dukeries and attending the races at Doncaster. I remember Gracie Fields staying there when she was appearing at the Nottingham Empire.

The White Hart was at the centre of the village opposite St Giles' church, which stands on a mound. The public house was a very busy place, meals were served and visitors could hire waggonettes to drive them around the Dukeries. They also had a farm which backed up to the churchyard.

On 1st May Ollerton had a fair. In times past it had been a cattle and sheep fair, but the fair I knew was a funfair, and was held in a grass paddock and entered through the farm-yard. Three or four large steam engines pulled the big waggons into the field and the power from the engines drove the roundabouts, flying-chairs and dodgems, played the music and provided the lighting.

The church of St Giles had been a chapel of ease attached to the parish of Edwinstowe but was now the parish church of Ollerton. I went with my parents and attended the Sunday school, which was held in the day school. At this time the day school was on the Wellow Road and had been built by the church. It had been opened in the mid 1800s and was built of brick. There were three large rooms with three big windows in each room. It was heated by coke burning stoves in each room. On certain days, Ash Wednesday, St George's Day and Ascension Day we were taken from school to the church for the service. While we were attending Sunday school in the day school a bible class was being held in church. This was run by the churchwarden Mr John Baker. The majority of the men, young and old, attended. They all seemed to wear navy blue suits with white shirts and collars, and many wore bowler hats.

In 1925/26 they started to sink a colliery on land adjoining New Ollerton. New Ollerton was a suburb of Ollerton and consisted of two roads, Walesby Lane and Forest Road, which petered into heathland with lanes leading to Boughton and Walesby. On Forest Road were a number of houses, a shop run as a general store, a sweet shop, a stonemason, a plumber, a photographer and a public house, the Plough. There was also a Wesleyan chapel. There was a cemetery on land lying back from the road. On Walesby Lane were a number of small cottages. This soon changed, houses and shops were built on the lanes and surrounding land. Children started to attend the school and we heard that a new school was being built in New Ollerton. I remember one day a lorry came to the school as we were leaving to go for our dinners. We were told that it was to take the children to the soup kitchen as their fathers were on strike.

About this time the church started to take children who attended Sunday school to the seaside for the day. I remember going to Mablethorpe and Skegness. This was a great day out, we went by train from Ollerton station. The butcher, Mr William Germany, who was churchwarden, took a very large basket filled with potted meat sandwiches, these he handed out to anyone who was hungry. At this time you could travel from Ollerton to most places in England or Scotland, there were junctions near Tuxford and Langwith, and you could get on to the main lines at either.

The buses had started to run through the village. At first they appeared strange, large and noisy, but we soon got used to them. There were two services, one to Nottingham and Retford, and one to Nottingham and Doncaster calling at Worksop. Three bus companies ran to Mansfield, a half hourly service on Saturday and one to Newark.

By now the colliery was working and many houses had been built. The school was open and a church was being built, and a Scout troop, St John Ambulance and other organisations started for young people. A Boys' Brigade and three companies of Girl Guides and Brownies were formed. A musical society was started and the various chapels and churches had their own youth clubs. A billiard hall was opened, and a picture house was built. The miners built their own welfare hall. Ollerton became a very busy place.'

35

UPPER BROUGHTON

'Upper Broughton at the turn of the century was a quiet farming village with several shops and a post office. We shared a council school with our neighbouring village, just across the county boundary in Leicestershire, but it was on our side of the brook and administered by Nottingham County Council. There was a well attended church and chapel, two public houses and the usual craftsmen necessary to farming communities. The local brickyard was then nearing the end of its life. Many of the cottages in the village and the chapel were built with the attractive pinkish-red bricks made there. We had a railway station a mile from the village and a carrier's cart to Melton and Nottingham markets.

Two major changes took place in the 1920s. The turnpike road was widened through the village and electricity arrived. Mains water and sewerage came much later around 1960 and gas has only recently arrived.

Most families kept and killed a pig for home-cured bacon – these were memorable occasions. Hand-raised pork pies were made and these, together with pig's fry, were shared with neighbours.

Upper Broughton is a friendly place and welcomed evacuees in 1939. The first contingent from Sheffield didn't stay very long, country life was not for them, but the second influx from Great Yarmouth soon made themselves at home and some still live locally to this day.'

THRUMPTON

'I was born in Thrumpton in 1902. My family were farmers at Ferry Farm, beside the river Trent. My father used to row the ferry across the river to the Long Eaton side. It cost a penny per person and a halfpenny for a bike. He would even row someone on Christmas Day, but they'd have to wait until he'd had his dinner.

My parents made butter and sold eggs. In the summer they would serve teas to visitors on the lawn. A plain tea (bread and butter, cake and jam) cost ninepence. A boiled egg tea cost a shilling. Boiled egg and fruit and cream to follow was one

36

shilling and sixpence, and it cost two shillings if you had home-cured ham. We had over 300 visitors one year.

I left the village school at 14 to help my parents on the farm. There were two teachers, one for infants and one for the older children. One teacher indulged in a little whisky at weekends and was not at her best on Monday mornings. They took us for picnics and swimming in the river after school.

Thrumpton was noted for its church choir. Lady Lucy Byron would not employ anyone who couldn't sing. We had an annual festival at Southwell and an outing to Skegness.

The Thrumpton estate covered nearly 1,000 acres and all the houses were owned by Lord Byron. Local people worked at the Hall and lived in the cottages or at the Hall. There were seven maids, five gardeners, a cowman, a chauffeur, a cook-housekeeper and a butler, and a village woman made butter and cheese for the Hall. Lord Byron always gave a Christmas party for the village children at the Hall with a big tree and presents.

Gardens were given by Lord Byron for the village people to use, and there was glebe land for grazing down by the river, since sold. Four council houses were built in 1946 for £800 each and when some estate land was sold after Lord Byron died, some more new houses were built in the 1950s.

In the early days a cattle waggon was converted by the carrier into a motor bus for people who wanted to go into Nottingham. There were two buses a week. You cycled to Barton Land End to catch one and left your cycle in the hedge and it was still there when you got back. The nearest policeman was in Gotham and usually visited Thrumpton on his bike every day.

A village cricket team played on Saturdays. There were also darts and skittles teams. The old cricket pitch had been used for 95 years before the new one was offered by Mr George Seymour in Thrumpton Park.

In the winter of 1946/7 the village was snowbound. Every road had drifts up to six feet high. The milk had to be taken from the farms with two horses going alternately on road and field. The postwoman went across the fields on skis to Barton for letters. Eight days after the fall the first milk lorry was able to come on the main road from Clifton. Two men from

37

Army 'ducks' delivering supplies along the main road in Wilford on 18th March 1947.

Gotham walked over the hill with bread for the village. There were floods when the snow melted and Barton in Fabis was awash. People were rowing in boats through the streets.'

SNOW AND FLOOD

'In 1945 floods came into our house at Wilford, leaving behind filthy slime on floors and skirting boards apart from damage to furniture, the piano taking most of the damage, being far too heavy to move. However, the water drained away quite quickly on that occasion and Kent and Cooper fetched the piano for drying out and repairs.

And then the "fun" started. Saturday morning after Saturday morning I queued at the Central Market for wallpaper, but always when I reached the front of the queue the allocation had been sold, this went on for weeks. However, patience is rewarded and I eventually became lucky and very thrilled rushed home with my purchase – some dark brown wallpaper. It was horrible, but as my mother said, "At least it will be clean".

Well – in 1947 we had the floods again and much worse this time. We lived upstairs for five days, having one delivery of bread and milk through a bedroom window. For a treat we opened a bottle of strawberries, no treat at all because we did not bottle in syrup owing to sugar being rationed – they were almost as awful as the wallpaper. Talking of which, one good thing about the 1947 flood was the demise of the 1945 purchase of wall covering!

On the Friday evening my brother in law rescued us in the garage breakdown vehicle. I don't think I've ever enjoyed a hot meal as much as the one served by my sister on that occasion.

As compensation we were given some disinfectant, horrible scrubbing soap and a "Utility" blanket!'

'After weeks of heavy snow during January and February, on St Patrick's Day, 17th March 1947 a thaw developed overnight. We were living at 147 Ruddington Lane, Wilford in a house which had five steps to the ground floor level, and at 7 am on the Monday morning I could see the level of the river Trent from the bedroom window. The news was threatening and by 9 am water was in the greenhouse and in the hollows of the garden.

We prepared to move furniture as high as possible and to get food and fuel upstairs. We tore up and down the stairs. The two elder children aged seven and two helped, and Elizabeth was then a two week old baby. She was the first of our children to have been born at home. I'd had a wonderful midwife who had attended us through blizzards and snowdrifts from Ruddington, but now we faced floods.

By midday the water was in the houses on our lane and flowing as the river between the houses. The river Trent was now covering acres of farmland and gardens in Wilford, West Bridgford and lower lying land in Nottingham. Water in the Midland station meant that the tracks had to be raised so the trains could run. Some houses had a few inches, others were feet deep. On Wilford Lane the flood came halfway up windows, and some cottages had to be evacuated from bedroom windows by army "ducks".

We had bread and milk delivered by boat. We had to cook on a bedroom fireplace and keep the children warm, and to resort to candles when water rose above the electricity box for two days. We could speak to our neighbours because we had bay windows. One night, the son of a neighbour lower down the lane came home on leave, and had to swim up the path to his home. Not the usual method.

We had a greenhouse and had had a ton of steel coke delivered, most of which was washed away. Poultry was kept in a pen and my husband put boards across the pen with bales of straw and as much food as we had, and when he was able to get to them again they were very hungry, and he was able to take them a loaf to keep them alive. We had lost one, it must have fallen into the water. We calculated water depths of four feet six inches on the ground level of the garden. It was very worrying and not at all a normal life, with limited hot water and food. We could not wash many clothes, just look after the baby and the other two children.

Downstairs we had moved all we could above water level. We had a heavy oak table with a sideboard on top fastened to the window catches, the piano up on planks and bricks and the piano stool with an easy chair propped on top. Strangely the piano stool legs were perfect after its ill treatment, the piano suffered around the base but was otherwise unharmed. Fitted carpets were not the vogue so carpet squares could be rolled up and put as high as possible.

People who had pets had a difficult time. One neighbour had ducks and they were kept in the bath.

Fortunately for this area the Ladybower dam held, otherwise it would have been much more serious as the depth of snow in Derbyshire created even more havoc. "England awash" was a newspaper headline. Friends of ours in Germany at the time gave generously to flood appeals, and many Commonwealth countries sent tinned foods, soap, disinfectants and blankets. Some people even had new carpets, which we were allotted as soon as we were able to get out again and get to the church hall to collect these various rations. But it was hard work cleaning, scrubbing and disinfecting with windows wide open to dry properties out. Gardens were wrecked.

My family and I went to live at Mapperley with my sister whilst the house became dryer. It rained constantly even then, but we did the best we could.'

40

'In late 1946 we moved to a brand new council house that had big rooms, three bedrooms, running hot water, a bathroom and electric lighting. It was a very hard winter with low temperatures and snow – a real old-fashioned winter – but came the thaw and the river Trent flooded all the Beeston Rylands.

Mam and Dad and us three children lived upstairs for a few days with the council making deliveries of milk and emergency food by rowing boat, but after a few days the Beeston and Stapleford Urban District Council took my sister and me by rowboat out of the house to a rescue centre in Beeston and then we went on to stay with an aunt. My baby brother stayed in the flooded house with my parents. To us it was an exciting adventure!

A few weeks after an emergency nationwide appeal, money and goods were donated for flood victims. My sister and I each received a pair of shoes.'

'The severe winter of 1946/7 stands out in the memory of most people who went through it. My husband, who lived at Papplewick water works, talks about not being able to get to school for six weeks, milk and groceries being fetched on a four to five mile round trip by sledge, the baker bringing by tractor flour and yeast instead of bread and, after the main Mansfield road had been opened to traffic, of drifts at the side of the road higher than a double decker bus. However, we lived in The Meadows area of the city and the snow I can only recall as heaps along the gutters. City life was soon functioning again.

What lives in my memory are the floods which followed as the thaw took hold. As the Trent started rising and the water reached those houses nearer the river, I was despatched to the grocer's to collect the weekly rations, Mum being occupied with my three month old brother while Dad made numerous trips upstairs with the contents of the coalhouse; luckily there was a fireplace in the larger bedroom. Necessities for daily life went upstairs first, followed by as much else as there was room for and time for, as the water rose rapidly, with all the drains overflowing first, then creeping into the house and up stair by stair. Dad was still able to get water from the tap downstairs by walking across from stairs to sink on two chairs;

41

basic cooking was done on the little fire and bread and emergency rations came by rowing boat down the centre of the terrace and were hauled up in a basket on a string.

I have no recall whatsoever about our sanitary arrangements, but Mum talks about the dreadful smell left behind when the water went, and a depot was opened nearby for people to obtain disinfectant. Dad's salvaged wartime stirrup pump was put to good use!'

'The floods in 1947 were the highest we can remember at Gunthorpe, but in spite of all the troubles there was always the funny side. Several people went by boat to take food to an isolated cottage where an elderly lady lived with her animals. All that could be seen were dogs, cats, pigs and chickens through the bedroom window.

Some local folk assured motorists they could get through on the main road, hoping they would get stuck so the village children could increase their pocket money. "Two and sixpence a time" for a push and if they needed the tractor's assistance, it would be five shillings.

To ease the traffic problem in flood time, the A6097 was later raised and this has meant that flood water to the west of the A6097 is now much deeper than previously.

At the Cedars they had water through the windows and as it receded, it was followed out with hosepipe, boiling water and Jeyes fluid. The smell lasted for weeks.'

CHURCH AND CHAPEL

Sundays were special, a break in the hardworking routine of the week. Church and chapel were important parts of village life and most people went to services on Sunday, while the children attended Sunday school. How well we remember those Sunday school outings – perhaps the only outings some of us ever got.

CENTRED ON THE CHURCH

'In the 1920s Sutton Bonington was a small rural village of two separate parishes, each with its own church and resident rector, as well as three chapels. Life in those days centred very much around the family and the church. Sunday was a very special day when people put on their "Sunday best" and kept the day for worship and for rest from the toil of the week. Special celebrations were enjoyed at the major festivals of Easter, Whitsuntide, Harvest and Christmas when holidays and tea parties were enjoyed, and the highlights of the chapel year were the Sunday school Anniversaries when all the children sat up on the platform in their new clothes to sing songs which they had been practising for weeks. This was followed by the Sunday school and choir outing, by train for the day to Matlock or Alton Towers, or maybe, if we were lucky, to the seaside at Skegness, Cleethorpes or Rhyl.'

LOVELY MEMORIES

'Sunday was a special day at Laxton when the family would attend church in the morning, the children returned for Sunday school at 2 pm and often went again for evensong with Gran at 6 pm. On Whit Sunday the girls were expected to have new dresses or "The crows would mess on yer". Hair was curled with the aid of rags, and teenagers used curling tongs heated in the embers of the stove.

There are many lovely memories, such as Harvest Festivals when children from the Sunday school went round collecting fruit and vegetables. The garden fetes (pronounced "feets") were fun, where there was bowling for a live pig, a magic lantern show, and wooden swingboats for the children. There was the Sunday school outing each year which was nearly always to "Skeggy" (Skegness).'

RESPECTED

'The church was the mainstay of Trowell village and Lord Middleton and the Squire had their own pews. They and the rector had to be called "Sir" and were respected by the villagers. All the children went to church on Sunday morning and to Sunday school in the afternoon. The highlight of the year was the Sunday school outing to Skegness on the train. We were a very close community, everyone knew and helped everyone else. Soup was always taken to anyone who was ill.'

MOST WENT TO CHAPEL

'Most people at Hayton went to chapel as there had been no vicar there for a number of years when we came in 1930. We children mostly went three times each Sunday. Lay preachers came from other villages for morning and evening services. Prayer meetings and "cottage meetings" were held at people's houses during the week. About Whitsuntide each year the chapel Anniversary was held. The children would learn poems and hymns and sing on the stage at Hayton chapel, which would be packed with people. On the Monday we would go round on drays drawn by horses, the organ would be roped on, and seats for all the children, and we would sing at every house through Hayton, Clarborough and Welham and collect money for the chapel. We then had tea in Mr Beard's barn, which is still there today.

When Mr and Mrs Wardle came to Hayton to live in the vicarage some of us went to church. We always had the chapel trip to the seaside, when the buses were packed with stools down the aisle. Many people were ill on the bus as they weren't used to travelling so far. The church also came to have an annual trip. We usually went to Skegness, Mablethorpe or Cleethorpes.'

SIGNING THE PLEDGE

'We went to Sunday school at Sturton le Steeple. There were two chapels, one in North Street which was for Sunday school and the big chapel on the main road. We joined the Rechabites, which was a sort of club. I find in the dictionary they were descendants of Jonadab, son of Rechab who abstained from wine by vow, which is exactly what we did. We signed the "pledge" to say we would never touch a drop of alcohol. I shouldn't think many of us kept the vow.

There was also the Band of Hope, and a festival was held at Wiseton Hall each year. People went on horse-drawn drays from Sturton to Wiseton, travelling through Wheatley and up Awkward Hill to Clayworth and on to Wiseton. They had to get off and walk up the steep hill so the horses could get to the top.'

HAPPY TIMES

'The first Sunday after we arrived in Rainworth, the little girl next door, who was four years older than me, came and knocked on the door and asked if I would like to go to Sunday school with her. That was the start of a very long and happy time for me. Just about three weeks after I started it was the Sunday school Anniversary. There were two platforms, one for the primary children and one for the Sunday school – and these were both full. There was also the chapel choir who helped with the singing. We loved the singing, and those who could sang solos and recited poems. It was our way of raising money for the Sunday school attendance prizes. The chapel was always full of parents and grandparents.

We enjoyed our Sunday school classes. At the beginning of the war a family came to Rainworth from London who began the tradition that those children who wished could enter a Scripture examination. The preparation work was done on a Sunday and Mr Barnes, who started this, devised a "Coronation Ceremony". We used to have a concert for the first half of

Dressed up for Anniversary Sunday in 1934, three little girls at Wells Farm, Sturton le Steeple.

the programme, and for the second half, those who had taken part in the Scripture examination gathered to crown the Sunday school queen. This was usually the girl who had the highest marks in the examination. The other children acted as buglers, courtiers, ladies in waiting etc. They were super nights and one which I am sure we all remember.

For our Sunday school outings we used to go in the cleaned out coal delivery lorry to a local farm and have a picnic in the open barn and then games. It was a super day out. When we started having outings to the seaside, we thought we were in seventh heaven, as very few of us in those days used to have a seaside holiday.

We did a lot of things together from the Sunday school, and as we had a double tennis court at the back we had the opportunity to learn to play tennis, although some of us were not very good.

Our Sunday school teachers put in a lot of hard work with the children but I am sure they felt that their efforts were well worth while.'

SUNDAY SCHOOL ANNIVERSARY

'I remember the Sunday school Anniversaries at North Muskham Methodist chapel. Of course they are still held but are not quite "the day of the year" as they once were. We spent weeks learning special hymns and every child had to present a recitation, though some were inaudible to the congregation. The great day was quite a little fashion parade for the girls who just had to have a new dress and hat. In the schoolroom before the service, we girls were surreptitiously eyeing each other up and down, hoping our own dress and straw hat with daisies round were prettier (or posher) than anyone else's.

On the Monday afternoon after the Sunday services, a farmer brought his two horses with a waggon and a flat cart. All the smaller children were packed into the waggon and forms and the harmonium were hoisted onto the cart for the older children along with the organist. We then toured round all the houses in North and South Muskham, singing the Anniversary hymns and collecting. The poor lady organist got jolted and missed a few notes each time the cart stopped and started. I've often thought what hard work it must have been for the horses – stopping and starting every few yards. Back at the chapel, we were treated to a scrumptious tea with potted meat sandwiches and slab cake followed by sports in the field.'

'Methodist Sunday school Anniversaries were very special at East Markham. For girls it was the excuse for a new dress. Poems and hymns were learned and the Sunday afternoon service was given by the children. There was a special service in the evening and on Monday there was a tea served in the Sunday school (seed cake a speciality). Afterwards games were played in a nearby field and sweets handed out.'

CHURCH AND CHAPEL

'Woodborough in the early part of the century was a divided village between church and chapel. The schoolchildren had to sit separately and it was unheard of for a church person to marry a chapel person. Even in death they were divided and to this day there is a church side and a chapel side in the cemetery.

The Sunday school outings every year to Nottingham Arboretum were looked forward to for months. Passengers were taken on the carrier's cart, and on one occasion a village "wag" shouted as they went by to say that Sally Cheetham was coming from Derby Arboretum to Nottingham Arboretum to treat 'em! One lad hung about the entrance all day in case he missed her!'

SUNDAY SCHOOL OUTINGS

'I remember going to Sunday school in Daybrook in the huts near St Paul's church on Church Crescent. The church hall was not available during the war as it had been taken over as a "gas cleansing station". We had to take our gas masks with us everywhere we went but fortunately there were no gas attacks from the air. Our superintendent was dear Miss Beattie Barrow who also produced the Sunday school plays and concerts, which she was still doing years later when my children took part in them. Sunday school outings were usually to Sherwood Lodge where we enjoyed games, races and a big tea. We also joined in the Arnold Whit Walk of all the churches in the area with decorated floats and bands.'

'Sunday school outings in the 1920s from Southwell were to Hazelford Ferry (fancy taking small children near that water) and to Edwinstowe. We travelled in a charabanc and made paper streamers to hang out of the window.'

'The chapel at Gunthorpe is now closed but when I was a little girl in the 1920s I attended Sunday school there. On one or two occasions we went over the old toll bridge in a horse-drawn vehicle to villages in the Vale of Belvoir for our annual outing.'

'For as long as I can recall there has been a church, a Methodist chapel and a Baptist chapel in Ruddington. At one time there was a Wesleyan chapel, but Methodists and Wesleyans joined forces. My father had been a member of the Wesleyans but he changed his loyalties and went to the church where for years he was a chorister.

Sunday schools at each of the establishments were well attended. We had outings with picnics to places like Woodhouse Eaves in Leicestershire and went on the train, which was always popular. Prizes were given for good behaviour and attendance.

Families mostly went for walks together on Sundays as there was little else to do, but it was nice to go with Mum and Dad on a Sunday after church in the summer.'

'We went to the top chapel at Lowdham. They had lovely concerts there and it was full to capacity. On our Sunday school outing we would go to Carby's Mill (Lowdham mill) and Mr Carby would let the children ride on the dray. If it was fine we had tea under the trees and if not it would be back in the schoolroom.'

'Our Sunday school trips from Tresswell were to Skegness or Cleethorpes. We had to get to either Cottam or Leverton railway stations. Young ones sometimes got a lift, older ones had to walk. We used to get a few coppers spending money and we took sandwiches and ate them on the sands, then after a tiring day we had to walk home again from the station, which was two miles.'

GETTING ABOUT

We walked nearly everywhere, or used horse-drawn transport, in the days before the motor car. The first country buses were very popular and opened up new worlds to us, as did the steam trains, such a fond memory for many of us.

THEY HAD TO WALK

'The only time the children from Ranby went to Retford was when they needed new boots and then they had to walk.'

TRANSPORT WAS DIFFICULT

'Transport was difficult in the 1920s. A daily bus (Lewis's) left Gamston at 10 am and returned at 9 pm. Farmers used a pony and trap for visiting. On market days a larger cart known as a float was used to take pigs, calves and chickens to Nottingham cattle market. The animals were covered with a strong rope net so they could not escape. Market day (Saturday) was the farmers' day out.

There was also a carrier's cart. A man from Tollerton would deliver any item bought in Nottingham to our homes.

I remember the telegraph boys, with their navy suits and pillbox hats with chin straps, as they rode around the villages on special red bikes delivering telegrams and messages.'

50

THE FIRST AND LAST

'The first train ran from Edwinstowe to Mansfield on 20th March 1899. The line from Nottingham Victoria (Mansfield, Edwinstowe, Ollerton) saw its last train on New Year's Day 1956, ending 40 years of passenger service from county town to village.'

A SPARK FROM THE ENGINE

'My village was in a mining/agricultural area and there was also some industry connected with the coal mining, a tar works and also a gasworks supplying gas to Nottingham city, a distance of twelve miles by pipeline. Several fires raged at the tar works and these were usually started by a spark from a passing engine pulling a train.

I went to business college on the train and we were often locked in the compartment and on arrival in Mansfield duly unlocked.'

DANGER – POND!

'We so often arrange to meet the bus for outings at Pond Corner, East Markham, yet strangely there is no sign of a pond. Many newcomers to the village wonder why this site is so called.

A newspaper cutting of February 1922 states: "Work has begun on filling in the pond at East Markham. There are few of these old ponds left by the roadside and this one at East Markham has always been a picturesque feature of the village as well as a definite point in direction as to where a sharp turn in the Lincoln road occurs. In the old days of horse traffic there was no source of danger from this turn, and the pond served as a useful watering place. But other times, other manners: England must be made a fit place for motorists to scorch in, and recently some impetuous cyclists and chauffeurs have run into the pond." So the pond had to go!

However, the loss of the pond was to be compensated for by the provision of a drinking trough which the vet said was better for the cattle. The residents disagreed and said they preferred to see the ducks swimming and the cows cooling their legs in the water. They also commented that it was pathetic to see the village boys taking their final slide on the half filled pond where in every hard frost for generations the children of the village had found their piece of ice for winter sports.

The pond was completely filled in in 1941 but not before several despatch riders, through taking the corner too quickly, were plunged head first into it in the early days of the war.'

EARLY DAYS

'In the early days at Welbeck Colliery before buses, horse and cart and pony and trap were used to get people around. Before the village school was built children would walk to Warsop (only a lane in those days). They would take their lunch and walk back home again in the afternoon.

The first buses were used to transport miners to the colliery. Some men came by train stopping at Paddy station. The small platform is still there. It was also used when the annual trip to the seaside was run by the Druids Insurance Company, then the Miners' Welfare. The first bus fares were Mansfield return sixpence, to Warsop twopence. The hourly service was run first by Baker Bros then Beven and Banker who kept running whatever the weather. In fog the conductor would walk in front and my, how they filled their buses. We were like sardines in a tin sometimes during the day but they'd never leave anyone behind. They knew how many used the bus to get to work in the mornings and would wait around for a while if someone was late.'

'Buses would visit most villages on market days to transport not only passengers but poultry. Ducks, geese and chickens would be taken in crates on top of the bus and even a litter of pigs was penned in the back seats.

Transport between the villages was mainly on foot or by bicycle. In winter the bicycle lights were either carbide or paraffin, later followed by battery ones, then dynamos.'

THE FIRST BUS

'The first buses I remember at Hayton in the 1930s were the Silver Queen and Ne plus ultra, and of course George Hird's bus which took the market ladies with their baskets on Saturday to Retford. The buses would be packed with young people going to the pictures on Saturdays. The railway bus ran between Gainsborough and Retford, through Sturton, Wheatley and Clarborough and the fares would be a penny, twopence or threepence, but you could get a threepenny workmen's return ticket on weekdays.'

BUSES, MOTORS AND TRAINS

'Green Lincolnshire buses came through East Markham on the Retford to Laxton route in the 1930s. One of them intrigued me. There was a round hole cut out of the driver's side window to enable him to put his arm through and give hand signals. I used to wonder why the hole didn't allow rain to come in. Our local bus was a small blue Bedford owned by Mr Gilbert which went to Retford on Saturdays, on Wednesdays to Newark for the market and on another day to Lincoln.

Jack, the Retford Co-op butcher, drove his van around the village twice weekly. The Co-op milkman delivered bottled milk and had hot competition from Mr Brunt, who brought his milk round in churns carried in his Austin car and poured it from his measure into customers' jugs. Harry Start had a large newspaper round, and he would cycle to other villages too.

There were two threshing contractors in the village. The traction engines towing the threshing gear and elevator and sundry trailers made an impressive sight and I always marvelled at the driver's skill in negotiating some of the very difficult farm entrances. They always managed to drive through first time – but lots of us boys stood and watched, just in case!

The Co-op delivered milk to the school in a very old-fashioned looking Morris commercial van (even in 1939 it looked old-fashioned), but sometimes the driver gave us a treat even though we badgered him every day. He would make the engine backfire! What a fantastic bang and it never seemed to harm the engine.

A full load at Edwinstowe. The cover at the back could be pulled over if it rained.

The local builder, Mr Brett's transport was a 1938 Hillman Minx car. The interior was a strange grey colour from the countless bags of cement which were carried in it.

Like most things, bicycles were very scarce during the war and they were all black – very sombre and not much sought after. When Cliff College trekkers came to evangelise the village their cycles bore religious slogans painted on the steel sheet which fitted in the open part of the cycle frame.

In 1938 the *Silver Link* train hurtled through East Markham on its daily run from London to Newcastle. The cinderpath ran alongside the railway line and as a special treat I was sometimes taken to the edge of the village to see the beautiful streamlined silver train streaking past. Other famous engines like the *Flying Scotsman* also came past, but even though they were worth seeing they didn't have the same magic as the *Silver Link.'*

BEFORE TIMETABLES

'The first bus in Ruddington was an old army lorry bought by returning First World War soldiers Jack and Arthur Bullivant. It was most uncomfortable with bench seats down the sides but it was so popular they soon bought two proper buses and ran between Ruddington and Nottingham without any proper timetable. They also started trips to the Dukeries and other scenic places.

Soon others saw the potential of bus travel and a Gotham firm, the Ideal Bus Company, moved in followed by a Ruddington firm, Squires, who were also carriers of goods and parcels.

Then a farcical situation developed where all three buses left the church (the start of the journey) together and the first one could see passengers waiting at the first two stops so he judged which stop was the more lucrative and if the second stop had more people waiting he ignored the first stop in favour of the second. The two buses behind, not wanting to miss out on what could be a good third stop, also missed out the first one and this situation carried on all the way to Nottingham leaving many frustrated passengers in its wake.

Eventually timetables were introduced and companies were taken over until just before the Second World War only one company, Barton's, was left.'

TRANSPORT AT RANBY

'Mom had never learned to ride a bike, but decided it could be a real help to get into town when the need arose; so she learned – with much laughter, tears and hard work, especially on Dad's part, holding her up to get her balance. At last she could get on the bike and ride but not get off, she just fell off. At that time we were friendly with the horseman and his wife at Bilby and cycled over every Sunday for tea. When Mr Morris saw us coming he would run out and put the cattle pole across the lane and Mom had to brake hard and of course fell off. With much laughter he had to help her to her feet. I wonder who enjoyed it most?

About this time too Ancliffe's of Blyth started to run a bus from Blyth to Retford via Ranby on a Saturday morning. You just went out and stood at the gate, and when you saw it coming, stepped out into the road and it pulled up for you to board. It had two long seats from front to back, so sitting facing one another it was ideal for a good gossip on the journey. The buses, carrier carts and waggons parked in a long row in front of the town hall, in the Market Square. The carrier's horses were taken and stabled at the nearby hotels and inns. When cycling into town you could have the bike "stabled" too, for the princely sum of twopence a day. When your basket or bag was filled with shopping you returned to the bus and put it under the seat and went off again, and when tired and shopping done, went back to the bus and sat to wait until everyone returned, and then off home.

Of course other bus companies were formed to set up in opposition to one another. At one time we had four buses an hour through the village. I think the Silver Queen was the first to start, followed by the Blue Bus and Pioneer. The Railway Bus from Sheffield to Gainsborough did a brisk trade, especially at the weekends when the anglers took advantage of the easier travel to come into the country for a day's sport and fresh air. Previously they had come by train but it was a long walk from Chequer House station to the canal.

To the cottagers along the canal bank these anglers were a big asset, there were so many of them sitting only a yard or two apart. The children were sent out on to the bank to ask, "Any tea mashing, mester?" The angler then gave the child a twist of newspaper containing a mixture of tea and sugar which was taken home for Mom to put into a jug or milk can and boiling water poured in, with milk added and an old cup or mug supplied, which the child then took back to the angler who paid twopence for the service, returning the can later. This meant a lot, probably amounting to two or three shillings on a good day which was a great help when the husband was perhaps only receiving 25 or 30 shillings a week for his wage.

The one big thing that annoyed the angler was the interruptions caused by the boat traffic. It was quite a busy canal for barges. The chief cargoes were corn and coal. It looked a peaceful life, the slow progress through the water, the bargee or his wife at the tiller and the horse straining at the end of the

Cars were still few and far between when this snap was taken at Sturton le Steeple in 1929.

tow rope, head down, plod, plod, plod. They looked sometimes as if they were asleep – unless the rope broke. The sudden stop, with surprise at the strain having gone, with the new life and the feel of freedom, a jump, a gallop and then a fast trot – everything getting out of the way, we kids included, backing into the hedge or to the top rung of a fence to see better. The bargee would be trying to get the boat to the side to get his bike off and ride off after the horse as fast as he could. This did not happen very often, but was exciting when it did. There was a bike on nearly every barge, carried on top of the tarpaulin over the cargo. This enabled the boatman to hurry on ahead to the lock gates when they had a deadline to meet on the cargo's delivery. I expect it was a help too to get to the nearest pub when he had tied up for the night along the bank.

The canal bank made a good playground for us too, bird nesting, tadpoling and fishing. We were threatened what would happen if we played there and fell in – either we were drowned or had a good hiding, so we just had to learn not to, or how to get out quickly. I think we all fell in at some time, but there was always someone else there to help us to get out.

Mr Baines was an employer in the village with his threshing machines. These were huge steam engines and threshing drums which travelled from farm to farm, belching steam and black smoke. He had purchased a piece of land between the canal and road, the other side of the playground wall. The old headmistress grumbled as it would spoil the school view. We did not think so, and would rush to the wall, leaning over it, to watch them lumbering down the canal bridge to enter the gate into their yard. We could not believe that the brakes, or whatever stopped them, would hold when they reached the gate, but the driver always kept in control, turning the wheel round and round and getting it backed up in position in the shed. We loved them when they were in the farmyards. It was a hive of activity, threshing corn, all hands were occupied, jerking the sheaves onto the drum, the drum itself clatter-banging away, sorting out the grain, chaff and straw into the sacks attached to it, and others jerking the straw into a new stack. The men swinging up the full bags of grain on to their backs and carrying them up to the granary. The boys and dogs waiting to chase the rats and mice escaping from the stack. The men had binder twine tied round their trousers below the knee to stop the mice running right up. Thomas the Tank Engine would not stand a chance against Charlie Baines' Threshing Tackle.'

HOUSE & HOME

THE HOUSES WE LIVED IN

From farm cottages to terraced houses, our homes were colder and darker in the days before 'mod cons', but we look back with affection to the coal fires and the oil lamps of just a few decades ago.

WE WEREN'T WELL OFF

'As a small child at Oldcotes one of my vivid memories is of sitting in front of a large coal fire with the flames making all sorts of patterns and shapes. We had no electricity in those days and Mum saved on the gas as much as possible but we didn't complain because Dad would tell us stories of his childhood.

Each house proudly owned a beautiful black polished fireplace – such a fireplace was the pride and joy of any house. A box-like tank was on the side of the fire which was the only means of getting hot water. On top of the box was a hole with a hinged top flap and you could ladle the amount of hot water needed. On bath night a tin bath would be placed in front of the fire on a pegged rug – one lot of water bathed many bodies. As kids we were then sent off to bed with a fire brick wrapped in a piece of blanket on which to warm our feet.

There was no such thing as television and only in the late 1920s was radio around. Although radios were considered portable they were about 76 inches at the base and about two feet high. Families were well off if they owned a gramophone; these were spring wound with a large horn and sixpence was the average price of a record. During the long winter nights we would play at games such as dominoes, cards, draughts etc.

Water toilets were still a luxury. Our toilet was outside and earthen with a wooden top over a box with an open back for emptying. The buckets often overflowed. In many cases two or three people could sit side by side over the same box.

Our floors downstairs were made of tiles and concrete and

covered by linoleum – well worn in parts – and pegged rugs on top. These pegged rugs were made of cut up pieces of any material and pegged by the whole of the family sat round a piece of sacking. The finished results were warm to the feet, but awful dirt holders.

Our beds were made of feathers and lovely and warm to snuggle into. Some had mattresses of flocks and some had palliases.

My grandfather was a joiner and undertaker and he made our table, chairs and sideboard. I can remember when visiting their house going to his yard and work place and seeing coffins, large and small, lined up against the wall. Also I sometimes went with him to collect money owing to him for funerals. People were paying him threepence and sixpence a week until it was paid off.

There were not many tarmac roads around and the main purpose of the old steam roller (which we loved to follow) was to keep the roads in decent order and free from potholes.

Our milkman would come round every morning and deliver milk straight from the churn. Also the lamplighter would come round every evening lighting the gas lights and early again the next morning to put them out.

With only a little money in their purses, housewives had to be careful shoppers. Clothes were handed down from family to family and from child to child.

We had tinned foods only on special occasions. One of the most popular shops was the pawnbroker's which used to loan you money on the goods you took in and then when you could afford it you bought them back, which wasn't very often. Lots of our food came off the land, rabbits, hares, pheasants, partridge which were caught by poachers who then sold them cheap.

Saxon's carrier's cart would pick up passengers at Oldcotes on its way from Worksop to Tickhill; this was later followed by petrol buses. The drivers would also collect groceries and medicinal goods for people of the outlying villages and deliver them to the nearest point.

There was no National Health Service in those days and it was well known that people died because they could not afford to pay for a doctor or medication.

One of the highlights of the week was Mr Metcalf's travelling shop, pulled by horses. He used to deliver paraffin and many more extras that could not be bought at the local shop.'

ON THE FARM

'I was the second child of a large family and my first memories in 1918 are of a large farmhouse kitchen with a whitewood table and an open range with side oven where all the cooking was done.

All meals were eaten there too, the floor was red bricks and only covered in front of the fireplace with a large pegged rug. We had a pantry off the kitchen with scrubbed shelves and a meat safe. This was just a cupboard with mesh sides and door to let in the air but to keep out flies. The butter churn was kept there and the large pancheons which held the milk until the cream was taken off for making the butter. We had one cow which was milked morning and evening and we had a pony and trap which was used to take us to Newark market. The farm belonged to my grandparents but my mother had gone home when my Dad was fighting in France. I was too young to remember the war but I remember the family grieved about Uncle Walter who was Dad's brother, killed just before the armistice.

On market days, any cattle or sheep which were sold had to be driven there by the men along the main road so everybody had fences and gates to their fields and gardens. The farmers went to the cattle market and did their business whilst the womenfolk, with the children, sat in the butter market and sold their butter, eggs and fruit in season. I was told I went as a baby in the clothes basket.

We moved to a similar house, still on a farm, when Dad came home. We had to walk a long way to school and back in the afternoon. We took sandwiches and if we had a drink it would be water.

There were no taps in the houses. There was a pump in the yard and barrels which caught the rainwater from the roof. We had a zinc bath which hung in the washhouse and was brought in front of the kitchen fire on Saturdays and we took turns. The girls had their hair done in curling rags then so we had ringlets on Sundays. We always went to Sunday school

A family group outside their terraced house in Worksop during the First World War.

but weren't allowed to play on Sundays or read any book or paper except the Bible. Grandma was very religious.'

IN A TERRACED HOUSE

'When I was a child we lived in a terraced house in Worksop, with two bedrooms and an attic. There was a living room and a front room (which was used only on Sundays and special days), and we also had an extension which was used as a kitchen. We had a tin bath that was brought in and used in front of the fire. The water was heated in the copper in the washhouse. My mother always washed on a Tuesday – it was a communal washhouse for four houses, so two washed on Monday and two on Tuesday. We also had an outside toilet which was shared with another family.

My mother made her own wine, such as rhubarb, elderberry, or parsnip, and also made nettle beer. We used to go along the hedgerows collecting the ingredients. She made bread three times a week. Some of the neighbours kept pigs and I remember going to see one killed, they just slit its throat, it was horrible and I never went again.'

NO HEAT

'Washday every Monday, copper lit at 5.30 am for boiling sheets and whites. Dinner always bubble and squeak, cold joint and rice pud! Washing not finished until 3pm. The scullery cleaned up. Tuesdays and Fridays baking days. Dough put to rise in large bowl in hearth. Ironing Tuesday night, irons standing on trivet in front of fire. A quick spit on them to see if hot enough! Range blackleaded twice a week and tongs and poker etc cleaned with steel wool. No electricity yet. Two gas mantles either side of fireplace above high mantel. Toilet down the yard, candle needed to light the way. Bath night Friday. Big tub in front of fire until one grew bigger then relegated to long zinc bath in scullery. No heat.

The fishman with horse and trap came about once a fortnight. Then bloaters for tea. The pikelet man came about once a fortnight. The Co-op baker had a cart horse and covered dray, and funerals were horse-drawn. Beautiful black horses and a black and silver coach for the coffin. Milk came by pony and trap in big milk churns. We took our jugs and the milkman used half pint and pint tin measures to pour the milk into our jugs. Sometimes he put in an extra drop for me!

Kidney beans from the allotment were sliced and salted down in stone jars. In the summer elderflower drink was bottled. Old overcoats and winter dresses were cut into small strips, a piece of sacking was then pegged with them to make a hearth rug. The only warm spot on the lino! Chimney swept twice a year, everything moved. Furniture beeswaxed, curtains changed. At bedtime the oven shelf from the oven at the side of the fire was wrapped in layers of brown paper to warm the bed, which was iron with brass knobs! At the sign of a cold the chest was rubbed with camphorated oil and a dose of sweet nitre (horrible) was put in a cup of hot water to sweat it out.

My father was brought up on a farm. He remembered fetching water from the stream by yoke and his mother having a bread oven outside which she heated by putting a fire inside for a whole day and then raking it out to put in pies etc. They had oil lamps and he walked over three fields to the village school. He took a potato to put on the iron stove to cook for his dinner.

Then came electricity. No more gas mantles popping and we could go upstairs without a candle. Life was good. Our parents worked hard for small wages but we were fed and clothed and had loving homes. Then – war. Sharing school with London evacuees. Air raid warnings – ration books. Seeing the devastation of bombs and the list of dead posted upon the town hall notice board. So many sad memories of schoolboy friends first and then boyfriends killed. So young to die. So long ago and yet it seems only yesterday at times.'

THE LUXURY OF GAS

'My mother's family moved to a new bungalow in 1911 outside the village near the farm where her father worked. At the time there was neither gas nor electricity in Ruddington. In the bungalow there was cold water on tap and a brick copper for boiling bath and washing water. Lighting was by candle or paraffin lamp and cooking was done either on the fire or in the side oven. Her father would light the fire when he got up to tend to the horses and on his return he cooked the breakfast bacon in the now hot oven.

In 1924 the family moved back into the village, where they discovered the luxury of gas, which had been laid on. My mother's younger sister, who was still at school, had been taught how to use gas so for a time she took over the cooking until their mother became more confident.'

THE GOOD OLD DAYS?

'You have heard of the so-called "good old days". Well, it was not so comfortable like it is today, I must say.

Our Mam was always up early blackleading the hob grate before lighting the fire and filling the side boiler for our only supply of hot water. We children got out of bed onto cold lino, downstairs to the scullery for a quick splash, and hastily dressed in front of the fire.

When it was Monday washing day (regardless of the

weather) Mam filled the copper in the scullery and lit the fire underneath. The mangle was outside in the backyard. Mam was only five feet tall; I don't know how she lugged all the wet washing outside to the mangle and turned the big wheel at the side. I do remember it was an all day job!

Dad was a milkman early morning and a farm labourer the rest of the day at Trent Vale Farm, Beeston Rylands, and when I was eight years old I started to help him deliver milk to the customers at 7 am before school. I was made of sterner stuff then! The milk was in churns and was measured into the customers' own jugs and cans: I had never seen a milk bottle.

Our house was terraced with gas mantle lighting, no bathroom, a scullery, and an outside lavatory. Friday night was bath time in the tin bath in front of the fire. Yes, we children shared!

Although a small house, the front room was kept for "best" – I only remember it being used for Christmas. During air raid warnings we sheltered in the "glory hole" which was a cupboard space underneath the stairs.

Dad had a small piece of ground on Grassy Lane on which he kept a very large pig called Bertha and it was my task every evening to take her for a walk up and down the lane, armed only with a stick for protection from her! When she produced a litter, Dad always registered with the Ministry of Food one less piglet than Bertha had produced; the unregistered piglets were our private supply of meat during wartime food rationing and swopped with neighbours for their new laid eggs. Animals were fed to produce fat meat in those days which absolutely nauseated me and I used to gag just looking at it. Dad was very strict and insisted that this horrible fat pork was served to me every meal until I had eaten it. Today, I am almost vegetarian.

No, it is not the "good old days" to me.'

OFFICIALLY OPENED

'I was born on Carsic Lane at Teversal, in a bungalow which belonged to North's farm. I remember the first house on the Carsic estate being built and officially opened by someone. We all traipsed round to have a look and the proud new owner

At Hayton vicarage in Rev Wardle's time, about 1937. Looking after such a large house was hard work and a maid was an essential member of the household.

spent most of her time telling us to keep our hands off the walls of her nice clean staircase!'

THE COAL FIRE

'Welbeck Colliery Village was the name of our village until about 1974; it was changed then to Meden Vale, taking the name from the river Meden which runs through it.

Our memories of home life were of the coal fire, as coal was a part of a miner's wage and was delivered once a month. It was tipped on the street and had to be brought around to the coalhouse on the yard by bucket or barrow and anyone willing to help, sometimes a man, would offer to get in the coal for a shilling – if you had a shilling to spare. On one side of the coal fire was the oven, on the other side a boiler to heat the water. This was filled and emptied by a ladle; there was a mantelpiece to stand photos etc and a fender. The fireplace itself was blackleaded, it really shone – the wife's pride and joy. All the cooking was done on this fireplace, and bread was made two or three times a week, a lovely smell to greet the children coming home from school. Cakes were all home-made. There was always a fireguard around the fire, this was also used to dry and air the washing.

On washday the water had to be heated in a coal-fire copper, which stood in the corner of the kitchen. The washing was done by hand with a rubbing board or posher. The copper was sometimes used to boil the puddings for Christmas. The first washing machine was worked by hand; ironing was done with a flat-iron, heated on the fire. In some houses the kitchen was called a scullery. In these there would be a dark coloured stone sink with one cold water tap and also a mangle with large wooden rollers.

Rugs for the floors were made out of all cast-off clothes, pegged through hessian. We loved to have a go at pegging when we were sat around the fire at night. One thing I remember though, those rugs collected a lot of dust. They had to be taken outside for a good shake – no vacuum cleaners then! Walpamur was used to decorate the walls during the Second World War, sometimes stippling was done with a sponge or hairbrush. Most beds had metal headboards and bottoms, the base of the beds had coil springs. Mattresses were either flock or feather filled. These needed a regular, good shake up to remove the lumps.

Our houses had no bathrooms but eventually a bath was installed in one corner of the kitchen. When the bath was not in use it was covered by a large board – the bath board we called it. One good point; it was lovely in the winter having a bath in the same room as the fireplace. The toilet was outside, on the backyard. In the winter all the pipes would get frozen up. Rents for the houses were parlour-type 12s 6d a week; non parlour-type 11s 6d.

People grew most vegetables themselves in their gardens, wine was made at home from elderberries, rabbits were plentiful for making stews and pies. The electricity we used in our home came direct from the pit where it was generated. If extra power were needed at the pit down would go our lights. Power cuts were a regular happening; the more lights we put on, the dimmer the light. We had gas street lighting down the main road to Warsop, none in the village.'

GREAT EXCITEMENT

'There was great excitement in our house in the 1920s when new wallpaper was chosen. There was only one book to look through, and we always had a border. White lime was used for the ceilings. I don't remember anything being cream.'

A COBBLED ROAD

'I lived as a child during the 1930s in a cobbled road at Trowell of 23 old houses. This was called "The Forge" as there was a working forge at the end of the road. We had a small kitchen with a stone sink – the taps for cold water were outside and we had no hot water but a copper that had to be lit and the water heated before clothes could be boiled. Washday was a full day's work with a tub and mangle. Clothes had to be dried inside on a wooden clothes horse on a bad day. We had a living room with a fire grate next to a hot water boiler. The fire had to be lit even on hot days whenever hot water was required – the grate had to be blackleaded every week! There was a parlour but this was only used for visitors. This was all very "proper" with a brown leather sofa and chairs and a wicker stand under the sash cord window – complete with aspidistra.

We had no bathroom or toilet inside. Water had to be boiled and the zinc bath brought out in front of the living room fire. The toilet, in a block of four down at the bottom of the yard, was an ashpit one that had to be emptied once a week and taken away by horse and cart.

We had one corner shop until the Co-op opened one about a quarter of a mile away. This was something entirely new – you could have an order of groceries and pay for them the next week! We soon got money back in the form of "divi" on our purchases. A milkman with his milk in a churn filled a jug for

A mischievous group outside 'The Forge' in Trowell in the 1930s.

us, a baker called and a greengrocer with his horse and cart. Butter was made in the farm kitchens. I remember tripe and onions was a favourite meal in those days.'

A FARM COTTAGE

'I was married in 1941 to a farmer's son. We lived in one of the cottages on the farm with two up, two down and a dairy. The living room had a blackleaded grate with an oven one side and a boiler for water the other. In the middle of the room was a well with a big concrete slab over it, and we always knew when it was raining as we could hear the water running into the well. The floor covering was pegged rugs, made mostly by my husband when he was sitting up all night at lambing time.

In 1947 my father in law retired and we moved into the farmhouse, where we had a bathroom and indoor toilet – but the water was provided by a mill and if the wind did not blow we had no water. We also had a generator to make electricity but it was only strong enough to provide lights. We did have a small iron but it never got very hot.'

SHOPS AND HOUSES

'Ruddington had a number of very presentable houses. In the Manor Park area, they were well built and most had gabled fronts, nice gardens and a private road.

A number of houses were three storey and there were a lot of cottages. One row, off the High Street were one up, one down with a very small kitchen at the back; toilets were also in the garden. The cottages were ten in number and known as 10 Chimney Row; large families were raised in this type of place.

The High Street was the hub of the village. The house I was born in was one of six, three each side of an entry. The first house was a secondhand goods shop (all these houses had a type of shop front). The next one was a post office which also sold sweets, biscuits and a little fruit and was open all hours! The next house was ours, my father was a ladies' costumier and worked there. The next had at some time been a butcher's shop but my memory of it was as a watch and clock repairer's, later it became a ladies' hairdressers, and the house next door

71

to this was a haberdashery and the husband went around with a pack-case. Finally the sixth house was a chemist's shop and still is.

The sitting rooms in the houses were on the first floor and the top floor was bedrooms; we had no bathroom. We managed with a swivel bath under the sink in the kitchen, this was pulled out on bath night and a copper with a large gas ring underneath supplied the hot water which was filled from a soft water pump. Off the kitchen was a larder with a cold slab in it. The room between the shop and the kitchen was the living room. The toilet was up the yard and was serviced by the nightsoil men. Woe betide if the washing line was left out, it was duly cut by them. Who could blame them!

Barclays Bank had the shop front of our house, one day a week at first, later two days. It is now open all week and the property belongs to them.'

WATER AND WASHDAY

We were careful with water when every drop had to be pumped up or carried in from a well or spring. No running water meant no indoor sanitation of course, and the little house at the bottom of the garden is a lasting memory! Washday was a real day's work then too, from the fetching of the gallons of water to the final mangling, drying and ironing. Were they really the good old days?

WASH AND BATH

'In 1920 my father took over Grange Farm (200 acres) in Gamston. The farmhouse was a large rambling place with no electricity or running water. We were lucky having a small iron pump beside the kitchen sink. All the cottagers had a pump on the village green and they carried water to their homes in buckets and bowls.

Monday was washday. We had a large kitchen with a little brick copper in the corner. Early in the morning the fire was lit and out would come the dolly tub and ponch. Mum would slave away all day – I really think that she enjoyed it. Sheets were boiled up in the copper and pillowcases and tablecloths starched with Robin starch and rinsed in dolly blue, a little bag of blue dye which was supposed to make everything look really white. Then the big heavy iron mangle would do its bit. As one of the children turned the handle Mum would guide the washing through. Then it was hung outside or on lines across the kitchen to dry. When the washing was dry it was neatly folded and put in a huge wicker basket ready for ironing.

Tuesday was ironing day. The flat irons were heated up on the fire. In those days we had a huge black iron range with a fire in the middle, an oven on one side and boiler on the other. The big black kettle was always boiling on the fire and by removing the iron plates on the hob we could cook in the large black iron pans. I don't remember a cooker until much later.

Friday was bath night. Dad would bring in the old tin bath. Water was ladled from the boiler and we children had our baths. No fancy smelling bath foam, just white Windsor soap. How we managed not to smell I will never know. I'm sure that our friends would have told us! Dressed in our long sleeved winceyette nighties we would drink our cocoa and so to bed. No electricity so we took a candle upstairs. The living room was the only room with gas lights, one on each side of the fireplace. I remember going to the village shop for inverted mantles for the lights.

On Saturday I could buy four little packets of sweets for a farthing each. That was my weekly penny gone.

Every house and cottage in Gamston had an outside toilet. It was awful in winter walking across the yard with a hurricane lamp. Snow, wind or rain, if you had to go you had to go! Our first inside toilet came in the late 1940s.

Furniture in those days was big and cumbersome. Large padded armchairs and horsehair sofas with a head rest. The kitchen table, a large wooden one which would seat ten or twelve, had to be scrubbed every week. Most of the floors were stone so a lot of lino was used and there were rag rugs and home-made pegged rugs. The kitchen floor was stone with coconut matting which was taken up on washday and when the washing was done the floor was scrubbed. There were no cleaners, everything was swept with brush and dustpan. Panshine was the main cleaning agent for sinks.'

PRIMING THE PUMP

'I lived at Sturton le Steeple in the 1920s, where we had a big garden with raspberry canes and gooseberry bushes. Of course the toilet was down the garden, as it was a midden and would be emptied by horse and cart. The water pump was in the middle of the garden and in the winter it had to be primed by pouring rainwater into it to melt the ice. In the summer the same would have to be done when the water was too low.'

NO NEED FOR DUSTBINS

'Water was not laid on at Woodborough until 1931. We had a pump outside the kitchen door and people from nearby cottages came and fetched buckets of water just for drinking and cooking every day. Rainwater was used for washing clothes.

We were very fortunate as we had a one-seater toilet down at the bottom of the garden, but most cottages had two-seaters, which they shared with next door, taking it in turns to scrub the big wooden seat once a week. These toilets drained into ashpits which were dug out and carted away periodically.

There was no need for dustbins as most rubbish was burnt on the coal fire and vegetable excess was fed to the pigs. Every cottage had a pigsty with one or two pigs.'

A REAL CHORE

'Washday was a real chore. It started at 7 am, first filling the copper and then lighting a fire under the copper to heat the water. A dolly tub and dolly legs were used plus a rubbing board. After, whites were boiled in a copper, then they were

74

Helping with the wash at Sturton le Steeple in the 1930s.

taken out, rinsed three times and then blued and starched. I remember my father's dirty overalls being soaked over the weekend before being washed on Mondays. We had to cross the yard to go to earth closets. We used oil lamps and candles until 1934 when electricity was installed.

Another Ranby resident can remember, as a child, having to fetch water from the canal for washday. Common soap and soda was used for washing the clothes, they were dollied, then scrubbed in a wooden tub. White clothes were boiled for 20 minutes and they went through several rinses before being mangled and hung out, or placed on a clothes drier in the house, overnight. All clothes were folded and then rolled, the rolling being done after starching and to make the ironing easier. The clothes were ironed with a flat iron which was heated in front of a glowing fire.

Furniture was scrubbed-topped tables. Mother had a rocking chair and father an armchair. All chairs were spindle backed and scrubbed.

Toilets were buckets which were emptied into a hole, dug in the garden. The bath was a tin bath which was hung from a hook outside and covered with sacking. All grates were black-leaded and at night either a brick was heated in the oven and then wrapped in a blanket and used as a hot water bottle or the oven shelf was wrapped in a towel or newspaper and again used to heat the bed. If you had a temperature the brick was wrapped in a blanket which had been soaked in vinegar and a cold cure was hot milk with suet. The water pump was a long way from the house and was shared between six houses and therefore they used mainly canal water. All coal was delivered by horse and cart and left in a heap by the gate, all the family co-operated in taking it in. Lighting was by oil lamps which had to be trimmed every day.'

WITHOUT FAIL

'Without fail, whatever the weather Monday was wash-day in my mother's house. I was born in the 1930s when a woman's place was still at home.

Early in the morning my mother would light the fire under the copper. This was situated in the washhouse at the top of

76

the yard. It was part of a row that contained the coal sheds and lavatories. While the water came up to boiling the clothes were ponched in the washtub and dirty bits rubbed on the washboard. They were then taken to be boiled in the copper.

Back in the house to be rinsed and "blued". They were then hung out to dry if fine, otherwise on the wooden clothes rack in the kitchen cum living room.

I remember Monday lunch, the remains of the weekend joint served cold with "pip and squeak" followed by rice pudding. When the water in the copper was cold it had to be emptied out. To this day I remember the silky feeling of the cold suds as I slid my fingers through them. This was a full day's work.

Now you just pop it into the automatic washer and get on with other things, or even sleep while the washing is done in the night.'

MIDDENS AND BATHS

'In the home there was always so much work to be done. Monday being washday the copper had to be lit very early for hot water. There were dolly tubs, scrubbing boards, starch and blue bags. I remember my Grandma drawing water from the well. One day a newt came up in the bucket, but it was quickly returned to "keep the water clean". Some at Laxton and New Ollerton recall having a pump in the kitchen. Flat irons were heated on the fire and spat upon to see if they were hot enough.

Then there was the blackleading of the stoves, usually on Fridays. The outside steps were "red raddled" (raddle meaning red ochre – sometimes used to mark sheep).

The toilets were outside, some in the village being earth closets one, two or even three side by side. The "midden men" came by night to empty them and they carried a lantern on a pole (the word midden meaning a dunghill or muckheap). In between the visits from the midden men, cinders were put down to cover the contents and help disintegrate them. Those who came from the colliery village remember that there were no pit baths so Dad came home in all his "muck". Turns were taken to wash Dad's back, but he only did his top half in the kitchen, his bottom half was always washed in privacy upstairs.

77

Baths for the family were taken on Friday night in a tin bath in front of the fire. Again the copper had to be lit to produce hot water. After all the children had been bathed they were lined up for some Scott's Emulsion or syrup of figs, whether they needed it or not. If any had a cough or cold goose grease was the answer. The farmers' wives plucked and dressed a goose and saved the grease and the feathers. With the aid of a feather the grease was applied liberally to the chest.

Feathers were also used to make feather beds which were warmed in winter with a shelf from the oven wrapped in a blanket.'

FOOD AND SHOPPING

Our diet may have been more limited in the past but we enjoyed home cooking and home-produced fruit and vegetables – and often, home-cured ham and bacon too. Killing the pig was a part of life and everything was used but the squeal, so they said. Small local shops catered for our everyday needs and traders called at the door with meat, bread, milk and much more.

PIGS, APPLES AND BREAD

'Gardens provided most of the fresh fruit and vegetables. Many people at Ranby kept poultry and my father kept the pigs, one to be killed at Christmas and the other about March. These provided sausage, brawn, home-made pork pies, bacon and ham. Fatty bacon was hung from hooks in the kitchen after being preserved in brine. One kitchen had 365 hooks in the ceiling. The meat was often covered with bluebottles and if it went maggoty that portion was cut off but the rest was still eaten. The houses had cellars underneath in which game, milk and eggs were stored. In the loft space was an apple chamber where the apples were stored on open shelves, the heat from the house keeping the area frost free. The apples were usually Bramleys, Newton Wonder and Russets and kept until well into the new year.

All bread was made at home because in the early years there were no local bakers. Milk was collected straight from the farm and in 1911 cost a penny a pint for skimmed milk; in the 1930s the cost had risen to threepence halfpenny with a large white loaf costing a penny more. Eggs were bought by the score and were carried in baskets, often looped over the bicycle handle-bars, so a sudden turn could result in the eggs being dropped!'

TWOPENCE A PINT

'My brother and I would fetch milk from the Fox and Hounds pub at Sturton le Steeple. Mrs Crookes would milk the cows wearing a man's flat cap back to front, to protect her hair from the cow's side. It cost twopence a pint.'

FOOD AND DRINK

'We grew most of our potatoes and vegetables. Also Dad slaughtered a pig now and again and cured his own bacon. We had what was known as a dairy, nothing to do with milk, with brick slabs around it and the bacon was laid on them and treated with saltpetre. After so long the hams were wrapped in muslin and hung from the ceiling.

All the baking was done in the range oven. Bread, cakes and even the weekly joint were cooked in this way. I am sure that they tasted much nicer than the cakes we buy today.

Our usual drinks were tea, cocoa and Ovaltine. Coffee was not thought of in our house until much later and then it was Camp coffee essence. We had lemonade and raspberryade from the village shop in bottles with a marble in the top.

Mother made a type of beer with Mason's Herb Extract which she put in a pancheon with yeast and liquid and left to ferment for two days. When it was ready we all gathered round for a sample before it was bottled. Most of it would be drunk by the men in the haymaking fields, very refreshing. We never had alcohol in the house until Christmas and then just a bottle each of port and sherry.'

FLOUR BY THE STONE

'We cooked with a kitchen range that had a side oven. Mother used to know just how much coal was needed for the right temperature. As most people did, she baked her own bread. I remember her buying flour by the stone from Rampton Co-op. When the weather was hot and we didn't have the fire alight she had a contraption of two primus stoves with a framework over and an oven over the top. I don't know how she did it but she could produce Sunday dinner for seven without much trouble.

One of my brothers worked at Popple's at Beck Farm and when cows calved we had a jug full of "beestings" (the first milk) and Mother made beestings custard.

Like most people who lived in the country we kept hens at the bottom of the garden. After the harvest we used to go gleaning the corn for the hens to eat. After the war we also kept pigs and we had a busy time "getting the pig out of the way". The job I disliked most was cleaning the sausage skins. We used to cut up the fat and render it down for lard and eat the scraps that were left. One of my jobs was taking the fries out to friends – they wouldn't wash the plate because that would have washed away the luck. I was always allowed to make myself a pork pie and these were taken to Rampton to cook in the bakery.'

'When I was twelve years old, on my way to school, I used to get my wheelbarrow and put some paper in the bottom and then put in the bread tins, each with two pounds of dough in. My Mam would tear off a bit of white paper and write her name on it, then push it in the dough and I took it to Baker Bros at the bottom of Moorgate in Retford to be baked. It cost a halfpenny per loaf. I collected the bread after school.

My mam made a stone of dough at a time, as there were seven of us. Sometimes Mr Baker would give us a bag of cakes that had been damaged, either tipped over a bit while baking

or a little burnt. He would charge us sixpence – we thought it
was a real bargain.'

ICE CREAM IN SEASON

'We lived in a house at Southwell in the 1920s, with a shop at
the front which sold groceries and sweets. In the summer I
would wake up in the early hours of the morning to hear my
mother making our own ice cream in the back garden. This
had to be churned for what seemed like hours, packed with
ice. The ice arrived periodically on a lorry and had to be kept
in a big hole in the garden. The ice cream was wonderful and
made with real strawberries when they were in season. It was
very popular and people travelled quite some distance to come
and buy it.'

'We had two ice cream makers at Welbeck Colliery, both
very good. A bell was rung to let us know when the horse and
cart was on the street, and it cost a halfpenny a cornet.
One lady in the village used to make dandelion and burdock
and nettle beer at home. When the kiddies took back the
empty bottles she would always give them a sweet.'

KILLING THE PIG

'Life could certainly be hard on the farm. When pigs were
killed they were laid on a cratch and a so-called humane killer
was used to shoot them between the eyes. After this the throat
was slit with a knife to release the blood, keeping the flesh
white. Boiling water was poured on and the hairs scratched off.
The pig was hung with the aid of a pulley and cambrel. Some
of the blood was caught to put into black puddings. The pig
would be killed on Saturday, cut up on Sunday and on
Monday it would be salted. There were pork pies to make as
well as sausages, pressed tongue, bacon, chitterlings and pork
scratchings. There would be a "fry on a plate" for a friend or
neighbour and "Don't wash the plate or you don't get more".
On Tuesday the big oven was made hot with "brashy sticks"
(hedge-cuttings tied into bundles). The heat of the oven was
tested with flour. When the pies were baked they were taken
out with long-handled forks. Lard could be kept from one year

to another. It was kept in the pig's bladder and would be rendered down.

Then there was wine making and so many varieties like may-blossom, dandelion, cowslip, parsnip, potato – both the latter being very strong, and wheat wine which resembled whisky.'

'When a pig was slaughtered at my grandparents' home, sides of bacon were salted and hung on the staircase walls and we walked upstairs between them to bed.'

FUN TO PUT THE PIG AWAY

'It was 1943, wartime and my father had died leaving my mother and six children aged from three years to eleven years. My father was a farmer and the only help on the farm were land girls so Mother had to sell up and the seven of us went to live with Gran and Grandpa at Sibthorpe. We took with us two cows, a calf which belonged to my brothers and a dog. Gran and Grandpa lived on a smallholding and the only animals they kept were pigs and chickens. As we had taken our own two cows we had a constant supply of fresh milk so Mother and Gran used to make butter. We all helped with the churning. It made your arms ache. Gran used to finish the butter, making pats with special tools.

Grandpa kept pigs but they were not like the ones we had on the farm. His were for eating whereas Sally, Sarah and Susan (yes, they had names) were kept for breeding. Twice a year Grandpa applied for a licence to slaughter a pig. The butcher came to the smallholding one day to kill the pig then it was hung up and the next day he came to cut it up. The sides and the hams were salted and placed on the stone shelf in the larder where they remained for several weeks before being hung in the kitchen or living room where they stayed until they were needed. The rest of the pig was made into sausages, pig's fry, pork pies and scratchings. We helped to clean the sausage skins (which were the intestines) and fill them with minced meat, flour and lard made from the pig's fat. Special wooden moulds were used to shape the pie then they were filled with meat and tops put on them. We were allowed to cut the fancy decorations for the tops. The pies were then collected by the local baker to be baked and returned. The belly fat, kidney and liver were made into fry and put on plates, some to be delivered to friends and neighbours. We queued up for the job as it was an easy way to make extra pocket money. Each friend would give the plate back unwashed as it was unlucky to give it back clean and with it we would get sixpence. It was fun to "put the pig away".'

VILLAGE SHOPS

'There was a good deal of poverty in Ruddington, the families tended to be large and took some keeping. Farm work was in abundance but not too well paid.

A corner shop on the High Street sold greengrocery, sweets and tobacco, and several front-room shops sold sweets. We also had a cobbler's shop and a corner shop on Church Street that sold drapery. The owner of that shop went round with a case selling his goods. There were two butcher's shops and a baker's shop where the bread was made on the premises. A fishman pushed a barrow from town each week selling fish and rabbits. He was very popular.'

'Woodborough was self sufficient as a village with a CWS and three corner shops, as well as four butchers and many little cottage shops selling anything you may have wanted, such as "a ha'penny knot o' narrer tape". Many traders came to the village weekly selling hardware, shoes, drapery, fish, oranges on Pancake Day and hot cross buns on Good Friday. Everyone grew their own vegetables. There were three decorators and joiners, three undertakers and two cobblers. We didn't have a policeman or a doctor, which says something for the state of our behaviour and our health.'

PACKAGING THE GOODS

'My father had a grocer's shop in Nottingham up to 1931 and I remember the neat way he used to package the goods for customers. He just had squares of blue paper and would scoop up and weigh the required amount of tea, currants, raisins, sugar etc, put it in a little heap in the centre of the square, deftly tuck over the edges of the square into a cylinder, tip one end and fold and tuck in the top end. He would then reverse the package to tuck in the other end, all done in a few seconds without spilling a grain of sugar. Butter and lard were sliced off big blocks, weighed on a piece of greaseproof paper and packaged up in the same way.'

CALLERS TO THE DOOR

'Miss Disney, who lived at Wysall, cycled round villages as far away as Langar and Cropwell Bishop. She had a large portmanteau strapped to the carrier of her cycle, which she took to each house and opened to reveal a quite amazing selection of drapery of all kinds. Our greengrocer, who came from Upper Broughton to Willoughby, was often still doing business after midnight on Saturday evenings. We were very well served at Willoughby – apart from the village shop we had traders come from Wymeswold, Aslockton, Upper Broughton, Asfordby and Loughborough. We also had two bakers, apart from the village baker, who came from Wymeswold and Quorn.'

'The milkman at Lowdham delivered twice a day as housewives wanted their milk fresh and there were no fridges then. He would come early in the morning and again at lunchtime. That was on his bike, and the milk was in an enamel jug with a lid. Everything was delivered in those days: there was a fish man, two greengrocers and even a shoe van came round. There was a good spirit in the village and nobody locked their doors. Nobody wanted for anything at Christmas, not even very poor people. The butcher made sure people who couldn't afford it got a bit of meat. Mrs Kirkbride from the Old Hall would come round with a basket during the war, with food for people who needed it.'

'Father went to Retford for most of the shopping – seven miles on a bicycle. He would buy in bulk, things like seven-pound jars of jam. Bread could be bought in Rampton, and a horse-drawn fish and chip van came twice a week. On rare occasions we would spot the ice cream van in the distance and race across the fields to catch it. Ginger beer was delivered in large stone jars from Markhams of Gainsborough.'

FROM THE CRADLE TO THE GRAVE

We were more likely to be born, to suffer our illnesses and to die in our own homes in the past, and in the days when the doctor had to be paid for, we often relied on home cures for all but the most serious of illnesses; many villages had locally organised benefit societies that helped to insure against the cost of illness or accident.

HOME CURES

'Every household had a jar of goose grease on the pantry shelf and at the merest hint of a cough out it would come and chest and back got a really good rubbing. It was awful stuff but it did the trick. Other basic medicines were Fenning's Fever Cure if we felt sick, or Lung Healers, a long orange sweet for coughs and sore throats. There were Aspro, liver pills and of course Beecham's pills and powders. No NHS in those days. If you called the doctor you had to pay.'

'One local remedy for a cough was a swede hollowed out and filled with sugar to make a cough syrup. Very good it was too. For toothache everybody went to the dentist in Warsop. He would pull out the teeth and if you needed new false teeth, these were made in the back room of his house.'

'When a doctor's fee had to be paid many people looked to their own remedies. One that was handed down to my mother was the "brown paper vest" and she used this treatment on my eldest sister and on me!

It was used to clear congested chests. A vest shape was made of brown paper and smeared with either goose grease or hen fat which had previously been warmed, then it was wrapped around the child, who was to be kept warm. Eventually the paper rotted and then it was removed, but not before. The result was the child was sick and brought up the offending phlegm. My mother said this was due to the awful smell of the fat!'

'Cures for illness were very basic. There were no antibiotics of course, so tormental tea was used to relieve high fever. Pearl barley for kidneys, syrup of figs, brimstone and treacle, and cod liver oil as a tonic were the medicines used. Poultices were often used to draw out poisons. I remember a fried salt poultice being used over the ears to treat a mastoid.'

'When I was a child in the early 1900s, when a girl had her period she had to use a napkin pinned to her underclothes, and used ones were soaked in a bucket and washed by the girl herself. When she had bad pains she took raspberry leaf tea to relieve them. The first period came as a shock because mothers were often too modest to tell us what was happening.

My mother made rue tea, and if medicine was needed it sometimes came from Kegworth via the postman who was given twopence for bringing it.'

AWFUL MEMORIES

'Only as an adult did I realise and appreciate that the childhood which I thoroughly enjoyed and delighted in, was not only a very comfortable one but one that was indeed, privileged.

In the early 1930s we had a car, albeit with celluloid windows; it sometimes had to be pushed up hills and always had to be crank-started. We had a tennis court: a gardener; a charlady and a maid – "two blue and white morning uniforms; two black and white afternoon uniforms: live-in with own room, half a day per week off; one weekend per month off plus 2s 6d per week pocket money!" To justify most of these "perks" of my father's job we did have to live, almost literally, in the pit yard.

However, my most clear memories and strongest emotions are of unpleasant "health" situations, which contrast most strongly with an otherwise idyllic childhood. These incidents influenced my adult behaviour, attitudes and reactions to my own body and health matters – they continue to do so. The following memories don't need to be recalled, they are so vivid.

Combinations! How I loathed them and was never convinced that my disdain of them would lead to horrors untold in "later life" – they haven't. But I was never shown, or told, how to "drive" them when I went to the outside toilet at the infants school. I thought I had to take them off and I couldn't. I remember so vividly the clamminess of wet combinations – only one morning perhaps, but a life-time experience.

Sun-ray treatment – I can still taste and smell those awful clinging, cloying, acrid fumes of the sun-ray lamp and see the blue light through the shades we had to wear – at the Cripples Guild of all places!

The smell and feel is still with me, also, of the awful iodine locket stitched into a small oilskin bag and worn around my neck on a piece of tape. To ward off? Who knows what! The derision of the doctor when he saw it and my shame as I looked down at the stain it had made on my liberty bodice.

Hospitalisation to remove a TB neck gland was pretty awful for me at the age of seven, but the horrendous thing was being given a small sealed tube of blood (not my own) which I had to rock constantly between my thumb and forefinger for what seemed hours on end. Whenever I stopped a huge starched, strident ogre bore down on me. I hate the sight of blood now and I was totally unimpressed if I was, then, being involved in the advancement of medical science.

Ipecacuanha was an emetic, a diaphoretic and purgative. My brother, five years my senior, shares with me, now with some hilarity but certainly not then, the memory of the two of us kneeling on the cold kitchen floor, either side of a galvanised bucket, strategically placed! A spoonful of ipecacuanha was about to work wonders. My mother had good intentions, but little medical knowledge I fear. "It" was supposed to get something or other off our chests, but I suspect that she was greatly or fearfully influenced by my father, who was a great bowels man! He was a great believer that bowels opened regularly and a cold shower were the panacea for all ills. The daily inquisition of "Have you had your bowels open today?" left me totally bewildered. What on earth was he asking? It was years before I knew. Perhaps I should have learned more quickly and answered an unconditional "Yes" and been spared the most embarrassing memory of all – soap suppositories. The maid and my mother at some mystic hour washed themselves thoroughly in the upstairs bathroom and changed out of morning work clothes into their more gracious afternoon wear. This, before I went to school, I watched with fascination which turned to horror and dread as I saw my mother rolling, surely miniscule but, to me, rock-sized torpedoes, from the toilet soap – oh the ignominy of what happened next! I have never dared to be constipated since!

All these attitudes and attention to health matters were pretty basic and insensitive, but could be interpreted as "preventative" and "positive" so perhaps I can thank my mother for my own, almost paranoid attitude to alternative medicine and positive health. Bless her though, I feel that she never really did sort out her diarrhoea from her constipation in her two children!'

THE DOCTOR

'A lady in Woodborough, Mrs Robinson, made a special punch which was a cure-all for illnesses. She charged sixpence a pint and the carrier used to bring the ingredients from Boots on the cart once a week. Sadly, the recipe died with her.

There was only one doctor in the early years of the century, and he came from the next village when necessary in his pony and trap. He performed minor operations with a penknife and pair of scissors, and also acted as a dentist.'

'Before the NHS we were fortunate at Sutton Bonington in having a resident doctor and district nurse. The doctor's services were mostly on a private basis, but there was a club which one could join for a small contribution for the benefit of his services, and the district nurse was financed by annual subscription to the District Nursing Association, of which most families were members. Most babies were born at home with the help of the nurse – the doctor was only called in difficult cases.'

'Going to the doctor was very different when I was a child, as you went to his home where he held his surgeries. He would also make up the necessary medicine while you were there.'

'My parents contributed sixpence a week to the local doctor, whose representative called to collect the money each Friday evening and signed a payment card. The doctor also dispensed any medicine prescribed at the back of his surgery. He was one of the few people to own a car.'

'Before phones were installed at Bunny, you had to cycle to fetch the doctor. I had my tonsils removed by our local doctor on the dining room table.'

BEFORE THE NHS

'There were two doctors in Ruddington who also served surrounding villages and we had a district nurse (a very much respected person). She was very small and my memory of her was when she was getting on in years. She had a cottage to live in and did midwifery as well as general nursing. When she retired, another single person took over the job and lived in a cottage off the village green, with similar duties to her predecessor.

On her retirement, surgeries were being formed with both doctors and nursing staff under one roof. As people had to pay for the doctor, he wasn't called unless all else failed. Home remedies were used, eg rue tea for tummy upsets, camomile put on an aching tooth or a small amount of whisky. The centre of a hot onion was put into the ear as a cure for earache. There was also a remedy for chilblains, quite cheap, a dip in the "gazunder" first thing in the morning!

The patients with scarlet fever or diphtheria were removed to the fever hospital, but measles, ckicken pox and whooping cough were isolated at home. Goose grease on brown paper or a flannel was applied to the chest and back for a bad cough and chest.

Vaccination was available in my early childhood if your parents allowed you to have it. There were one or two sick clubs in the village which members paid into and got help to pay for the doctor, which helped the less well-off families.

Minor operations were usually carried out by the doctors, otherwise the patient was sent to the general hospital.

A dentist came into the village and used the front room of a house on the High Street once a week. Usually there was no dental nurse, just the lady of the house would be present.

There were one or two women who could be called in to help with sickness, childbirth or laying out of the dead and this was a service much called for and much appreciated.'

BARTON'S FEMALE FRIENDLY SOCIETY

'I belonged to the Female Friendly Society which was formed in Barton in Fabis in 1821 for the benefit of women aged 14 to 30 years. The rules were strict. The purpose of the society was to provide a doctor's services for any woman who fell sick although this specifically excluded pregnancy and childbirth.

Subscriptions had to be paid at each meeting (every second Saturday evening of the month) and non-attendance for more than four consecutive meetings meant exclusion and no chance of being readmitted. Members had to have subscribed for two years before they could claim benefit.

The entrance fees varied according to the age of the members but subscriptions were usually sixpence for the box and a penny for the surgeon. The doctor in my time was Dr J.M. Hunter of Ruddington who received a yearly fee. In 1914 this was £8 8s for attending 24 members. I remember cycling to Ruddington to fetch medicine for my family.

When a woman was sick two appointed Stewardesses from the society saw the patient, fetched the doctor and awarded a sum such as £4 a week for the duration of the illness. Benefit was also paid out for death money (£5); three shillings for members who attended the funeral of a member; five shillings for a three-month stint as a Stewardess; salaries for the Honorary Secretary and Treasurer, both apparently men; a fee for auditing the accounts; rent of the school room for meetings; cost of coal, candles and paraffin; and a small amount for the member who looked after the funeral pall and tea urn, the "Paul and Ern" account.

On Whitsun Thursdays the Gotham Temperance Band

would come over the hill to Barton at about 2 pm. I still recall the excitement I felt at hearing the drum. The two Stewardesses with the Hon. Sec., who was at one time my father, walked in procession to the church. All the ladies dressed up. The two Stewardesses wore sashes and carried poles decorated with lilac and laburnum flowers. After a service they walked around the village, stopping at all the farms where they were given refreshment, then back to the village hall for a business meeting, then tea, and later everyone was invited to a dance.

The Female Friendly Society finally ended in 1948 when the new National Health Service was introduced, thus making such organisations redundant. The remaining money in the account was divided amongst the few last members.

My strongest memory of life in the old days is of the sense of community. For instance when all my family were ill with flu, the butcher's wife would make a big bowl of soup for us all to keep us going.'

BIRTH AND DEATH

'When someone died at Southwell in the 1920s, a local lady came to lay them out and the deceased remained in the home until the day of the funeral. When a baby was born there was usually a local person whose job it was to come and look after the mother, baby and the rest of the family, living in if necessary.'

'Most babies were born at home. Very rarely was a mother taken into hospital to have her baby. Sometimes the midwife would be a local woman, who with the help of neighbours and friends would look after the mother and see to meals. In those days, the midwife at Welbeck Colliery was often called to deliver the babies of the gypsies who camped out on Budby common just outside the village.

When anyone died a woman in the village would lay them out, washing and dressing the body, which would lie at home until the funeral took place. The hearse and carriages for the mourners would be horse-drawn.'

'At the birth of a baby, the mother would stitch a penny in

91

the end of a crepe bandage, place it on the baby's navel, and make the bandage into a binder.'

'There was a district nurse living in Ranby and most babies were born at home with the nurse in attendance. Mothers stayed in bed for ten days following a birth. in the 1940s some women bound a linen roller towel round their stomach following a birth and this remained until they got up and it was replaced by a corset. The idea was to help them get their figures back more quickly.'

'My little brother was born at home in the 1930s. a midwife qualified only by experience attended Mother. A roller towel was tied to the bed railings for her to pull on.'

THE TROUBLE WITH SIXPENCE

'I opened my eyes to the sun streaming in through the window of the small back bedroom I shared with my sister Barbara. We had been enjoying an Indian Summer that October (1939) and it looked set to continue. We usually dressed to calls of "Hurry down or you'll be late" but today was a school holiday. "Potato picking" we called it but it's now half term.

We lived in a farm cottage at Boughton and although we were a large family with six children, I don't ever remember feeling overcrowded. We must have had some spare room too as we often had relatives to stay. The last ones had been Aunt Nell (who we did not like very much) and Cousin Joan (who we didn't like at all). We always had an iced cake from the baker's van on Friday and before it was even on the table she had pinched the cherry off the top. She was horrid!

However, back to "the day". When I went downstairs I was very surprised to see my Dad standing at the range cooking the breakfast. He said Mum was having a lie in and not to disturb her. As Mum never had a lie in I knew something odd was going on. Another odd thing was Mrs Bullivant's bike leaning up against the washhouse. She was Mum's friend but she never came at this time of the morning. The four younger ones were already sitting at the table and after we had eaten and cleared away Dad told Barbara and I to get the push-chair ready as we were going out. The bad news was that we had to take the four younger ones with us. He gave us a large hessian sack and sixpence and told us to go to a certain farm in Kirton and ask the farmer for sixpennyworth of apples. We kept telling Dad that there was an orchard just down the lane but it made no difference. He insisted that we hurry.

There were two ways to get to Kirton, we could either go by road, which was rather a long way or over the fields, the entrance to which was just down the lane. The trouble with this was there were three stiles to negotiate and we had a push-chair and four children. It was no contest, the fields won. Just as we left the lane we saw the midwife on her bike. I was a very naive twelve year old at the time and had seen lambs being born as we lived on a farm but I didn't know a lot about human babies other than that they seemed to come with alarming regularity. However, I did know that the midwife had something to do with it.

Off we went then, giving Doreen and Brenda a very bumpy ride, Ted and John running alongside. When we got to the stiles it was "everybody out" and Barbara and I had to man-handle the push-chair over. Believe me it was no easy task. They built things to last in those days and as a consequence, that push-chair was very heavy indeed. About halfway across the fields there was a stream running through, it was known as the beck and we often went there for a paddle or to pick watercress. After our efforts with the push-chair we decided that we'd earned a paddle. I can feel that lovely cool water now as I think about it. It was so clear and it really gurgled as it flowed along. We held the little ones while they dangled their feet in the water, dried them on the long grass and went on our way.

The farmer was very kind, he didn't seem at all surprised that we had a large sack and only sixpence. He took us into the orchard, showed us which were eaters and left us to fill the sack. When he came to see how we were doing he brought a length of string with which he tied the top. He showed us which two ends to pull when we got home (which was a big mistake) and told us to put a couple of apples in our pockets to eat on the way. I didn't have any pockets so I put some up my knicker legs.

Now we had a very big problem. We not only had a push-chair and four children to get home but we also had a large sack full of apples. It was going to be no easy journey. We solved it at first by putting the sack in the push-chair and making the little ones walk. When we got into the fields, Ted and I dragged it while Barbara pushed the push-chair. There were some bruised apples as well as bruised shin bones but we pressed on regardless. I can't tell you the shenanigans involved in getting those apples over the stiles. We had to haul and push and sort of roll them over. By the time we reached the beck again we were exhausted and hungry. It was hours since breakfast and we'd eaten the apples from our pockets so we decided it was time to test the theory regarding the string – had he been right in which two ends to pull? He had. After we'd collected all the rolling apples from all over the field, eaten our fill and had another little paddle we headed for home.

My Dad was waiting for us at the end of the lane. Mrs Bulli-vant's bike was still there but the midwife's had gone and I had been right in my suspicions – we had a new baby sister and she was to be called Margaret. So all the little oddities of the morning were explained and we now knew why Dad had wanted to get rid of us. Mrs Bullivant had prepared a lovely tea for us and after we'd eaten and had all been in to see Mum and the new baby I went to sit on the back gate. I did most of my thinking there. Barbara and Ted came out to join me, I think we were all wondering the same thing – what were we going to do when Grandma came to see us? She always gave us sixpence and until now it had worked out at a penny each but how were we going to split sixpence into seven? We were still trying to figure it out when Dad called us in for supper.

I dreamed that night that I was trying to lift a giant push-chair over a ten foot stile whilst surrounded by hordes of screaming babies.'

CHILDHOOD &
SCHOOLDAYS

GROWING UP IN NOTTINGHAMSHIRE

So many different experiences of childhood, but we all look back to days of freedom sadly unknown to today's children. Families were often large and times hard but we found pleasure in simple games and treats.

TIMES WERE HARD

'I was born in 1916 and came to live in Nottinghamshire when I was four years old. My father was a farm foreman and we lived in a farmhouse. The farmer had one room in the house as his office and Mother cleaned and looked after it. I started school when I was four and a half years old and had about a mile to walk with my older brother and sister. I can't remember much of my early days at school but I know we had slates and slate pencils and kept our few things we had in sweet boxes which we used to get from the shopkeeper who came round with a horse and cart. When I was about six years old my mother was ill and was badly burned when she fell into an open fire. She was in Lincoln Hospital for a very long time and I remember walking with my nine year old brother three miles to Collingham station to visit her. Father would get us ready and start us walking and then he got ready and followed on his bicycle and would then give us a ride before getting on the train and having another walk to the hospital when we got off the train at Lincoln.

Times were very hard but we were always well fed and well clothed. There was Father, my sister (who was only 14 and looked after us all), my two brothers of three years and eight years. I say we were well fed and these were some of the things I remember. We always killed a pig so we had plenty of bacon, bread and lard, and plenty of fruit and vegetables from our own garden, and for a treat a sandwich spread which was butter, sugar and cocoa mixed together and we always called it "Beauto". Purely because it was beautiful, I think. A tin of fruit on a Sunday was a great treat. We had plenty of milk on the farm. We had cake most days, just one piece which was mostly home-made but we loved going to the baker's cart when sometimes he would give us a little iced bun. The butcher, baker and grocer all came round delivering. I remember my father saying the butcher used to say to him, "Don't let them kids go hungry, have the meat and pay when you can", but Father would have nothing he couldn't pay for. Money was very scarce and there was no National Health Service. Father had a bill from the doctor for £100 which he paid off when he could. Mother was by this time out of hospital but still very ill, she had skin grafts and all sorts of treatment.

The farmer decided to get married and we had to move to a smaller cottage. Mum was carried across the small field in her bed when we "flitted". The cottage had two bedrooms in the main part and another one to which you went up a ladder in the kitchen and through a trap door. By this time we had two farm lads living in and they slept in that room. My sister had gone into service and was away from home and the rest of us fitted into the two rooms. The lavatory was a pit right away from the house with a wooden seat with two holes, one big and one small, and every so often it had to be emptied.

One highlight was Father used to take me on the bus to Newark on a Saturday teatime to get fruit being sold off cheap and then we used to stand and listen to the Salvation Army band which played in the Market Place and we all joined in the singing.

On Sundays we went to Sunday School morning and afternoon and then as a family to evensong, and after the service in the summer we would walk by the Trent but in the winter we would have a sing-song at home.'

RECOLLECTIONS

'Recollections of early days at Ollerton include, at five years old, attending the infants class and being taught by Mrs Carter, who always dressed in black. It took me some years to realise

97

why she sobbed on her desk on Armistice Day. The loss of her only son.

Summertime brought the chapel Anniversary. New silk dresses and a new straw hat from Mrs Osborne's shop on Station Road. Mr Viner the postmaster who peered over his spectacles, Mr Germany the butcher, Mr Mettam the miller, Mr Buckingham the ropemaker. Ollerton then was a tranquil village.

Being brought up on a farm, one learned early of life and death amongst animals and birds, also of the work needed to care for them. Young as we were, we had to help.

Each season brought the work. The garden to be set for all kinds of vegetables. Corn to be drilled in the fields. My job to shoo off the marauding jackdaws eating the precious seed. Summertime came and the soft fruit to pick. My father set up bees – not favourites of mine, only the honey.

As wintertime approached, the awful day to me. Pig killing. I remember making myself scarce, that is until the carcase was cut up and Father did the mysterious process of salting the hams, sides and sundries (no deep-freeze then). Helping Mother to cut up the fat for lard. Next item – pork pies, sausages, brawn.

The year rolled on to Christmas. All hands on deck to help pluck and dress cockerels and ducks for Christmas. In between all this, cake making, Christmas puddings all ready for Christmas Day. Festivities went on in spite of having to consider the outside animals' welfare. We made our own entertainment, a sing-song round the piano, dance around the table, ate our hearts out with all the goodies. Boxing Day continued with friends too. Then back to business and the New Year nearby. All to start over again.'

WE ENJOYED LIFE

'I remember, I remember the house where I was born. It was 22 Park Row, Mansfield Woodhouse – some octogenarians would know the address as Hospital Row as I understand the first three used to be a cottage hospital. The first house was occupied by the landlady, a spinster by the name of Miss Stevenson, who always appeared so dignified clad in a black dress. The Hill family occupied the second house and we, the Banks, the third one. I still remember most of the twelve tenants, as families tended to stay put during and immediately after the First World War.

We only had paraffin lamps for lights plus candles for bedroom use, as I well remember. Later on, the attic became my bedroom and I enjoyed reading by candlelight but one night I must have dozed off and was aroused by a blazing wicker chair. Fortunately for me, the contents of the chamber-pot under the bed were sufficient! We didn't have indoor toilets in those days. A coal fire provided heat for cooking in an oven and a side boiler provided hot water for bathing on the hearth in a large zinc bath. Happy days! We didn't have to worry about locking our doors then.

We had a fair-sized garden at the front which had two large apple trees, one of which supported a swing as well as providing us with beautiful crisp juicy apples. When I was nine years of age, I took charge of the garden and made a few coppers from the produce. We always had an allotment. Around 1919 I remember climbing up large stone steps off Welbeck Road to an allotment on the "rec" and surprising a large hare. Next we had a garden in Woodland Grove, later still an allotment on Longyards which ran alongside Park Avenue and beyond. It was there that we kept poultry which ensured we always had something to eat. At home, on the backyard we always kept a pig. At the appointed time, Harry Boole from Alcroft Street would turn up with his equipment and provide us with bacon, sides, hams and all the bits and pieces. Alongside the pigsty we kept pigeons which provided excitement on race days and occasionally a pigeon pie.

Before starting school at five years of age, I had a speech problem and only my mother could understand me. However, one day it was decided I could visit my aunt and uncle, Esther and Wilf Kitchem, at Dallas Street (Mansfield) which was at the back of the shoe factory. I was put on a tramcar at the Woodhouse terminus with two halfpennies for the return journey, a note saying where I was going and, most important, a live pigeon in a large ventilated flour bag. On arriving at Mansfield terminus, I found it to be market day and very busy. I remember showing my note to a very tall lady clad in an ankle-length costume surmounted by a very large hat – they still wear them at Ascot. The lady had two young girls with her but agreed to take me to Dallas Street after she had finished shopping on the market. I've often wondered what the girls thought of the little ginger haired lad trailing along with them, clutching tightly at the flour bag containing my little dark hen. I duly arrived at my aunt's home and without a moment's delay the pigeon was liberated from a bedroom window and within a few minutes was back at Park Row confirming my safe arrival.

There was a time before electric lights and telephones when we enjoyed life and the fact that a child of five could travel alone speaks for itself.'

A DIFFERENT CHILDHOOD

'The children of today have a very different childhood from mine in the 1920s. I lived in a farmhouse with an orchard, pond and field – all our own private property. There were very few cars on the road and until I was about 14 no buses. A day out to Nottingham meant over two miles to walk and although we were only about 14 miles north of Nottingham, it was considered in a similar way to going abroad today. I had a wonderful childhood and at that time it was considered a privileged one.

We all had our chores to do. We would deliver milk in cans on our way to school and collect them on our way home. In the winter we had to pulp the turnips and chop the hay which were mixed together to feed the cows. In the summer the mowing machines would start at 4 am and it was a very anxious time, weatherwise. We would use the wooden rakes to turn the hay over by hand so that it would dry. In the evenings the vicar and church choir would all come to help as my father was secretary to the Church Council. They didn't expect any reward but after the last load was brought in they would all gather round the dining room table and the vicar would carve the ham. There would be fruit pies and cream, all homemade, to follow and we always had a barrel of beer. They really enjoyed it as many of them were miners and a meal like this was a real luxury. The children would ride down in the

100

A children's party at Edwinstowe in 1910.

haycart, pulled by a horse of course – such a jolly time.

All our entertainment revolved around the church and in our case, some round the chapel. During Lent we all paid a penny and we would go to the church hall for the magic lantern. The vicar would read and explain the story to us as the titles were shown on the screen. I remember we had *Little Nell, Oliver Twist* and *Pilgrim's Progress*. We thought it was wonderful.

Everywhere we went we had to walk. We would go for long walks in the summer and picnic. We would gather wild flowers and press them and write underneath where it grew and the time of year it flowered etc.

For many years we only had oil lamps, no gas or electricity. In summer we still had to have a huge fire in the kitchen to heat the water and the oven, also to get the irons hot for ironing. In winter we often had three huge fires, kitchen, dining room and lounge. Once the fires went out the rooms soon went very cold.

I was 18 before I ever heard the word "divorced" and had to ask what it meant.'

JUST A BUS RIDE AWAY

'I was born in a small village in Oxfordshire. My mother died when I was only three years old and I lived with my Grandad and aunts until I was eight years old, when my Dad remarried and I was brought to live in Lenton, Nottingham with him, my stepmother and sister.

The change in my life was enormous. From being a country girl, I was now a towny; where I had been used to a bucket privy down the garden, we had a yard with a "real toilet" with a chain; instead of water fetched in buckets from the spring, it came out of a tap; and we had a gas cooker instead of an open range. All very new and exciting!

We lived close to the Raleigh cycle works, which at that time was producing munitions for the war effort and in the mornings we would wake to the sound of hundreds of men and women marching down the street to start their shift. It was all very noisy and there was a great deal of dirt from the factory.

Our games of whip and top, hopscotch, hide and seek, etc were played in the street amongst the brick and concrete built air-raid shelters, but oh how I missed the fields, streams and flowers! I soon settled in but I was still a country girl at heart and sometimes longed for the open countryside so much it hurt. Until, one day, a neighbour and her son asked if my sister and I would like to join them for a picnic.

We went by trolley bus to Wilford Road, and paid a half-penny each to cross the toll bridge over the river Trent into Wilford village. We walked through the village and along the banks of the Trent and there they were – fields! We picnicked, played games and paddled in Fairham brook and I had one of the most memorable days of my life! I had rediscovered the countryside just a bus ride away!

During the next few years we revisited Wilford village often and also found many other places where we could roam, not too far away, for outings and picnics.

Even now, when I cross Clifton Bridge on the busy A52 and see all the houses built where once there were "our" fields, I still feel so grateful to the neighbour, and so thankful for the pleasure of that particular day, when I realised that I could still enjoy being a country girl, even though I now lived in a town.'

102

LIFE AT WHATTON IN THE VALE

'My childhood memories are of Whatton in the Vale where I was born and lived until I married in 1962.

We had a little village shop which was a wooden hut built onto a bungalow. It seemed to sell everything. We also had travelling shops – greengrocers and butchers. The milk was delivered in milk churns and measured out into your own jugs. We didn't have fridges but when the ice cream man came round we bought blocks of "hot" ice to keep things cool. Most houses had cool larders with stone benches in them. To keep milk cool we stood the jugs in bowls of cold water.

My father kept hens so we always had plenty of eggs. When the corn had been cut we used to go gleaning. We would spend the day in the cornfield going up the rows of stubble picking up any ears of corn which had been left. These would help to eke out the poultry food. We usually had a picnic lunch. We didn't go away for holidays but enjoyed trips to the coast. The church had a day out. We had Sunday school outings and we could walk to the station at Aslockton and catch a train to Skegness for the day.

Because the village had only one shop, there wasn't a barber's so on a Sunday morning our front room became the village barber's. From 9 am to 1 pm a steady stream of village men came to have their hair cut by my father who had bought some hairdressing shears during the war and found he could make a good job with them. He sometimes cut hair in the evenings and we often ended up playing cards with some of the customers.

Saturday mornings were always spent doing our chores. We had to keep the hens cleaned out. My sister and I had to clean our bedrooms out, sweep the yard and scrub the front doorstep. Then I had to go to an elderly couple to do their shopping for them. The list and bag were always ready for me and when I had been to the shop I would be given sixpence to spend. Once a month I was given their sweet coupons as everything was still rationed.

On Sundays we would go to the Sunday school and then go for a walk. We would be able to take either a roll of fruit gums or a Mars bar with us. The Mars bar would be cut into four pieces and we would take it in turns to have the end pieces. (How anyone can eat a Mars by oneself I don't know.)

We used to play cricket and rounders in the street outside our house. Cars were a novelty round our roads and only occasionally did we have to stop play to let one go through. We also played whip and top and hopscotch. In the summer we would go to the river Smite and paddle and catch sticklebacks and minnows in jam jars.

We all went to the village school: there were just two classrooms – the seniors and infants. The children who lived in Aslockton used to walk over the fields to school. The headmistress was very strict and even out of school hours you wouldn't dare to do anything wrong in case she saw you. I can remember of a Saturday afternoon playing with a friend and trying to knock conkers down from a tree with bits of wood. She saw us as she was going to catch the bus and had us in front of the class on Monday morning telling us off. I think she gave us a stroke of the cane for misbehaving.

After leaving the village school, I went to the West Bridgford grammar school and had to walk to Aslockton to catch the special bus. The footpath between the two villages went by the side of the churchyard, over the river and over the old river bed, across a field and over the old railway line into Aslockton. There were no street lights and you could trip over a cow on the way home at night.'

WHEN SMARTIES WERE NEW

'Monday – washday – copper lit early morning – kitchen full of steam all morning. Sheets, pillowcases, handkerchiefs, tea towels etc boiled then starched. If the weather was fine and the washing dry my hated job was to polish the serviettes when I got home from school. Each one had to be perfectly square, stiff as a board with starch and shiny – the iron as hot as it would go. In the summer the kitchen was like a baker's oven but I couldn't go out to play till I'd finished so hated it if we'd had visitors for a meal and there were extra ones to do.

Frost on the insides of the windows in winter; a window open in all weathers; getting dressed under the bedclothes and then a mad dash to the old bathroom. Yes, we had a bathroom

104

with an inside toilet so we were privileged. I can remember when very small, someone coming to visit my mother especially to look at this house built with inside conveniences and electricity at the touch of a switch. The year was approximately 1930.

First day at Holy Trinity school in 1933 and I was collected by two "big" girls aged seven. I spent the first day looking at cards with the alphabet on – A for apple etc. I thought this was silly as I already knew that and could write my name. Twelve o'clock dinner time and a walk home for something to eat and then back again for the afternoon session. Each journey was about a mile in distance.

The only time my mother took or fetched me from school was Friday afternoon when we went shopping and I had twopence pocket money. One week Smarties (chocolate beans) were new and I spent the whole lot on them. Another week I bought a pair of sunglasses!'

COMPLETE FREEDOM

'My parents lived in a small village south of Nottingham called Owthorpe. There were only about 17 houses, and they were mostly farmhouses and tied cottages.

The whole village used to belong to a Major Davey. He had inherited the estate from his family who were from Scotland. Eventually the estate was sold and most of the tenant farmers bought their farms. My father worked on a farm owned by Mr Chapman and spent 52 years of his life on this farm until his retirement when he was 67 years of age.

The most vivid recollection of my childhood is that all the children had complete freedom. We would play wherever we wanted and I'm sure our parents never worried like parents of today. I used to love harvest time the most, the whole village would help each other and I can remember trying to catch mice, there were always hundreds of them amongst the chaff. Afterwards the whole village would organise a harvest supper which used to be held in Mr Chapman's barn, but later when a village hall was built it was held there. Afterwards there would be dancing which I loved, this was quite an event in those days as going anywhere else dancing was unheard of.

Christmas time was always magical. We would walk miles in the evenings carol singing. We would go to all the outlying farms and cottages, and when we went to Major Davey's house we were always asked in and he would open a huge box of chocolates. I thought this was the epitome of luxury. The older boys and girls used to frighten us smaller children with ghost stories, but I can remember those Christmases so vividly.

My sister and I would write a letter to Santa Claus and we would leave the letters on the lead stove which was in our kitchen. We would also leave a glass of sherry which was quite an extravagant thing to do as my parents lived on a very tight budget, and a mince pie. I remember being really pleased that Santa had taken the time to have his sherry and pie. Our stocking always had fruit and nuts in the bottom which were not so plentiful then, and I wonder if today's children get as much pleasure with all their expensive toys.

But we always seemed to have plenty to eat. My father had a very large vegetable garden, and this would keep us in vegetables all the year round. Also we had apple trees and plum trees, it was fruits such as bananas and oranges which were so scarce soon after the war. My father also kept a pig at the bottom of the garden and I used to hate it when it was taken away to be slaughtered. I would go and hide under the front room table as the poor pig used to squeal so much. It was slaughtered at Mr Chapman's farm and everyone in the village would have a small joint from the pig. It was my task to take the offal and pig's fry to our neighbours, and I used to love home-cured ham. I wonder what EEC regulations would make of that practice now!

Owthorpe had no shops so if my mother ran out of anything which was urgently required my friend Christine and I would either walk to Kinoulton or Cropwell Bishop. We really enjoyed this as we would stop and see friends on the way. I often wonder if my mother had an easier way of shopping than we do now, then everything was delivered to the door. We had the Co-op grocer, the butcher from Cotgrave, the papers from Colston Bassett, and we also had fizzy pop delivered by Redgates in the summer. Milk was plentiful, my father would bring a jug of fresh milk straight from the dairy.

We had no shops or pub in Owthorpe, but we did have a church. Most of the villagers went to church in those days. I would go to evensong every Sunday, and also Sunday school. We would have an outing every year, and go to places like London Zoo and we once went to Norwich. We also had a choir, and a nativity play in the village hall every year, and once we all performed in a play at Cropwell Bishop Memorial Hall. I remember I was an angel one year and I used to think it so exciting going to Cropwell Bishop for rehearsals.'

SWEETS AND SLOGANS

'We played hopscotch and marbles on the pavements at Hucknall in the 1930s, and spent our ha'penny pocket money on kali, gobstoppers and liquorice sticks. My brother and sisters and I were "railway children" and we had a garden and an allotment on the other side of the track where we also kept chickens. Our Dad was the signalman at Butler's Hill box and we were known to all the train drivers fetching coal from the Hucknall pits.

During elections we used to go round the streets banging dustbin lids and chanting slogans such as:

Vote, vote, vote for S. . . . C. . . . .
He's the winner of the day.
If you don't let him in, we'll kick the door in,
And drive all the . . . away.'

A BUSY LIFE

'What a busy life I led 70 to 80 years ago. Transport was important then because one memory was "my first bicycle" at age ten years. I had to learn to ride it with two wheels – what a thrill.

All children attended church or chapel Sunday school at Cropwell Bishop every week, and enjoyed their Anniversaries and summer outings. Sunday was considered a "day of rest" and devout people were not allowed to indulge in knitting, sewing, read novels or newspapers. We would take a walk after

107

church service where it was hoped your special boyfriend was doing the same. Then home for supper, the remains of Sunday dinner – beef, Yorkshire pudding and certainly apple pie.

It was a pleasure to look forward to Easter, the Easter concert and party afterwards. At this time of the year there were wild flowers, violets, cowslips, daisies and buttercups and a host of dancing daffodils. Then bird watching, with blackbirds, thrushes, tom-tits and wrens to find and look for birds' nests. We knew their habits and the colour of their eggs.

It was the age of innocence when we were told babies came from under the gooseberry bush. We accepted this with a certain disbelief but were too busy with our other interesting activities and didn't get deep into investigating this wonderful performance until later.

There was Pancake Day which was a half day from school when whip and top, battledore and shuttlecock appeared, and there were skipping ropes and much swapping of marbles, black alleys, blood alleys and snobs, hopscotch and so many more.

Of course, growing older, fancy clothes became a great interest and we had a new outfit for Whit Sunday and of course for church. It must have been about this time when the opposite sex became interesting and doubt set in about the gooseberry bush theory.

In my day we did not expect to go for a week's holiday but thought it wonderful to go to the seaside for a day. We would talk about it for weeks. We would take sandwiches with us and buy a pot of tea. There was always good solid food at home as mothers were resourceful cooks and could make a joint of beef go a long way.

Children led a happy busy life according to the seasons and Mother was always at home when we returned after school. Of course there was a certain amount of mischief but we were scared of the village policeman who walked the beat every day. I don't remember any vandalism or burglary. We got our sweets and toffee from a lady who opened her parlour to oblige and had our clothes made by the village dressmaker, and they appeared very important people to us.

Town children would sometimes visit us and would behave as though they were better than us, but we didn't care as we

108

knew milk didn't come in bottles, how lambs were born and didn't just say "birds" – we knew them as blackbirds, thrushes etc and where their nests were, but we had to admit the toilets were at the bottom of the garden – three seaters, two for Mum and Dad and the small one for us.

Every so often my father would have a session with me about what he called "manners". Table manners and what to do with all those knives and forks which appeared on the Sunday table, not to put my knife in my mouth, also how to behave when his elderly relations came as they didn't like cheeky children and didn't like children who told fibs and told secrets – I remember worrying and thinking growing old did have problems.

Yes, I must have enjoyed my childhood and now I have the benefit of country lore and city amenities and count my blessings, although I cannot leave my front door open and chat with strangers.'

CUSTARD AND COCONUT

'I was born at Gedling, the daughter of a farm labourer. It was the weekend of the Munich crisis and the Second World War was imminent. Father had been firewatching and air raid shelters were being built.

I was educated at Gedling church school. I remember coconut ice creams from the shop at the bottom of the twitchel and the school meals van which was always late as it came from Lambley. It swayed so much that it always spilled the custard.'

FATHER WAS THE BUTLER

'I was born and brought up at Brackenhurst. My father was butler to Sir William Hicking who owned Brackenhurst Hall and we lived in one of the cottages on the estate. I loved it up there but I suppose life for me and my sisters was a little different from some children. For example, when we met Lady Hicking in the lane we had to say "Good morning M'Lady" or "Good afternoon M'Lady" as the case may be.

All the families on the estate were friendly together and we used to have Christmas parties in each other's homes, culminating in one at Brackenhurst Hall (when the Hickings were away!). On this occasion my father would be the host and the cook the hostess and a great time was had by all.

Our particular friends were the Townshends and Mr Townshend was Lady Hicking's chauffeur and drove a rather splendid maroon Rolls-Royce. The children on the estate were told by our parents never *ever* to wave to Mr Townshend while he was driving until we were absolutely certain that her ladyship was not inside. Then we waved like mad! The same thing applied to Mr Roberts when he was driving Sir William in his Packard.

Washdays must have been quite hard work for my mother who used to stoke up the boiler in the washhouse which was just across the yard from the house. She would then get busy with the dolly stick and tub. We had no water in the house and on bath nights my father would carry buckets of hot water from the Hall. We had our bath in front of the kitchen fire.

It was a mile to walk to school and we always walked home for dinner. I never felt hard done by, in fact I felt rather sorry for those children who didn't have such a nice walk.

When the war started we had evacuees from Southend at first and later on some came from Nottingham. Some of us had to sit three to a desk instead of two but we soon settled down together. I joined a party of evacuees being shown round Home Farm at Brackenhurst and the farm manager was much amused when one of the youngsters said, "Well how do you milk a cow? Do you pull its tail?" It amused me too! There were evacuees from Worthing boys' grammar school too and they went to Southwell grammar school. When the air raid siren sounded Mr Davies, the headmaster, would open the big wooden partition so that he could be heard by everyone and say "Scatter". We all went off to prearranged houses nearby until the all clear was sounded. I don't remember feeling worried. It all seemed a bit of fun.'

Paddling in the river Trent at Laneham in the 1920s.

DOUBLE SUMMERTIME AND SLEDGES

'Only born in February 1939, one of my wartime memories was having to climb into the back of an army lorry to go to Retford, presumably because no buses were running. We used to play hopscotch in the middle of the road, only having to move when the odd bus or lorry hauling coal to Rampton Hospital came chugging up the hill.

My mother and I used to spend a day picking blackberries for jam, pies, bottling etc. We carried a milk can and a large basket – the basket to carry them home and the can to carry the juice dripping from the basket.

I went to Rampton primary school. For the first few years I was there we had no water toilets – it was the wooden seat jobs. Also we had paraffin lamps. We were modernised in the late 1940s. A new kitchen was built and we had hot dinners. Before that we had a very small dining room next to the head-

111

master's house with lovely open fires in the corner. Mr Hunt, the caretaker, had the kettle boiling to make our hot drinks to have with our sandwiches. If we made too much noise the headmaster's wife would open a little window and tell us to be quiet.

I enjoyed our nature lessons at Rampton school with Mrs Allsopp. We had charts on the wall and we used to collect wild flowers, press them and then fit in a slot with its name at the side. I also remember Mrs Allsopp reading a chapter either daily or weekly of *The Water Babies* which was one of my favourites.

I fetched milk for the rector and his sister at Treswell. One milk can was left at Popples, Manor Farm and I collected it after school, delivered it to the rectory, collected an empty can (along with two apples for me) and took it back to the farm ready for the next day. I got threepence a week. I also used to practise whistling on these errands and one day old Miss Day, who also lived in the village, commented on the fact that she enjoyed hearing me whistle and had always regretted not being able to do it herself.

Mr Wright lived at Orchard House and his sons delivered the papers. If a new comic came out he would let me have one to see if I liked it. I already took the *Dandy* and *Beano* and he sent me an *Eagle* but I didn't like that – it was more a boy's comic. One which I did take for a number of years was *School Friend* and my father used to read it from front to back. I still kept taking it for him when I had left school. Another I took was the *Children's Newspaper*.

We listened to the radio a lot. Saturday night was *Music Hall* and *In Town Tonight*. That was the one where they used to "stop the mighty roar of London's traffic". Sunday night was *Variety Bandbox* and *Grand Hotel*. I seem to remember Tuesday was the only night I went inside without being told because of *Just William*.

Tuesdays and Saturdays were the days Thackers from Retford delivered groceries and bread. Roger, who lived next door to me, and I couldn't wait to go and choose our quarter pound sweet ration so we would meet them as they came into the village and tell Mrs Thacker all the news and events that had happened during the week.

Going to school from the age of five, we had to cross the beck over two planks; they are no longer there now, they were washed away with the floods. We walked up the jitty on to the Grove Road then walked along the road to Rampton school with a satchel and sandwiches and a bottle of home-made ginger beer. If the bottle was shaken the top used to fly off.

When it was double summertime, evenings were spent playing hide and seek until late at night and if the moon shone we were even later. Also we played whip and top and marbles on the road.

In winter snows makeshift sledges were made from any old wood to hand. Then we used to sledge down the "ungle" – a hill on a narrow lane. We would also get a wooden box about 18 inches long and pack snow in and make igloos which lasted for weeks.

We would get a willow pole about ten feet long and two inches in diameter, then "lope" (leap) across the beck and hedges. One lad got stuck in the middle of the beck when the pole sank in and was left stranded in mid-air. He had to slide down into the water to escape. Tree houses were made in two trees then we used to attach a piece of string from each house with a tin fastened on it to pull from one house to the other with messages in.

We had two weeks' holiday to pick potatoes and I went to Mellors at Rampton. If you were over the age of twelve you could get extra time off school during the war to work on the land – as long as the form was filled in. After the potatoes we got up mangolds and swedes and loaded them into carts to be put in "pies". We also got up sugar beet in cold wet weather.

Holidays were spent at Grandfather's farm at harvest time. He opened up the fields round the edges with a scythe and I used to go round with a taking-up rake after him and make sheaves with a straw band to tie them up. They were then reared on the hedge and the horse-drawn binder finished cutting the rest of the field and we had to go round stooking the sheaves to dry and then stacking them to be threshed later.

For Retford Saturday market I used to collect fruit and vegetables from various people in the village on an old wooden wheelbarrow and then caught Applewhite's bus to the Butter Market. After the market, empty boxes were collected from the bus and returned to owners. Sometimes I was paid threepence or even sixpence from each person.'

VISITING GRANDMA

'Grandma and Grandad Lewis lived in a two up, two down cottage on the main road at New Ollerton.

The parlour was crammed full of furniture including a piano that only my mum could play properly. At one time the cottage had been a shop, so it had a very large window in the parlour. The sill was full of plants, as were all the window sills in the cottage, but I remember that window the most. It was full of geraniums, all different colours. In one corner of the parlour behind the door to the kitchen was a tall table with Gracy sitting on it. Gracy is an aspidistra which we still have. I can remember sitting on the horse-hair sofa looking at the big framed photo of my Great Grandma and Grandad wondering why Great Grandad was sitting down and Great Grandma stood behind him. I thought it should have been the other way around. My Great Grandma had had twelve children but she was a slim woman. My Grandad was the eldest and the only thing he ever told us about his early family life was that he had to help look after the younger ones and as he rocked the cradle he would sing to them, "Die you boggers die".

Above the big photo was Grandma's clock, which is now mine. How I love that clock! It strikes the hour and half-hours. As a child it fascinated me, the pendulum swinging in the glass case, that lovely old face smiling at ten to two, frowning at twenty to four.

The parlour had a large fireplace with a high mantle shelf. The shelf was a shrine to my Uncle Ernest killed in the war, with his photos in silver frames. When it was his birthday or Remembrance Day flowers were put at the side of the photos.

The kitchen was always warm and welcoming. The black range took up most of one wall, with the big pan of potatoes and potato peelings boiling on the fire for the pigs. Grandad kept two pigs, rabbits and chickens to supply them with meat and eggs.

I remember the teas we had with Grandma. She did not have much money so could not afford to go to town with the expensive foods, but I always enjoyed the things she gave us; even the bread and jam tasted great at Grandma's.

In the school summer holidays my brother and I would go and spend a week at Ollerton with Grandma and Grandad. Those were lovely days. I was a right tomboy and was always ripping my clothes. Grandma would "mend" them for me so my mum would not know, but Grandma was as good at mending as I am! My mum would re-mend them when we got home and never let on to Grandma.

When it was my birthday Grandma could not give me much but I was not bothered because I knew she would take me into the flower garden and fill my arms with lovely smelling flowers. She knew I loved flowers, and right up to her death she gave me flowers from her garden.

Bedtime at Grandma's was fun; our Jimmy and me slept in the attic until we were too old to sleep together. Then I slept on a camp bed in Grandma and Grandad's room.

The bed in the attic was a large brass frame with a shake-up mattress on top of the springs. It was smashing for jumping on. The attic smelt of drying herbs and Grandad's home-grown tobacco. If we stayed overnight in the winter we would put in the bed the shelves from the side oven wrapped in old towels to warm it up.

The loo at Grandma's was down the garden; it was a flush toilet but toilet paper was a luxury. Old newsprint was torn in squares, put on string and hung from a nail. It was okay in summer but gosh it was cold in the winter! We would put off going to the loo as long as possible.

When it was time to go home Grandma would give Jimmy and me a glass of ruby port to keep us warm on the way. Even in summer we would still get a glass, if we asked nicely. She would laugh at us and say "I shouldn't really".'

LIFE ON A COUNTRY ESTATE

'I have fond memories of growing up on a country estate in the Retford area, where my father was a gardener. Though far from wealthy, life itself was rich, for as a child there were few if any responsibilities and I was allowed to roam the estate at will, though I had to make myself scarce if the gentry were around. The estate owners were kind people and gave good presents at Christmas. I especially remember the Christmas tree which stood around 15 to 20 feet high and was decorated with lighted candles from top to bottom.

The gentry travelled in style and a brand new black, shiny Daimler would transport the Squire and his family to their shooting lodge in Scotland, while a six-wheeler van laden with supplies and servants would prepare the lodge for the visitors. No such luxurious travel for me though, seated on a wicker basket on the back of a donkey was more likely to be my mode of travel. The donkey's life came to a sad end when he ate some yew berries and died. He was taken away to the knacker's yard – oh, how I cried.

Our living quarters were in the stable yard. The house only had cold water which was pumped up from the estate lake and was unsuitable for drinking. The home had the added advantage of an indoor water closet which had a wooden seat. To flush, there was a brass handle beside the pan which had to be pulled up. When I caught scarlet fever, the closet was condemned and the house fumigated.

At the tender age of ten I spent six weeks in an isolation hospital. Those were dark days as young people around me were dying and there was little reassurance that all would be well. The hospital food was abysmal. One lunchtime spinach was served and I could not eat it for the grit that was still clinging to the leaves, so I left it. Little did I think it would be served up again the same evening for tea. This time I had to eat it or it would have appeared again at breakfast. With no visitors allowed I could only look from the ward window to the street below and wave to my mother and sister. Those were desolate days – almost Dickensian.

Life changed dramatically in the 1930s. The estate owners were caught up in the slump and subsequently many of the estate workers lost their jobs. My father was one of them and he never recovered from the shock and died shortly afterwards, leaving my mother to bring up two small children. We rented a council house at 13 shillings and fourpence when our total income was 18 shillings, made up of ten shillings widow's pension, five shillings for the first child and three shillings for the second child. Mother supplemented her income by going charring. It was all she knew as she had been in service all her life.

Like everyone else, we had our good times and our bad times and you saw them through and got on with life as best you could.'

A NEW LIFE

Moving house in the 1920s left vivid impressions on one little girl.

'I knew my mother had married because I had been her bridesmaid and had been left at home to a bread and butter scramble with my cousins instead of going to the reception. It seemed a long while later that Mother came back for me. No grown up had told me what was going to happen. Granny said, "Come here, dear, put on your hat and coat and go with Mamma" – for all I knew we were going to Southwell just on a little trip.

My woollen bonnet strings were tied, my gaiters buttoned to the knee, my navy pilot coat fastened and a huge hairy scarf tied into a Scotch waistcoat that hardly left room for breath. You never see a Scotch waistcoat these days but they were quite common at that time on toddlers and often grown-ups wore them too. You simply tied a long scarf around your chest and fastened the ends behind your back in a knot if there was enough scarf – with a large safety pin if there wasn't. I did not have gloves but Auntie Jossie's fur muff which I promised to look after and return. It was a treasure in its own right with a tippet – a fur tie for the neck – similarly made in real sealskin which had been brought from Newfoundland by Auntie's grown-up stepson who was a sea captain. Auntie had been a widow for many years but wore the furs every winter. I loved

117

to stroke the greenish black-brown fur and imagine the seals gliding through great icy waves and towering icebergs on the other side of the world.

When we reached the garden gate Mother was there, wearing knee-length Russian boots (very fashionable), a leather coat loaned by her ex-army brother and a cloche hat I hate to this day. Fully expanded it held about two gallons and was striped in brick, black, violet and white. Many a nest of laid-away eggs I've carried home in it and many a morning's dewy treasure of mushrooms. It's still around somewhere. Outside the gate stood a horse and dray. Nothing unusual about that, there were horses everywhere at that time, but I knew this horse, his name was Owd Paddy and I did not like him. He had a nasty habit of blowing in my hair and when you are a very small seven year old, this was unnerving. Then the dray was covered round with sacking and from within came squawks and rustles that meant hens and I didn't like hens. It was my own fault, one of Granny's had pecked my inquisitive hand very badly a week or two earlier as she did not like me to investigate her nest. George was driving Owd Paddy – I didn't like George either. He was young and very different from us all and it was small wonder that Granny didn't approve of Mother's marriage to him. (He didn't like me either and this journey was the beginning of a 20 year war between us.)

Mother hauled me up onto the "box" of the dray. It was a long rail-backed seat which formed the lid of a large roomy box holding all sorts of things, grease, odd straps, string, crayons, market cards, frost nails for Owd Paddy's feet in bad weather, nails, hammers and more. Now I was by no means a fastidious child, or a sybarite but it struck me that the seat was very hard, very high and very cold but just then George slapped Paddy with the reins and we moved off.

It was a long drive by such transport and in those days although only about 20 miles, it could have been across the world. Paddy trotted heavily, lumberingly; he was what was called a clean legged horse but his great fiddle head and powerful body were all shire and his legs were Suffolk Punch if anything. The roads, away from the main road, were not neat, tidy tarmacadam but could be "mended" for nearly half a mile at a time with egg-sized flints – far from smooth and pot-holed here and there. The dray had iron tyres on the wheels and they made a trundling noise like an iron-hooped barrel being rolled – a noise that has gone forever; very conducive to headaches, particularly as the dray had the most primitive of springs. The fowls smelt, and as time went on it grew worse. The journey took about six hours. We stopped twice on the way, once for a cup of tea while Paddy got his wind after a long hill and once for me to stretch my legs.

We slowly approached the village of Syerston, past the russet-leaved oak, the bare horse chestnut, the huge elm, the overgrown blackthorn hedge. It was almost dark and here and there were small lights twinkling – very small lights because many of the cottages only had candle light or a Kelly lamp and set it on a window sill to light the wanderer home. We had turned into a narrower lane, there was a tiny light flickering over to the left and we were stopping. Mother lifted me down and I immediately fell down as I had sat on that box for so long I had become cramped.

All the garden hedge was made of lilacs with an arch of wedded white and mauve lilac over a tiny green gate. I went through the gate past the pump in the yard and on the door-step sat two rabbits – real live rabbits. The door was green with a fuchsia growing on one side, an everlasting sweetpea on the other but what really captivated me was an enormous Virginia creeper which covered the whole house to one side of the door and an apricot tree climbed up the brick wall at the other side.

Mother had lighted the hanging paraffin lamp and as she got a hasty meal ready I sat by the fire and looked around. The wallpaper was sombre, I remember – large crimson medallions, each containing a basket of flowers, patterned it from floor to ceiling. A dark wood cupboard seemed to cover half the fire-place wall; the fireplace was huge with an opening of about six feet wide and five feet high with a side boiler and an oven and a high grate. The fire hole was so wide I looked up the chimney, following the leaping flames of the logs which blazed below and I saw, far up, a crane. I had only seen a crane once before, it was a bracket up the chimney from which an iron chain with a hook hung to take the kettle or the stewpot.

119

When we had had our cup of tea and a sandwich we went "up the fields". We went through a five-barred gate and along a cart track. It was almost too dusk to see more and I stumbled on into the next field holding on to the dray with a rope until we came to a huge wooden hut. This it appeared was to be the home of the fowls. They were duly unloaded. When I asked what I could do I was sent to pick some mushrooms for supper, so I picked up the hem of my pinny which I always wore over my few frocks. It kept them cleaner longer; that meant that one bath a week and a clean dress every month in winter was sufficient. All I knew about mushrooms was what shape they were and that they grew in fields. I gathered some very pretty ones, brown, blue, green, red, yellow, spotted and all shapes and sizes. I was most offended when Mother took one look at them and emptied them into the dyke and took me to wash my hands at the pump with carbolic soap. We didn't have mushrooms for supper, we had one egg each and a small piece of bacon with a lot of fried bread to fill up the corners.

We sat round a very old kitchen table that had belonged to Auntie Jossie who had given it to Mother for a wedding present with several other pieces of furniture. George sat at the head of the table in a beautiful antique chair with a rush seat. That made me like him even less because it was my favourite chair. Mother sat on the piano stool so that she could turn round to the fire and I sat on a kitchen chair and also on the dictionary, a massive tome six inches thick, because without it I couldn't reach. One consolation was the drawer in the table was at my side and it was very handy for slipping in crusts if they were too tough. It took good muscular jaws to chew the bread in those days and quite a long time to digest it. A good "doorstep" spread with lard was plenty to keep one going from breakfast to dinner.

Against one wall stood Mother's bureau, walnut veneer with brass handles. Over it hung the "mystery cupboard". This had a canvas front painted to look like a bookcase full of books but really it unlocked to reveal a little strong cupboard which was home to the cash box, the cartridges, the unpaid bills and one or two things which were safest out of reach like incubator capsules, calcium carbide, permanganate of potash, copper sulphate, red-lead, Paris green. They were really do-it-yourself days.

When the table was cleared and pots washed I was told it was my bedtime. My face was flannelled and then I followed Mother upstairs. The bedroom was large and cold; a dressing table across one corner and a marble-topped washstand in a recess were all its furniture. There was a tiny iron grate with a fire basket only about six inches square. The washstand held a bowl, jug, a soapdish, toothbrush dish, two large chamberpots and a china slop pail in a little cupboard. I don't remember a carpet but a velvet prayer rug was by the bed and a little bedside table for the candle. I was a very small child and it was a very large bed. In spite of the stone hot water bottle in its flannel bag I felt even smaller and very lonely. I was not afraid of the dark and I was so tired after such a day that I soon dropped fast asleep. About two hours later I was awakened by the most dreadful scream I had ever heard which was repeated soon after. I called Mother to tell her someone was being killed. She came to my room, quite unmoved by the blood-curdling sound to assure me it was an owl but I said my prayers again just for safety's sake.

The next morning it was quite light when I awoke. I washed in the ice-cold rainwater from the jug, dressed myself carefully in woollen vest, liberty bodice, long cocoa-brown hand knitted woollen stockings, navy bloomers with a pocket in one leg, flannel petticoat, serge dress, pinafore and rather heavy buttoned boots to go out and explore my new surroundings.'

TO A COTTAGE IN THE COUNTRY

From town to country, a change in pace and in experience for the blacksmith's daughter.

'It is when looking back on life that one realises how things have changed. I suppose the Industrial Revolution and the Great War changed the lifestyle of thousands – the slump after the Great War certainly changed mine. All my relations were busy working in industry. I was born during the war in Smethwick with uncles and cousins working in the iron foundries and my father as a blacksmith and farrier. Farriers were much in demand to shoe all the horses needed for transport, which had not then become mechanised. The slump came and he was "suspended" which meant that the firm did not pay him; there was no dole then, but they could recall him when work became more plentiful. He applied for a job advertised in the *Standard Mercury* and got it. It was for a country blacksmith and farrier, here at Ranby.

From a home in a typical town street, bay windowed and about two yards of blue brick path and garden between it and the street, where when I lay in bed I could hear the clip of heels on the pavement, the chimes of the Council House clock and the hum and clang of the traffic on the main Dudley Road into Birmingham, I was transported one cold February day, by a seat at the front of a lorry, along with all our worldly goods, to a cottage in the country.

I suppose the difference in the environment makes my memories so vivid. I was used to a shop next door but one, which sold more or less everything, with a bicycle shop, a baker's and a fish and chip shop opposite, street lights, and Birmingham a twopenny tram ride away. Here we were, without any means of transport to the towns, and nearly a mile to walk to Mrs Clark's shop and post office. The Co-op from Blyth did a delivery once a fortnight, and mother's catering had to be reformed. I can remember Mom asking for a bag of flour, meaning two or three pounds and they were going to send her a sackful. She soon learned to buy dried goods in half or one stone bags.

She made friends with the joiner's wife whose husband also worked for Mr Haunch. Every Saturday Mrs Brown put Reg and Geoff in the high wheeled perambulator (with me sitting in the middle, part of the way) and off we went to walk to Retford. At Babworth we sat on the bench opposite Ordsall Road end to rest and change into our "best" shoes. We changed again on our way home to save our shoes and ease our feet – oh, the bliss! In those days working people could not afford to ruin their good shoes by a long walk, only the rich could afford walking shoes such as brogues. We were lucky to have more than one pair but we were "tradesmen", which was then a bit up in the social strata from labourers or farmhands, as our wages were higher.

We could walk to Chequer House station and get a train to Retford or Worksop, but to walk there was about halfway to either place and a train ride cost money. Not that anyone in the village was desperately poor, far from it, as things were in those days. The poorest were those who moved from farm to farm not staying long. All cottages in the village had large gardens, in which a year's vegetables could be grown. My mother never bought a vegetable after coming here. Dad always had a good supply, ready all the year round, including potatoes. Farm workers usually got those, and milk, as part of their wages, along with their tied cottage. The farmers were good to my parents. I think my father's work was appreciated, as we often found a sack of potatoes or a swede, or a couple of rabbits, put over the garden gate. Everyone too had their few hens, providing eggs and an occasional bird for the table, which were fed on scraps from the household (and a bit of "pinched" corn!).

Most cottages had a pig sty, so when the cold weather came there was a supply of fresh pork, offal, sausages and pork pies. All neighbours had to be given a "fry" for which the donor's child was given one penny and the plate returned unwashed; if this custom was not followed it meant bad luck for the salted bacon. The salted chines, bacon and hams lasted well into the next year. I had always been taught that I should not accept payment for doing any little kindness, so I was absolutely dis-

123

traught when the penny for luck was pressed on me and took to my heels, and ran with the irate, flustered, neighbour chasing after me. She explained to my mother and I had to accept the coin. Oh dear, rules in the country were so different to those in the towns.

My parents always kept two pigs, one to kill and the other to sell to provide the money to go "home" for Christmas. We had to set out before daylight a day or so before Christmas and walk to Chequer House station. Dad with the wicker hamper on his shoulder, and Mom with a bag containing a pork pie, some sausages, a salted chine and a piece of ham (from the pig the previous year), with a cockerel fattened up for the feast, still feathered, tied to the side by its legs with the head dangling. Thus we would travel by train via Sheffield to Birmingham.

I think my parents must have had a good long strain of yeoman blood in their veins, for them to adapt themselves so well to country life, after their town upbringing. One story that Mom used to tell against herself was that when they went to the local cattle market to buy their first pigs she listened to the auctioneer and then nudged Dad and said, "George, I can't see where he's lost a spot can you?" and Dad replied, "Shut up you silly fool, he's saying that they are Gloucester Spots – a breed of pig."

There was another country custom which at first I could not understand; when certain people visited school everyone stood and then bent their knees and did a little bob saying "Good afternoon my lady or sir". Even if they passed in a car we did the same but that seemed to die out after a time. When Mr Mason of Morton Hall came to school in early February it meant an invitation "to his house for tea", known to us as Mason's Party, usually on a Tuesday before Lent.

All we school children rushed home at dinner time to change into our Sunday best, going back to school and then walking in a long crocodile up to Morton Hall. On reaching there, the teachers went into the Hall, and we were let loose in the grounds at the back, where we galloped about exploring, poking and prying in outhouses and woods where we would not normally have dared to go without the fear of being chased off by the gamekeeper. Then we assembled in a long upper

124

room for tea. This always made me think of the Last Supper. The tea by today's standards was, I suppose, quite plain, bread and butter, sticky Swiss buns, jam and lemon curd tarts and buns, but they were all bought ones from the bakers and this was a great treat as we were only used to home baking! After tea we reassembled in the garages to sit on forms, the parents by now arriving, who sat on the chairs brought up from the church. After each Sunday school pupil had received a prize we were entertained by a conjuror or Punch and Judy. On leaving we were all given an orange, usually eaten on the way home. The drive must have been littered with orange peel next day. The adults seemed to enjoy the walk home in small bands and there was much gossip, dropping the men off at the Chequers as we passed.

Another biannual event was the gift of a jersey from Lady Bingham, red for girls and navy blue for boys. We children did not really appreciate this as it made us all look alike. One year a very poor family came about a week before this event to live at Bilby, and the eldest boy watched with wide eyed envy as we all walked up to the headmistress's desk to receive the gift, did our bow and said, "Thank you, my lady". His name had been added at the end of the list and when it was called out he could not get to the desk quick enough, took it tight to his chest and said, "For me? Thank you Mrs." Lady Bingham said it was the best thank-you she ever had, so we heard afterwards. The year we did not have the jerseys we went up to Ranby House for a party in the summer. I can't remember these very well. I think we had tea in a marquee at the front of the house on the lawns, and we just played in the gardens and ran races on the cricket pitch. We enjoyed running down the sloping side of the ha-ha and banged into the wall, much to the detriment of the rock plants growing in the crevices; we just thought this was a dried up ditch not realising its true use.

The school was so different too, there were less children in the whole school of all ages than there were in my town class, and three teachers too. No traffic to contend with. I could skip down the middle of the road all the way to school; if you were skilful enough you could keep your top spinning the entire way, and if you had plenty of time there was always marbles. The only flat surfaces for games like hopscotch were the road and the school playground. We did not play in the gardens as every inch was cultivated, no lawns, that was a waste of growing space, so all play was on the road. Country children were not allowed to play in fields and woods, to do that provided a constant battle between us and the farmers or gamekeepers as a gang of children could make a mess of his mown hay or young growing corn, and could disturb the game birds. A "low bag" of birds in the shooting season could mean the loss of work. The appearance of a farmyard and corn stacks were certainly not improved if a ladder was left leaning up a stack and three or four children used it as a helter skelter, but oh the thrill of the slide down. The scratched and prickled legs were not felt until we had run out of reach of the irate farmer.

Word spread like wildfire when a farmer had got a supply of locust beans for his sheep, they were delicious, all the better for being "pinched". No children were over-indulged with sweets, so we devoured anything edible, "bread and cheese" from young green hawthorn, blackberries and scrumped apples etc. There were two carrier carts that visited the village when we all had some coppers to spend (twopence being a fortune). Mr Gagg came from Sutton and Mr Cobb from Retford, they both sold more or less everything in the hardware line, paraffin and sweets. I loved the cinder toffee and the lucky potatoes which usually contained a "jewelled" ring.

I had a swing in the old apple tree, how I loved that swing. When I was cross or upset I swung and swung until the mood passed. In winter, while swinging, I looked up through a tracery of twigs to the sky, spring was a canopy of pink blossom, summer a tent of dark green leaves, and autumn a shower of apples to dodge as they fell with the movement of the swing. It was a very prolific tree, perhaps due to the "muck hill" at its base. The swing was on a tree branch between three points, the earth lavatory, the pig sty and the muck hill, not the most healthy of positions. We weren't so hygiene conscious in those days. At school, the water for drinking had to be carried from the pump at the cottage on the canal bridge. Two of the oldest children were allocated to fetch it in a white enamel bucket. This was a coveted chore, it was surprising what mischief one could get up to out of sight behind the hedge. The full bucket was placed on the stone sink in the boys' cloakroom, and when a drink was needed an enamel mug, of which there were three or four, was unhooked off a coat peg and dipped in the water. After the drink, it was replaced on the peg. I think they were perhaps washed once a week or probably once a term, the same applied to the bucket, all the germs were probably too busy attacking one another to attack us.

All the children in the village went home for dinner. The only ones to eat their sandwiches at school, with no hot drink, were those from outlying farms, Bilby, Morton over Chequer House station, Forest Lock and Low Farm. There was no school bus, they had to walk unaccompanied or cycle if they could afford a cycle, which was a luxury. Miss Blackburn took no excuse for absenteeism or lateness, that meant the cane.

I had to fetch the milk before going to school, there were no deliveries then. We had ours from Hayles, Chequer House Farm, and the milk was still warm when we got it. If the maid was busy, and we were waiting when the cowman brought in the two buckets of milk, we set about filtering it and then separating it. The milk was put into large containers, usually pancheons, something with a wide top, and left until the next day to settle and the cream to rise, then the cream was skimmed off. This was known as skimmed or "old" milk and was sold for one penny a can full, the cream being saved for butter making. We also bought one pint of new milk, before skimming, for twopence. Often when the maid came we had all the milk attended to, saving her a lot of time. We bought our butter from Mrs Taylor at Low Farm.

I did not do badly education wise, we had good grounding by teachers who knew their job and did it to the best of their ability, getting the most out of us. We stayed at the village school until the age of 14. At the same time there was much to learn about living, working and play. Children had to help around the house, farm and garden, there was nothing else to do and when we were free we made the most of our environment, birds' nesting, paddling and fishing with a stick, cotton and bent pin.

But the world was changing, things were becoming more mechanical, more people were acquiring bicycles and motor cars. The buses were running between Retford and Worksop, even to Sheffield. The world was opening up to us. We were heading for another upheaval, but we had all our teenage and early married life before that, and that's another story.'

CHORES AND GAMES

We all had our chores to do before and after school, and pocket money was not always readily available. Our games were simple and went in seasons, and we used the roads as our playgrounds, untroubled by motorised traffic.

SIMPLE PASTIMES

'Our pastimes were simple ones – walks and rambles round the country lanes around Sutton Bonington, looking for wild flowers and birds' nests (without stealing the eggs), climbing trees and making houses in them. What could be better than a picnic in the fields on a summer's day, or a drive out by pony and trap? At home on winter evenings we played board games such as snakes and ladders and ludo, dominoes and tiddlywinks. We had sing-songs round the piano and played the old wind-up gramophone, and the cat's whisker wireless with headphones was just coming in. On the way to school we played whip and top and bowled our hoops. It was quite safe as there was scarcely a car to be seen on the roads.'

OLD ROGER IS DEAD

'Everyone seemed to play together, skipping to rhymes, whips and tops, marbles, leapfrog and hopscotch.
    One of the games we played at Hayton in the 1930s was about Old Roger:

128

Old Roger is dead and lies in his grave
Lies in his grave
Old Roger is dead and lies in his grave
Ee-ay, lies in his grave.
They planted an apple tree over his head
Over his head
They planted an apple tree over his head
Ee-ay, over his head.
The apples grew ripe and they all fell down
All fell down
The apples grew ripe and they all fell down
Ee-ay, all fell down.
There came an old woman a-picking them up
A-picking them up
There came an old woman a-picking them up
Ee-ay, a-picking them up.
Old Roger got up and gave her a clout
Gave her a clout
Old Roger got up and gave her a clout
Ee-ay, gave her a clout.

This was acted out in a group, all with appropriate actions of course.'

FUN AND HARD WORK

'I was one of nine children and we lived in an isolated cottage at Rampton, a long way from the road. At five years old I had to walk two miles to school, with my older brothers and sisters, across three fields and a "ginnel" between two houses. One field had been excavated for bricks in the past, which left hollows that filled with water and froze, so that we could slide on them. We took packed lunches, and the caretaker would boil our eggs and roast our potatoes for us. Children who lived in villages further off could come in by bus.

We played football in our kitchen with a rolled-up pair of socks (until we hit the paraffin lamp!) We played hide and seek in the open fields, and sought water-hens' eggs in the many ponds, and took them home and fried them – which was a treat for us as we did not get many hen eggs. Indoors, when we had finished our chores we would play board games like draughts.

In our family, at five years old your job was to get the sticks in for the next day's fire. At seven you would get the coal in. Then you would progress to helping on the land (we had a smallholding) hoeing, or putting plants in, even being kept from school if the weather was right for the job. We all had a little plot of our own at seven, where we grew peas, potatoes and greens, and Father, who had a vegetable round with a pony and cart, would sell our produce for us. We also had a Saturday penny for sweets. The pony used to work the land, ploughing and hoeing, harrowing, and fetching coal from the station. Father would meet us from school at the crossroads with our teas, then we would go round the Rampton Hospital estate selling vegetables. We used to ride the pony by putting a carrot on the floor, and when he bent his head to eat it we would straddle his neck so that he picked us up and could then be harnessed. When there was not much work we would ride him round the field. A blacksmith from South Leverton used to shoe him all round, as he did a lot of road work, and he had half inch square holes on the shoes into which "frost studs" could be knocked in icy weather.

When you left school on Friday, you started work on Monday on a farm: you got ten shillings and sixpence for a 50 hour week, and only Christmas day for a holiday. If you didn't want farm work you had to bike seven miles into Retford.

Boys of our class wore jerseys, summer and winter alike, and short trousers, which got handed down as you grew. You never wore "longs" until you left school. Girls wore frocks. All wore boots, laced for boys, buttoned for girls: sometimes a lace at the top of the boot used to fasten round hooks, to allow for different thicknesses of leg.

A Sunday school trip by rail from Cottam station to Skegness was our treat. Cottam was two miles away, you either walked across the fields or if you were young a horse and cart would take you. Parents came too. From your potato-picking money you would save for a secondhand bike and could ride to school. At 14 you could have your own paper round, and in the war we could be messengers to the Home Guard at 15.'

JOBS AFTER SCHOOL

'Father, Mother, five brothers and I were part of three generations farming on the Seely estate in Woodborough. We lived in an old farmhouse which knew nothing of modern conveniences. With a large family plus two farmhands to feed and care for, Mother worked hard from morning 'til night. I can remember Father buying Mother her first washing machine. It was like a cradle and we kids used to love helping to put in the clothes and turn the handles.

We had our jobs after school too. Mine was scrubbing out the two large milk churns with soda and water and longhandled brush – I couldn't reach the bottom without that. The milk was put into the churns and taken, twice daily, by pony and trap to the dairy in Sherwood, the driver collecting groceries and supplies on the way back. My Saturday job was to clean all the family's shoes ready for church the next day, when we all wore our best clothes and smelt of mothballs. We had to have learnt the collect for Sunday school and our parents made jolly sure we were word perfect. Saturday was bath night. Water was heated in the copper, the hip bath filled and put in front of the kitchen fire. Everyone had their bath, water being constantly emptied and replenished.

Our day began with a good breakfast of oatmeal porridge, fat bacon and bread with cocoa and at 8.15 we started walking to school. In all weathers we crossed eleven fields, wearing clogs, changing into our school shoes at a friend's cottage, near school. Doing, of course, the same in reverse on the way home. The school rooms were heated by cheerful fires and we were allowed to sit at the front because we had come so far. The teacher made our cocoa at lunchtime and we ate our sandwiches. Before I left at the age of twelve, I had to be able to sew a pair of boy's trousers, a blouse or shirt to fit myself and knit a sock. The second sock never was made and the first was the cause of many a tear.'

STREETS OUR PLAYGROUNDS

'My family moved into Nottinghamshire in May 1934, two months before my tenth birthday, and as my father was a pub-

A little Worksop girl on her birthday in 1920. Dolls were rare treats and very precious.

lican by trade we took up residence in the newly refurbished Denman's Head Hotel which occupied the whole of one side of the Market Place in Sutton in Ashfield.

My elder sister, two younger brothers and myself were quickly installed in various local schools and settled in well, and our parents began the mammoth task of improving the image and reputation of the pub which was the only residential hotel – or commercial hotel as they were more commonly referred to in those days – in the town, but which nevertheless enjoyed the doubtful honour of being known locally as "the cow sheds".

Life as a child in the early 1930s was a happy, innocent time, in my experience. There was little vehicular traffic on the roads then other than an excellent bus service (threepence return from Sutton to Mansfield). We came too late to enjoy the trams, they were discontinued in 1931.

In my school days we walked to school for nine o'clock start, walked back home for dinner (not lunch) between twelve o'clock and one o'clock and ended our school day at four o'clock. We had no school dinners, but a third of a pint of milk was served to us at morning break. This was paid for by those who could afford it, and given free to those who could not. We took our "milk money" to school every Monday morning, tuppence ha'penny. Another custom for me and my friends was that on our way back to school, after dinner, we would call at "Auntie Pat's", a small, dingy, not very clean (by present day standards!) sweet shop, and there we would purchase a ha'porth of sweets priced at two ounces a penny. These were always put into a cone shaped bag and were usually all eaten well before we reached school.

The streets were safe to walk in then and were our playgrounds. The year was divided up into "seasons" too. I can't now recall exactly when each season fell, but I remember there was a season for whip and top, a season for marbles and a game we called "snobs", a skipping rope season, a ball season and a conker season. Nothing was ever written down or published, we just seemed to know when to put away our skipping ropes and bring out the whip and top!'

'There were lots of skipping games and if you were lucky you could beg a good skipping rope from the greengrocer. We used to do "Dutch skipping" with two ropes.

We played snobs, which was played with five cubes on the hand. A great favourite was whip and top and we decorated the top with coloured crayons or chalks to make a lovely pattern when it was spinning. This could be played on the road as there was little traffic coming through Southwell. We played various ball games up against the walls of the house.'

SING ALONG

'When I was young in the war years my friends and I would have lots of fun playing in the air raid shelters and around the static water tanks in Mansfield. We also used to play on the market stalls. We went to the Granada cinema on Saturday mornings for threepence, to the Grenadiers Club. The organ would come up from under the stage and we had a sing-along before the pictures started. The song I remember most is *Any Old Iron*.'

SCHOOLDAYS: THE BEST YEARS OF OUR LIVES?

Fires or stoves in the classroom, long walks to school and wet clothes drying on the fireguard, all age schools and strict discipline – memories shared by generations of village children. Schools changed very little until the 1960s, but many of us have cause to be grateful for the hard work and dedication of our teachers.

NO FEAR

'School was a mile away and if not taken by my father in a pony and trap we had to walk. We had no fear of walking on the lanes alone. School was heated by a black stove and at dinnertime we ate our sandwiches in school. When we moved to senior school we cycled two miles or walked if the snow was too deep. There we had to wear uniform. In winter a tunic, blouse or jumper, black stockings and velour hat; in summer a panama hat, lisle stockings and dresses made by Mother in specified material, and a blazer.'

OPEN FIRE AND BORSTAL BOYS

'When I started at the village school at Lowdham there were open coal fires and a teacher who seemed enormous and was all dressed in black. There were washbasins with cold water only and carbolic soap. The older girls made Horlicks in mugs with nursery rhyme characters on for the younger pupils, and we paid a halfpenny a mug.

In 1930 a schoolmaster named Mr Barker took us to the school gate where we lined up to watch a group of boys march past. They were all wearing navy shorts and jackets and had taken over a week to march from Feltham in Middlesex. They were going to build the first "open" Borstal in the grounds of Lowdham Grange and live in tents while it was being built. Before it became an institution, a family named Gibbs lived at the Grange and we used to go there for maypole dancing and tea.

The villages were not at all dismayed to have Borstal boys nearby, they were very well accepted. We used to walk up to the Borstal for dances in the gymnasium about once a month, run by the Church or the British Legion. As the Borstal was an experimental venture (run on public school lines) the officers were very pleasant and hand-picked. Quite a few romances were born at these dances and two or three local girls married officers.

The boys marched down, in groups of "houses" to the church on Sundays, and to night school in the old school. Occasionally they would misbehave – once they took the

135

vicar's car and another time they pinched the milkman's float, loaded up with milk for delivery. They found the float, milkless, in Leicestershire, eventually.

At Christmas the boys, together with an officer or two, would deliver logs and holly to the old people. They also used to bring a lorry with a piano on the back to sing carols. In later years the boys came out, unsupervised, to help pensioners in their gardens or with a bit of decorating, or to help tidy the churchyard.'

A LONG WALK

'I went to Trent Boulevard school in West Bridgford, which was a long walk from Gamston. There was no transport and in those days the A52 was no more than a lane. School uniform was optional but most wore it: black gymslip with white long sleeved blouse, black stockings and shoes and a black beret with black and white tassel. There was no gabardine in those days but a black or navy reefer coat or blazer in summer. Underclothes consisted of all in one vest and pants ("coms") with buttons down the front and an opening at the back for obvious reasons, and on top of that a liberty bodice, a sleeveless vest of flannel with buttons down the front and very warm. Classes in school were large, 40 to 50 children, and the teachers were strict.'

GUNTHORPE SCHOOL

'There were only two classrooms and during the cold winter months the school was kept warm with stoves. The boys' and girls' toilets were outside in the backyard and hands could be washed in a basin with cold water at the back door.

I started school when I was five in 1921. I was left handed and the head teacher tied the pen or pencil to my right hand, but when she was not looking I got a friend to untie it. If the teacher saw what was happening she would creep up and slap me across the neck. This went on until I was twelve years old when we had a new teacher, Mrs Pilgrim, who let me write with my left hand.

The highlight of the week when I was twelve was to go on

136

the bus with the rest of the girls and those from Lowdham to Carlton chapel schoolroom where they had a cooking range. We went for the whole day and learned to cook. We also went once a week for nature walks by the Trent side and East Bridgford side of the river.

In 1927 when the old toll bridge was blown up, the whole of the school stayed to watch the divers at work. After the dinner break we went back to school to find the teacher standing behind the cloakroom door, and we all got the cane for being late.

We played with marbles, snobs, whips and tops. On Shrove Tuesdays we played battledore and shuttlecock. In the village street we played at bowling hoops, as there were only horses and carts, or the occasional carriages with four horses.'

JUST ONE SCHOOL

'Welbeck Colliery school was built in 1923. We started when we were five years old and there was just the one school, which we left when we were 14 and ready for work. We had very good teachers and had to do as we were told, but enjoyed ourselves with parties at Christmas, games days, plays, singing and dancing. At the May Day celebrations with the May Queen and maids of honour and page boys, the children danced round the maypole, with the girls in white dresses if their parents could afford it. Mostly we wore tunics, gymslips and blouses as there was no real uniform.

We played lots of games such as whip and top, battledore and shuttlecock, cricket and football. We learned to swim in the river Meden running through the village.'

'Little girls would arrive at Welbeck Colliery school in their clean pinafores and all wearing undergarments of liberty bodices with rubber buttons and fleecy-lined knickers, often with a pocket for the handkerchief. The teachers made an inspection to ensure each had a hanky and stars were given for clean teeth and nails. Discipline in schools was very rigid and, in some cases, really harsh. Joan recalled the teacher nipping her neck and wriggling the flesh. Margaret could remember having soap put into her mouth for swearing. During playtime milk was distributed. It came in third of a pint bottles with cardboard tops, having a hole in the centre for a straw. These tops were often collected as they made useful bases for making woollen pom-poms. In winter it was often so cold that the milk froze and rose above the neck of the bottle.

The lavatories were in a row and it was quite common practice to avoid the end one, referred to as the "Fever Toilet". Nobody seems to know the origin for this, but we were assured it went on for years. At the end of each day sawdust was scattered on the school floor before the caretaker swept it. If you did not attend school it was not long before the "School Bobby" appeared at your home wanting to know the reason. If you made a full attendance there would be a prize at the end of the year.

In the mining area they also had a "Lawn Bobby" to stop children walking on the grass in front of the colliery houses. If you were caught doing such a thing it would result in a note being left on your Dad's miner's lamp and a fine.

The village policeman was a regular sight and if you were in trouble with him for such offences as scrumping, then there would most certainly be trouble from your Dad as well.

Joan could remember that her Gran's upbringing had been even stricter. Gran was expected to be in by nine o'clock, even when courting. One night she was late and her father locked her out and she spent the night in a chicken coop. After that iron bars were put across the windows as a precaution from anyone letting her in from inside.'

TEACHERS

'I lived at Sturton le Steeple until I was seven years old. There were three teachers and a pupil teacher at Sturton school. Mr Cheeseman was head, Miss Atkinson the infants teacher who wore long black skirts and had to lift the top one to get her handkerchief from her petticoat pocket, and Miss Birkinshaw who cycled from Everton on Monday morning and lodged in the village until Friday. I cannot remember learning to read but I do remember writing with our fingers in a sand tray. We also had slates and slate pencils.'

Back to school – a pupil from High Pavement School, Nottingham buying school uniform from the Co-op Stores in Parliament Street, September 1938.

ALL VERY POOR

'I went to the small village school at Trowell and used a slate and chalk to learn the three Rs. We did a lot of craft work – weaving, knitting and sewing. Pupils left at 13 and there was no higher education. We were all very poor and the boys wore old jerseys and short trousers, the girls anything that was secondhand or handed down through the family.'

QUITE A DISTANCE

'I attended a little Trust school for my first year at school, then moved up to the Trinity school at Southwell. I used to walk quite a distance to this school and always came home for dinner, except if it was very wet or snowing and I took my slippers to change into and my sandwiches. I thought this was lovely. I was about six or seven then.

After moving to the National school for the next three years, this wasn't quite so far and if we were well behaved and sat up straight, sometimes we were allowed out a little earlier. This was great, because if I ran home across Harvey's fields I could just make it before the Minster clock stopped playing the hymns. Then at the age of twelve I moved to Newark to go to the high school and we had quite a journey. We went by train on the old "Push and Pull".'

THE AIRSHIP

'As a young child I remember the whole class being taken into the playground at the Whinney Lane school at New Ollerton to witness the passage of the airship R101.'

HAPPY WHEREVER I WENT

'My earliest recollection of school is in 1924 when I attended Python Hill infants' school in Rainworth where the headmistress was Miss Clark. She always wore brightly coloured clothes and she had straight dark hair. She spoke clearly and slowly and everything about her made me think she was French though I learnt later that she was English. At playtime we usually played "tiggy" or skipping when the rope was turned by a girl at each end. From there I went to Python Hill senior school housed in the same building. The headmaster was Mr S Cogin and his son Alan was in my year. Miss Enzor taught the top class, the 13 to 14 year olds, and she seemed to be the deputy head though I don't think that she received any extra salary. The teachers had to sign a book every morning stating the time they arrived in school. Mr Cogin was always popping into the classroom to tell a joke about "Pat and Mike".

While I was at that school I went for three short periods to three other schools. In 1925 my maternal grandfather developed cancer of the throat and after an operation in a Sheffield nursing home, he went back home to Springfield Farm, Belph. My mother and her sister went there to nurse him until he died and during this time, my cousin and I attended Welbeck Abbey school, where the headmistress was Miss Bingham. The children sat at desks tiered up from the front of the class with the teacher at the lowest level. My cousin and I had to go through one of the famous Welbeck tunnels on our way to and from school and I didn't like that at all. Sometimes we walked the mile or so to school and sometimes we rode in my grandmother's cart, pulled by Kitty the pony. When my grandfather died, all the grandchildren were taken up to his bedroom to see him lying in a coffin. The youngest of us would only have been five years old.

Once when my mother was ill, I went to stay with her sister and I attended the school in New Ollerton. I always enjoyed school and I think I was happy wherever I went. I loved maths, especially mental arithmetic. Another time, when my mother was ill, I lived for several months with my other grandparents and I attended Whitwell school just over the border in Derbyshire. This was the only time that I was hit with the cane. Miss Baker, my class teacher, hit me with it several times across my open palm because I could not sing the song *Drink to me only with thine eyes*. I still cannot sing!

TWO SCHOOLS IN THE VILLAGE

'There were two schools at Ruddington. The Church of

England school took in infants of both sexes and girls, while the boys, when out of the infants class, went to the boys' endowed school on the village green. We didn't have uniforms as such but most had tunic dresses with jerseys underneath.

Sport for the girls was netball, played latterly on the village green but before that we carried the posts with nets down Vicarage Lane to a farmer's field and played on the flattest surface we could pitch the posts on.

WINTER DAYS

'There were summer days of sunshine and sitting on the school steps at Upton, playing cat's cradle and other simple games, but in the winter the huge black coke stove with its three-sided guard would belch out clouds of acrid smoke when the wind was in the wrong direction. The stove itself would have on it a container of milky-watered Horlicks which heated through during the early part of the morning and which we were given at playtime. The fireguard on snowy or wet days would be draped with steaming socks, mittens, coats, pixie hoods and the like, drying in readiness for "home time" and filling the room with steamy woollen dampness.'

STRICT BUT FAIR

'An abiding memory from schooldays at Upper Broughton is Empire Day, when we would sing patriotic songs. Discipline at school was strict but fair. Everyone had to know their tables and we learnt long passages from the scriptures by heart. We played the traditional games in their season, starting with whip and top in the spring through to snobs (five stones) in the cold days of winter. All the children walked home for dinner at midday, except the few at outlying lodge farms.'

ALL AGES

'At Hayton school in the 1930s there were about 40 children aged between five and 14 years. There were two teachers, Mrs Fretwell the headmistress and Miss Clark the infants teacher. The room was divided by a curtain and there was a combus-

142

tion stove at one end and the coal fire at the other.

The girls learned knitting, sewing, embroidery and crochet. At that time we all wore crocheted hats which we made ourselves. The boys did painting and drawing while we were sewing. It was a church school and we always had assembly with hymns and prayers each morning and at dinnertime we sang grace – "Be present at our table Lord" before dinner and "We thank Thee Lord for this our food" when we came back after dinner. We were fairly well behaved but sometimes had the cane for talking. My brother remembers being caned on both hands for "nettling" a girl on Oak Apple Day.'

LEARNING TO SWIM

'In 1930 the Newark bathing place down Tolney Lane on the river Trent was the only swimming pool in town. The teachers from the different schools would take us there in groups. In those days a man named Mr Taylor would give each child a chance to learn to swim by placing a strong linen belt round our waists. He would stand on a plank holding us up with the rope and tell us how to work our arms and legs. When the river was in flood we were not allowed to go as there were dangerous whirlpools while the water was so deep. It was not until some years later that they made the new bathing pool in Barnbygate in Major Appleby's garden (the former mayor).'

SPANNING TWO DECADES

'Blyth Top School was built in 1215 as a leper hospital. Centuries later it was converted to use as a church school for boys. The Education Act of 1885 required it to be used for boys and girls, education being free and compulsory.

In the 1930s the old men of the village used to tell us how they paid twopence a week to attend school, but in the spring would stay away to earn fourpence a day scaring rooks off the newly-sown corn.

The school moved out during the war because the army required the premises and would have commandeered the new building on Retford Road if the move had not been made. On an October day in 1940 the soldiers helped the children to

143

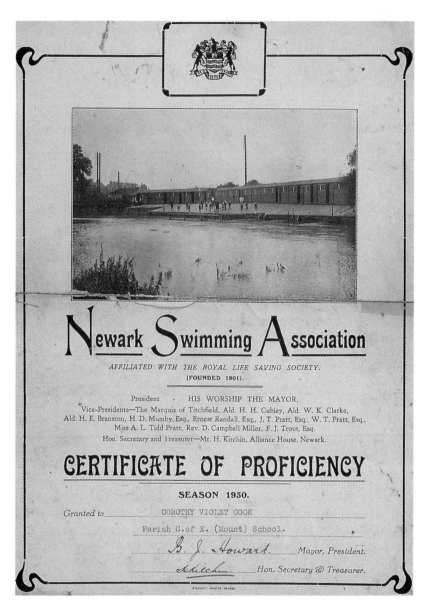

Newark Swimming Association

AFFILIATED WITH THE ROYAL LIFE SAVING SOCIETY.

(FOUNDED 1901).

President - HIS WORSHIP THE MAYOR.
Vice-Presidents—The Marquis of Titchfield, Ald. H. H. Cubley, Ald. W. K. Clarke,
Ald. H. E. Branston, H. D. Mumby, Esq., Ernest Randall, Esq., J. T. Pratt, Esq., W. T. Pratt, Esq.,
Miss A. L. Tidd Pratt, Rev. D. Campbell Miller, F. J. Trout, Esq.
Hon. Secretary and Treasurer—Mr. H. Kitchin, Alliance House, Newark.

CERTIFICATE OF PROFICIENCY

SEASON 1930.

Granted to _____ DOROTHY VIOLET COOK _____

Parish C. of E. (Mount) School.

_____ *B. J. Howard.* _____ *Mayor, President.*

_____ *Kitchin* _____ *Hon. Secretary @ Treasurer.*

STENNETT, PRINTER, NEWARK.

Many local children learned to swim with the Newark Swimming Association.

144

carry books and furniture across the fields to the present school.

Until the end of the war the Old School was the canteen and rest room for the soldiers at the camp in Blyth Hall Park, staffed by the village women. There were moments of drama when passing convoys stopped, needing meals from the limited rations. When a hundred men who had been rescued from Dunkirk walked from Worksop station everyone in the village was asked to give what they could spare.

For a few years after the end of the war the old building served as a parish room for social events and evening classes. Then the Memorial Hall was returned to civilian use and refurbished, so the Old School became neglected and dilapidated. In the 1960s it was "rescued" and skilfully converted into two dwellings, regaining its ancient name, the Hospital of Saint John.

Our schoolgirl memories span the two decades in which the Blyth Hall Estate broke up and motor traffic changed the village.

Inside the ancient building the long schoolroom was divided by a folding screen and heated by two round iron stoves. The cloakrooms had been built in 1885 with "yards" for boys and girls with standpipes and earth closets, and handbasins inside smelling of carbolic soap.

Although Colonel Willey (later ennobled as Lord Barnby) was our Squire, Henry Mellish of Hodsock and his sisters Miss Agnes and Miss Evelyn were managers and benefactors of the school. When the Misses Mellish came to visit and inspect the pupils' work the girls "bobbed" and the boys saluted. Occasionally Lady Barnby also came. She required a curtsy if one met her in the street. Patriotism was also compulsory. We celebrated Royal Oak Day and Empire Day, sang *God bless the Prince of Wales* and kept the two minutes' silence on the eleventh hour of the eleventh day of the eleventh month, usually out of doors.

Inside the school the first class to move up from the infants' school sat at one end of the building where the desks were arranged in tiers, so that the top pupils sat four feet above the dunces at the front.

In needlework lessons each girl made two garments a year, a

dress and a nightdress. These were entered in Blyth Show. The boys learned gardening in the plots across the road. They also produced vegetables and flowers for Blyth Show on Bank Holiday Tuesday.

In lessons the pupils sat at desks in twos or fours with holes for the inkwells, which were filled each Monday morning with reconstituted powdered ink. The pupil teachers issued the necessary steel nibs and blotting paper. A bell hung outside and each morning the first arrival had the privilege of ringing it for five minutes.

Being built on a green mound the school provided a sledge-run in winter. On the road we played hopscotch, whip and top, and shuttlecock and battledore in season. These customs ended when the old green lane which led to Ranby was widened and metalled as part of the A614, the main road through Nottinghamshire.

When Lord Barnby died in 1927 the children lined the street as the dray carrying the coffin under its bank of evergreen passed by, and each boy carried a wreath.

Soon after this the estate was split up and sold, men went to work in the pits at Harworth and Langold and bus services enabled people to travel into Worksop and Retford.

Doncaster races brought coaches and streams of cars. On a race evening the local pubs were crowded, and the cheerful winners handed out Doncaster butterscotch to the children. Violet Denton, a pretty crippled girl in a wheelchair, sold flowers to visitors charmed by her brave smile.

The great character of the 1930s was the vicar, Canon E. C. Kempe, who took the pupils to church for scripture lessons. He it was who insisted on the new school continuing as a Church of England school. He taught us many things – still passed on to generations of children and grandchildren – including this prayer:

God bless thy little child tonight,
And keep me safe 'til morning light.
Thy love has kept me through the day,
Thy love will lead me all the way.
In dark or light take care of me,
So I will sleep and trust in Thee. Amen.'

THE WORLD OF WORK

ON THE LAND

Farming has long been the backbone of Nottinghamshire life, and life on the land changed very little until after the 1950s. Horses were still the power on the farm, and haymaking and harvest were times of great importance in local communities.

HIRED ON THE TOWN HALL STEPS

'In 1916 a farmhand could be hired from the town hall steps in Newark on May Day. A boy of twelve would live in and be paid £9 a year. Any expenses he incurred during the year, such as new boots, would be deducted from his wages.'

I CAME TO THRUMPTON IN 1933

'I was born in Leicestershire but came to Thrumpton in 1933 to work for Farmer Frank Towers. I was to be in charge of a herd of cattle, but over the years I looked after horses, sheep, arable crops, and almost everything else.

My first cottage was on the farm, plagued with rats from the adjoining barn and by a smoky chimney. There was an outside lavatory over an ash pit. I later moved to a council house in the village.

My wife and I went by ferry to Long Eaton on a Saturday night to do the shopping, though a butcher called on Fridays. I had to walk over the hill to Gotham for a drink as Thrumpton has never had a pub. I kept a pig which the farmer killed for me, and I salted and hung it in the outhouse. I grew plenty of fruit and vegetables and there were rabbits to catch.

On a typical day, I had a drink of tea at 5.30 am followed by milking the cows. Breakfast was at 9 am (toast, boiled bacon and beetroot). Dinner was midday (cheese sandwiches in a hedge bottom if you'd been ploughing); tea between 3 and 4 pm (meat and vegetables, suet pudding) and at 8 pm some

Binding oats at Cropwell Bishop. Horse teams continued to provide the power on the land until the 1950s – these are Ginny, Actress and Jollity.

cheese and biscuits. I was rather partial to a couple of boilings of new nettles.

At first I worked with horses to plough, and was expert at sowing broadcast in the old fashion. I had my first tractor, a little Fordson, in 1940. I had 30 cows to milk before 7 am each morning. I could carry 18 stone of wheat; 19 stone of beans; twelve stone of oats and 16 stone of barley, often up a ladder. On a wet day I'd be in the loft mending sacks.

I also did shepherding and shearing; getting beet and mangolds up and potato picking, though women mostly did this for sixpence an hour. My wife helped with this and with sugar beet knocking, and threshing. She worked until the eighth month of pregnancy.

All the hours you worked on a Sunday paid your weekly

rent (roughly 6 shillings a week). In 1933 my wage was 31 shillings a week. The products of my garden were worth the equivalent of £100 a year.

I nearly always had a dog as a pet, and a ferret.'

THE FARM WAS OUR LIVELIHOOD

'In 1920 my father took over Grange Farm (200 acres) in Gamston. We had a waggoner for the horses and land work. One man ploughing with two horses from dawn until dusk was a very hard day's work. The cowman was responsible for all the milking and the cattle. We kids had our jobs too, feeding the pigs and sheep. Mother coped with the poultry.

I was mad about horse riding and wanted a pony. My father made a deal with me: milk five cows, then he would buy me a pony. It took forever. For weeks I tried and tried and after quite a time I managed it. The cows were very patient though at times they did get frustrated. However I got my pony.

Farm wages were poor. The cowman and his wife had a tied cottage on the farm. His wages were ten shillings a week plus milk and potatoes. His wife helped my mother in the house for a little extra. Gamston was a small hamlet consisting of four farms and twelve cottages and most of the men were farm labourers, though some would cycle to work in Tollerton, Plumtree and Radcliffe.

Every year we had a harvest supper in the large barn at Grange Farm. For several weeks beforehand the men would be busy cleaning the barn and bringing in benches. The women would prepare the food – home-made bread, cakes, pies, hams, beef, pork, the whole "Monty". There would be several barrels of beer and sherry for the ladies. We children were allowed to attend, no babysitters then, and a genial time was had by all.'

HORSES AND CALVES

'I was born and bred in Retford, the son of a cattle dealer and trader. June was always a busy month as it was haymaking. Back then we had to cut by scythe, turn the hay, cock it up then lead it out and stack it. This went on until dark, it really was hard work but enjoyable.

My Dad would buy horses in Manchester at Bradshaws Auction. He would leave Retford station on the 7 am train and book some horse boxes in Manchester for his purchases. He would return to Retford around midnight where my uncle and I would meet him. The three of us together would walk the horses through the town up to the farm on Spital Hill. People always knew when Bert was back home!

At 17 years of age I worked for Len Thorpe on his farm. I used to milk cows by hand and then go off to deliver the milk. The milk was twopence a pint and had to be measured out – no milk bottles in those days. I worked seven days a week and my wage was 15 shillings. To make extra money I used to buy a few hens that had finished laying, pluck and dress them and sell them to the customers on my round. If I got three shillings each I was doing well. I always advised my customers to either boil or steam the fowls first and then roast them and hope to goodness they came tender.

I remember 60 years ago, in July 1934 it was sports day at East Drayton – a big event then. It was held on a Saturday and my Dad and I had stood Retford Market with one week old calves and we sold five to Mr Laughton at Egmanton, two to Mr Price at Laxton and two to Mr Small at East Drayton. On our way home we called in at the sports field and my Dad entered me in a horse race which I am proud to say I won. The prize was either ten shillings or £1, I can't be sure but to me it was very acceptable.'

CATTLE AND HAY

'On our farm at Bunny my father, who had retired when I was one year old, fattened cattle as a hobby. They were grazed in the fields in summer, getting water from a pond or brook. When this dried up water was carried to troughs by buckets, on a yoke on one's shoulders. Cows were tented on the grass verges to keep them tidy.

Haymaking was done mainly by hand after the mowing machine had cut the grass, and teas were taken into the hay fields for all the helpers. Hay forks were used to turn the grass when drying, then it was put in haycocks to finish drying

151

At work in the fields at Springfield Farm, Belph in 1924.

before being gathered onto the horse-drawn cart to be taken to make into stacks. These were then thatched to keep the rain out. This hay was used in the winter to feed the cattle, along with cattle cake, mangolds and swedes. Hand-operated chaff cutters, cake breakers and mangold cutters were used to make a mixture.'

A FIT MAN

'My grandfather was an agricultural labourer and it was his job to walk with the cattle from Ruddington to Melton. He also slept with them along the way. A waggon was provided to transport cattle fodder and straw. He must have been a very fit man as he also walked over the moors to Gotham and Thrumpton where his relations lived.'

FROM THE PAST

'The foundations of the old cottage, built in the early 1800s, collapsed and we built a new bungalow on the site. On digging over the soil at the bottom of what was to become our vegetable patch, our neighbour told us it was the first time it had seen either a fork or a spade since he had lived next door, and he had moved in over 50 years previously. One day about five years later, we wanted some potatoes for lunch, so my husband went down to our vegetable patch and started to dig. Along with the potatoes up came a round metal disc which he threw on the path. On inspection it appeared to have something etched on the surface, so I decided to give it a good wash. Much to our surprise, it turned out to be a silver disc, two inches in diameter, beautifully engraved with the words:

Nottm Market
Bausor's Xmas Sale 1869
won by
Mr Thomas Richardson
Calverton
for the second best pen
of grey faced wethers
bred & exhibited
by him.

153

The *Nottingham Evening Post* archives turned up the information that the first prize for the grey faced wethers (which turned out to be castrated rams) was a silver plate valued at four guineas, and the second prize the silver medal we had unearthed.

Local enquiries did not elicit any information as to how the medal could have come to be in a garden some six miles from Calverton, and as we had unearthed it in 1975 it is possible that the disc had been in the ground for something like 100 years.'

DOWN THE MINES

Mining has been a way of life for many Nottinghamshire families. These memories of coal mining in the past include those of two men from Pye Hill Colliery, relatives and friends in that close-knit community.

MINING AND FARMING

'The work in our village, now called Meden Vale, was mainly mining and farming. New Hucknall Colliery Company purchased the land for Welbeck Colliery from the Duke of Portland in 1911. The pit was sunk in 1914. The first houses were built near to the pit – what we called the pit yard – about 1915. They had no bath. Baths were taken on the hearth in a tin bath, toilets across the yard, oil lamps for lighting.

The hut that was built for the housing contractors later became the meeting hall for the village, until the village hall was built.

Work on the farms was mostly done by horse-drawn ploughs, cutters and threshing machines. Women also worked on the farms picking potatoes, peas etc. The farm is now a Government Experimental Farm and has a small housing estate of its own. The old farmhouse has been taken down and replaced by a more modern house. Women also worked at home doing chevrons on stockings. Army camps were set up during the First World War at Norton, Clipstone, Cuckney and Thoresby.

Once each year the pit ponies, which worked down the mines pulling trucks and timber, would be brought up and set free into the fields near to the pit. Freedom and fresh air, sunshine and light! It was lovely to see; the kiddies would take little treats for them.

Before pithead baths, miners would go home in their pit clothes and get bathed at home. Everybody had a job working six days a week. We had some Bevin boys during the war; they came to work in the mines and lodged with families in the village.

At our colliery there was a distillation [sic] which produced petrol from cannelcoal, or "jacks" as they are known locally. It is rumoured that this petrol was used in the Second World War. Miners often took jacks home in their snap tins because they made excellent fire lighters due to the oil content.

Warsop Vale was a thriving mining village built by Stavely Iron and Coal Company. Rows and rows of three bedroomed houses were built to house the workers plus a row of cottages, and the manager's house (now a nursing home). There was a Church of England school, the rector of Warsop always on the governing body. Empire Day was marked with a parade around the village by the children who were then given a bright new penny and an orange. Sadly this colliery is now closed.

Our village had a small sub-post office with sweets and drapery. The sweets were always on show in large glass bottles. Next door was the general shop where everything you needed was on sale. Butter, sugar and cereals were all weighed by hand and packed in the shop. If you found you had forgotten anything, whilst the shop was closed, you could nip around to the back door and get what you wanted. The shops didn't stay open as long as they do today.

We had a branch of the Co-op where most people shopped,

sadly long since closed and replaced by a general store. At the cobbler's shop, shoe repairs were done in the shop and you could get a hair cut in a shed in the garden of the hairdresser. The doctor's surgery was held in the front room of one of the houses and later in the village hall or you could go along to Warsop or Church Warsop to the surgery there.

Doors of the houses were rarely locked. Everyone knew the village bobby who used to ride around on his bike. We were a bit nervous of him but he was always willing to help out, as were neighbours. One would mash a pot of tea and off would go the ladies with their cups for a drink and a natter. Children would spend many hours in the woods and common land around the village. There were paths through the woods leading to the Carburton lakes with some beautiful rhododendrons growing alongside. During the Second World War we weren't allowed to walk in the woods as the Ministry of Defence used it for storage and offices. A few of our local ladies worked in the woods at that time.

In 1947 our village looked as if it had been transferred from Austria. The village was cut off in deep snow for a while with no way down the lane. The colliery manager and his wife took to their skis on the pit tops and a local hill we call Wood Hill. The manager's house was a very large one with lovely gardens – it is now flats.

In 1960 a new village was added to house miners from Scotland and Newcastle and 380 houses were built on the site of the very old Eastland farm.

We were never really what you would call well off but had a happy time growing up.'

SON OF A MINER – JOE'S STORY

'The Crescent, Selston, is a small hamlet of about 36 houses, built on a hill. I was born there 11th July 1906 – the son of a miner. I was the fourth child. There were two elder sisters and a brother and later two more brothers. The earliest age I remember of my separate existence is about four, when I was still wearing frocks. Little boys wore frocks until they were about six. I started school at five – I didn't like it much!

We were poor children, as our family income was scant, but

156

The headgear at Rufford Colliery, near Mansfield.

we were always fed fairly well, with the emphasis on quantity not quality. We grew potatoes, (mashed, roasted, chipped!), and our own vegetables. Barm dumplings were plentiful and in summer we had "frommerty" [frumenty]. When the farmers had reaped their corn, we peasants were allowed to glean the ears which were left. The grain was threshed, stewed, and eaten with milk and sugar. Barm dumplings were balls of dough, about the size of tennis balls, boiled for 20 minutes and served with milk and sugar or treacle. Our meals were simple, tasty and filling.

There was entertainment for the village children all through the year: bird nesting, jumping brooks and climbing trees; Bonfire Night, when Clarry Coleman's firecracker blew off his cap tip and singed his hair; boxing matches between the older lads in the Dumbles – once two brothers, Cogger and Ben, gave an exhibition bout. Ben landed a nose-crunching blow straight away and Cogger didn't like it one bit. He sailed into Ben and soon there was blood all over the place. We all knew

157

that it wasn't right for brothers to fight like that but none of us had sufficient courage to stop them. Cogger started arguing with Ben about hitting so hard and the whole thing ended in argument.

Cogger was the tough guy of the village. He was a rough-headed individual with a head like a brick and no feelings at all. It was Cogger who had a dust-up with the rough youths who came each year to the fair or "Wakes". One year there was a lad with the Wakes strutting about like King Kong and challenging everyone. Cogger stood near the Wakes entrance looking as innocent as a lamb. When Wakesy came up he wasn't looking at Cogger and Cogger wasn't looking at him, but as he was passing Cogger shot out his foot, stopping Wakesy's ankle, and down Wakesy went into the mud. He jumped up glowering at Cogger and rushed at him like a bull. Cogger side-stepped and gave him a sizzling jab in the lower short ribs. Wakesy went out like a light, and his mother emerged from her caravan. She was about half a ton of woman, big and strong as a brewery horse. The local lads were cheering but Cogger had beat a tactical retreat.

Whilst we were out creating our own brand of mayhem, the womenfolk were house-keeping – and it wasn't easy. Their work was hard and exacting. Monday was washday. My mother and sisters used a tub, a ponch and often a kit brush. Then there was progress – a washboard of corrugated metal to rub the dirty clothes on. Of course they still used the ponch which exhausted the user and battered buttons to hell. There were more clothes worn out in the wash than on the wearer. On wet days the clothes were dried in the kitchen. We seemed to be ducking under them all day. Woe betide the child who threw a paper ball and knocked them down – women descended like spitting cats.

The cleaning was done every day but Saturday was special – blackleading and floor scrubbing was done then. We had a large cooking range in the kitchen. This had to be blackleaded and polished. The stone slab of the hearth was washed and done over with rubbing stone, the enamel hearth plate laid over the slab, and the fender and fire irons on top. These were brass or steel – brass were polished with Brasso, steel with bathbrick.

158

At 13 I left school and worked for my grandmother as a yard boy, looking after her prize pigs. Then I went to James Oakes' pipe yard and from there to Pye Hill pit. I worked there for nearly 50 years, becoming an underground official. One day the manager sent for me, saying that the fan had to be stopped for repairs. The fan creates the circulation of air in the mine, known as the ventilation system.

The fan was stopped for seven hours and then run for seven hours. During that time the pit had to be examined for gas, because of the previous lack of ventilation. There were two seams to be examined – Low Main and Blackshale. The manager asked who should be sent: there had to be two men to examine the seam together. The manager took Tom Richardson and I took Harold Brogdale, because when you are examining for gas you need someone you can trust, and Harold was, and still is, my best friend. When we got to the seam it was full of gas.

This gas is highly inflammable and a spark produced by a boot striking a piece of rock could cause an explosion which would blow up the pit. After reporting to the surface we made a hasty retreat.

Once when we had started winding coal there was a clatter in the shaft and a mass of rust, sludge and dirt fell to the bottom of the pit. We stopped winding and went to sort out the problem.

We were up 100 feet in the shaft when we found the trouble. Some of the staples holding the conductor to the side of the shaft had rusted, allowing ropes to fall down. Some were across the shaft and the cage couldn't get through. We in the cage signalled to be lowered – and one of the ropes slipped under the cage. We couldn't move. The ropes were made of steel and very heavy. If any weight fell onto the king plate it would release the cage and send it crashing to the bottom of the shaft. We hung like spiders in a web until we cut the rope and were lowered to the bottom.

I have known tragedy – my sister Olga died from rheumatic fever and the shock left my father a broken man, unable to work.

I have known great happiness – married to a charming lady for nearly 50 years, with three sons and three grandsons.

I have seen progress – brass ornaments, pictures and picture rails removed, coal fires discarded and I hear of houses without chimneys. Progress?

So there it is – just ordinary memories and no spectacular deeds. Looking back it all seems fresh and I don't believe the old fool who wrote that "life is just an empty dream, for the soul is dead that slumbers and things are not what they seem". [account written in 1982]'

HAROLD – PROUD TO HAVE BEEN A MINER

'I was born at 37, The Crescent, Selston on January 8th 1910. My cousin Joseph Lakin also lived in The Crescent. His grandmother was my grandfather's sister. We were friends when we were children, living in a close knitted community, and we remained friends until Joe died some years ago.

The houses in The Crescent, which were built to house the miners, had a living-kitchen, with a kitchen range to heat water and do the cooking. Off this room was a pantry. Then there was the best room, used only on high days and holidays. Upstairs, two bedrooms and a "box" room. At the end of the backyard, which was quite long, we had an earth closet and an ash pit. In later years the "privy" was made into a proper lavatory, and a bathroom was built onto the kitchen. For many years baths were taken on Friday evenings in the long tin bath, hauled in from the backyard and filled with water heated on the kitchen range. From the best or "front" room, there was a door onto a green and the long gardens. My father taught me to be a gardener, starting when I was three. Now I am 84 and still doing my own garden.

I was 14 when I started work at the Bull and Butcher pit at Selston. My grandfather had started work when he was ten, working on a farm, so I was lucky to continue my education until I was 14. I worked on the screens, picking dirt out of the coal. In future years this would be known as the coal preparation plant. I did that for two years and then moved on to "ganging" underground in the hard coal. Ganging was taking the tubs to our position, the "stall", loading in the coal with a shovel (hand-filled) and bringing out the loaded tubs to go to the surface.

At 18 I moved to Pye Hill pit with my father and ganged for him and George Barker. We gangers didn't send rubbish out of the pit. The slack was sorted out before the tubs were sent up. We put the slack at the side of the stall in the "gobbins".

When I was 23 I joined my father at getting coal in a stall for two years, and then, having studied at night school and passed the examinations, I became the youngest Deputy to be set on at Pye Hill pit. I was 25 and at that time I married Winifred and bought land on Wagstaff Lane at Jacksdale to build a house. The house looked over from the back over three fields to the pit. The land cost one shilling a yard. Now there are houses on each side of the lane, and a bus service! We waited years for pavements and street lighting and there was very little traffic on the lane even when our children were small.

The coal industry was nationalised in 1947, but before then, and for a number of years afterwards, there was no pit canteen or pithead baths. The miners took their food for the shift, or "snap" in a snap tin, along with a bottle of water or cold tea. Usually I took bread and jam; sometimes in the summer there would be beetroot sandwiches. My little daughters delighted in eating left over bread and jam when I came home. It seems that bread and jam tastes better when it's had a shift down the pit!

Before the pithead baths were built the miners went home in their dirt, hoping that their wives had hot water ready for them, and hot towels on the kitchen range. I washed in the scullery and it was the delight of my eldest daughter to take over the duty of washing my back, traditionally done by the wives.

There were some times at the pit which, looking back, are thrilling, but were emergencies. The time I went with Joe Lakin to test a seam for gas was one. That happened one Christmas Day, and we didn't tell our wives what we were going to do. It was a highly dangerous job – one spark and the whole pit would have gone up.

Then there was the Sunday evening when I was going down with just a cutting team to prepare for the Monday and we saw the screens on fire. Some men had been welding, and sparks had ignited the coal dust and caused a flash fire. We couldn't get water, so we made a barrier with sandbags to contain the fire. The screens were partly destroyed but it could have been a horrible disaster. Among the team were the three Scothern brothers: Bernard, Ernie and Lloyd. I had a letter of commendation from the National Coal Board for saving the pit, but we all did it, working as a team.

During my time as a miner, I have seen the introduction of modern mining. I started with wooden props and went through to steel, steel screw and Roofmasters. Trepanners brought a new way of winning coal – machine instead of shovel. Conveyor belts were replaced by pan and chain and the trepanner loaded the coal onto the chain to be delivered to the main belt.

Once we walked to the coal face – then a manrider system was introduced. Men going down at Underwood to get to the face rode on a manriding belt.

First, we had oil lamps, then Ceags, then Concordia and finally cap lamps, although there still had to be one oil lamp for every ten men to test for gas. We also had the Ringrose lamp, which showed a red light when there was gas.

Pye Hill pit always had a problem with water. I have gone down the shaft in the cage in winter, knocking off slabs of ice from the sides. The ice had to be cleared before the cage could deck and coal be brought up.

Eventually I became an overman, first on night shift and then senior overman. For many years I worked with my cousin Joe, but he had to retire due to ill-health.

We found fossils and iron pyrites in the pit. We had the jokers you find everywhere. The pest control man put down poison for the mice and a notice appeared saying "Dear Mice, don't eat this". There was one Polish miner whose name was so long we called him Dick Alphabet. We had a mines rescue team and an ambulance team. I was the captain for both. During the war we had a Home Guard company from the pit under Lt-Col Wright. I was chairman of the Pensioners Tote, which gave pit pensioners a summer outing and a dinner and parcel at Christmas.

In 1972 I retired. Now Pye Hill pit is closed. The view from my window shows a grassed spoil heap, with cows grazing. I am still a gardener, thankful for my memories, glad that I don't have to go down the pit, but proud that once I was a miner.'

LACE MAKING

The traditional craft of lace making kept many families fed when times were hard. Today machines do most of the work, but complicated patterns are still done by hand.

THE TRADITION OF LACE WORK

'In Nottingham the tradition of lace work runs in families. If Grandma was a lace worker usually a daughter then a grand-daughter took up the lace trade either in a factory or as a home worker if there were children to be looked after. That tradition still continues to this day.

Many lace firms have moved away from the city centre lace market to industrial estates on the edge of the city, or to the suburbs with their purpose-built modern units. The old build-ings and the road are unsuitable nowadays for the constant access to factories needed by delivery and collection vehicles.

The lace trade has always been a large employer of manual labour and it was considered the fourth most important trade in Nottingham at the end of the 18th century. Although Not-tingham remained the hub of the lace finishing and merchant-ing and lace machine building, during the 1860s the fancy lace manufacturers began to move out to Long Eaton ten miles away partly due to the formation of the Nottingham Lace Trade Union and the Nottingham Lace Employers Association who entered into collective bargaining, but also in Long Eaton they were outside the scope of the union and there were lower land rates and wage rates, also the chance to build new modern factories.

Edna was born in Sneinton in 1916, the youngest of three children. They lived in a two bedroomed house with one living room, a scullery, and an attic on Carlton Road. Edna's father served in the First World War but as thousands of men dis-covered on their return in 1918 and 1919 there was no work available, so, with his eldest son aged 13 years he emigrated to

Canada where he died and was buried. Edna never saw her father again after he emigrated. Mrs Coulton had to sign papers allowing her husband to go, and which stated she and the remaining two children would be supported financially by him and thus, no matter how poor they became they could not claim off the Poor Law relief even though money was only spasmodically received from Canada. The second son when he left school moved away to find work on the farms, eventually joining the army and serving overseas in India. Edna was grown up before she had contact again with her brothers.

A large number of women in Sneinton did home work for the lace trade and Edna's mother was a middlewoman, that is, a contractor who collected the lace from the factory, took it home and gave out to the women living in the surrounding streets. All the women knew roughly what time she would return from the factory and they gathered at the bottom of the street to wait for her so that they could all see that no one was given more work than anyone else.

The lace came from the factory in a big piece which had to be separated into parts. Each woman would be given two or three dozen or so parts to take home to strip. The finished lace had to be back at her mother's by 8 am the next morning. Work that was spoilt or dirty was not paid for, so if the factory, say, required 700 yards of finished work, and the lace measured, say, 720 yards, an overlooker would often manage to cut out the spoiled part. If this was not possible all the other women would chip in a few pennies to pay the woman knowing that this action would be returned when they themselves had mishaps. Very often the scalloping, drawing, warping and clipping of the lace was done into the night to be finished in time for return to the middlewoman. The children were often roped in to help.

The textile trade is always one of the first industries to be hit by economic turndown and the slump of the 1920s affected the trade badly. Edna's mother had to lay off her hands, just doing by herself what bit of lace work was available; she also scrubbed and cleaned at her employer's factory.

When Edna left school she worked as an errand girl and drawer of lace for a factory, but after three months she suggested to her mother that she worked at home with her as the

164

Elizabeth Baggaley working on lace outside her home. Generations of Nottingham women have worked at this most famous of local crafts.

lace trade was starting to pick up. At the age of 17 years she took over her mother's role as middlewoman to ease the responsibility and hard work required of Mrs Coulton, who worked for the same firm all her life until they sold out in the 1950s. Edna then contracted out to another lace firm in the city centre.

During the Second World War the lace trade factories turned to war work but the boom years for the lace took off again about 1948 when the export markets reopened. During the 1950s Edna used about 70 hands, but it was not unknown for a middlewoman to employ up to 300 hands. Today machines can do most of the work, but complicated patterns are still done by hand and the factories still use middlewomen. Edna continues to work for the same firm she joined in the 1950s, a prominent lace manufacturer in Nottingham.'

A STEADY HAND

'My grandmother, a widow, did outwork for a lace factory on Victoria Road in Sherwood. I often went with her to collect large bundles of lace inserts for underwear and blouses from this factory and remember the deafening noise of the lace knitting machines. Her job was to clip the surplus net off the inserts and neaten them ready to be sewn onto garments. This was skilled work that required a steady hand and good eyesight but the pay was very low. In later years I remember when the "Battle of Britain" lace panels were made and I saw them many times.

When my husband came out of the army he became a representative for a lace curtain manufacturer on Broadway in the lace market area of the city. These are now all listed buildings. I was also familiar with the famous Adam building on Stoney Street and have been in the chapel where the workers began the day with prayers and worship.'

IN SERVICE

For many young girls, going into service was the only option available to them when they left school. It was hard work for little pay – some liked the life but others couldn't leave fast enough!

I NEVER REGRETTED IT

'When I was nearly twelve we left and went to live in Lincoln-shire and I didn't come back until I was 15 and went into service as a housemaid. This was at Balderton. My sister was cook and there was also a parlourmaid, gardener and a chauffeur. It was a very good training for future life. Very strict but fair. We had two half days a week off duty from 2 pm and had to be back by 10 pm. For very special occasions we could ask to be a bit later. I remember one of the first jobs I was given to do was to clean the brass stair rods and fittings. I thought I had made a good job of them but had not thought to clean underneath the fittings and I had them all to take up and do again – it taught me a lot.

When my sister left I took on the post of cook. I was only 17 and had had no training and the first Christmas dinner I cooked was for 22 people. We used to look forward to visitors coming to stay and more so to the tip they gave when they left which was usually about half a crown. As my wage was then £2 a month, tips were very welcome. Out of our money we had to buy uniform. We wore cotton dresses in the morning with large white aprons and cap (any colour dress) and in the afternoon a black or dark green dress with small white apron and cap. We were really treated as the family except we had our own living quarters.

They were a very happy ten years and I only left to get married. I never regretted being in service or a maid as we were called. By the time I left, my wages were £4 a month and I had saved £81 for getting married.'

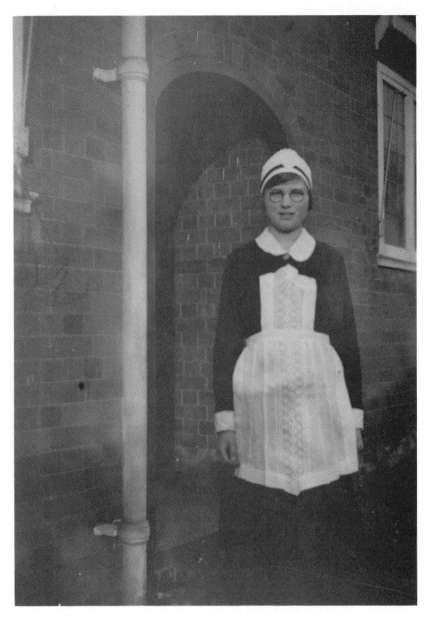

Rosamund in her afternoon uniform in 1933, which had to be bought from her wages.

I DIDN'T STAY!

'I left school at 14 and went as a daily maid in East Leake. I worked from 8 am to 5.30 pm for six days a week. Sunday I was required to set the tea and wash up afterwards. All this for ten shillings a week. I couldn't wait to leave and went to Greenwoods hosiery factory as a lockstitch worker on my own time and earned about £2.'

OTHER WAYS WE MADE A LIVING

There were, of course, dozens of other ways we made a living, often close to home when villages were industrious places of craftsmen and shopkeepers. From milkmen to stocking frame knitters, here are just a few memories of jobs of the past.

THRESHING AND ESTATES

'Women at Ranby were housewives except for the local school teacher and district nurse. My father, Mr Baines, had the local threshing machines and employed eight men. They had to get up at 4 am each day to prepare the threshing machines for the day's work and to get up steam. They worked at farms throughout the area – Darlton, Bothamsall, Wheatley, Clumber, Blyth, Scrooby, Morton Hill, Ranskill. The slack time of year for the machines was from June to September.

Other occupations in the village were farm workers, building trade, blacksmith, whilst a few men worked at Manton colliery, Mr Billyard was a winder and Mr Norman worked for 48 years on the shunting line on the railway. Due to the number of large houses in the area: Morton Hall, Ranby Hall, Ranby

House, Babworth Hall and Osberton Hall, many people were employed to work in the capacity of domestic servants, chauffeurs, gardeners, woodmen, gamekeepers and nannies.

When threshing was taking place the men had to tie string round their trouser legs because of the numerous rats coming out of the stacks. The children had sticks and would kill the rats and mice as they came out. Some of the boys would collect the mice and chase after the girls with them. Two men would work on the stack to feed the machine, one to bag the corn and the other to do the dirtiest job of all, which was moving the chaff. This meant that the men were covered in dust, from head to toe, from eight in the morning to four at night. At the end of the day the machines were moved to the next farm so that they were in position to start the next day's work. Lunch was bread and cheese with strong tea which was served in white enamel buckets and was ladled out using the drinking mugs.'

A VERY RURAL VILLAGE

'Sutton Bonington was very rural in the 1920s and there were no less than 15 farms, large and small, within the village boundaries, providing considerable employment for the menfolk. All the ploughing, sowing and reaping was done with the help of horses, and fresh milk was delivered daily around the village by pony and trap. There was a farrier, a blacksmith, a saddler and a shoemaker, but by then there was only one frame knitter left. The biggest employer in the village was the Hathern Brick and Terra Cotta Company. Some people travelled in to Loughborough to work, either by bicycle or by train from Kegworth or Hathern stations, or later on in the decade by the small bus which ran through the village from Kegworth to Loughborough.

There was the village bobby who pounded his beat every day, and the road sweepers who swept the whole of the village manually each week. There were six shops, two of which baked and delivered their own bread daily, and the Co-op also delivered their bread by hand-cart, but that was baked in Long Eaton. Groceries were delivered on a weekly basis.'

MILK AND MILLS

'My father was the milkman at Lowdham in the 1930s, and delivered the milk by a horse-drawn float on which stood the churns. The horse (Old Tom) was a former hunter so when the hunt was in the vicinity and he heard the hunting horn, he had to be restrained or he would take off!

Pearsons, seed merchants, were local employers and grew masses of tulips where the residential estate called Lime Tree Gardens is now. They were a colourful sight.

I remember catching the steam train from Lowdham to Nottingham to work. There was the 7 am train for Boots employees and a train at 8.19 for others. The trains always seemed to run on time. An old chap called Ike used to sweep the roads and whatever the weather, even if there was deep snow, he would have cleared a path for the early morning workers to catch the 7 am train.

Lowdham mill, on the Dover beck, was a working mill up until 1946. When I was a child I used to watch the miller, Mr Carby, grinding the corn and meal for local farmers. One day after very heavy rain, the beck was very full and the wheel was turning so fast that the whole place shook and pots were falling off the shelves!'

IRON, COAL AND FARMING

'Trowell had few houses in the 1930s and was mainly fields and farm cottages, along with one or two bigger houses. Farming was done by hand with spades, hoes and scythes being used. Horses drew the ploughs and other pieces of machinery and everyone helped to make hay and with the harvest.

Jobs were to be found in the factories, the mines, farming, the local ironworks or in domestic work. Trowell had a colliery in those days and the village had its own forge and blacksmith. An ironworks with tall chimneys belching smoke and dirt overlooked the village.'

171

FISH AND FORGE

'In the early 1950s I remember Cauldwell mill with its green lorries loading the flour from the hoist above the road at Southwell. The bags of flour were of linen with "Greet Lily Mill" and a Union Jack on them.

There were 13 pubs in Southwell, and two fish and chip shops – one in King Street and one on Westgate where Harry Taylor had his own greengrocer's. The old forge on Westgate belonging to Beckets opposite the Shoulder of Mutton and the smell of the hooves burning – I can smell it now.

Pat Frost ran a coffee bar down Queen Street, a real den of iniquity, it was a motorbikers' paradise. It didn't last long as there were too many complaints from the "old fogies" (I'm one myself now).'

MAGGOTS AND HORSES

'There were nine farms at Normanton on Soar until the 1940s, and 30 shire horses in the village which were used for working the land. There is a triangular piece of grass outside the Plough public house and this was where the blacksmith's forge stood until 1900 when it was moved across the road to one of the houses. In its original place was planted a chestnut tree!

A maggot factory operated alongside the railway line at the end of one of the village lanes, and tins of maggots were sent out from there all over the country. Villagers objected to the smell and the flies and many official complaints were made. All to no avail, since in 1937 the District Council Medical Officer of Health decreed that there was no problem according to the Public Health Act.'

MY FIRST JOB

'Armed with a reference and determination I started on my rounds every Monday and Tuesday morning visiting all the local factories looking for work. Huthwaite was the first call, arriving at eight o'clock and standing in dark small corridors outside the various departments, peeping to look inside the workrooms as the workers walked in. There would be about

172

eight girls waiting there, and after a while the manager of that department would arrive, we would stand in two lines with our backs to the wall to make room for him to pass.

If on walking through he said "Sorry, no work" we rushed to the next department hoping to join a line there and that the boss was a little late. If by any chance the manager walked past and didn't speak to us we knew he might want some workers and would stand with our fingers crossed hoping that our name would be called. We had already given our names when we applied in the first place. Again if unlucky we would dash for our bicycles and in groups pedal to the next factory, Simpson, Wright & Lowe and if their queue seemed a long one we would turn to Briggs & Greenwood and hope. By this time, about 9.30 am, we returned home as the places had been filled by then.

Tuesday was the far end of Sutton factories – they seemed to employ people on this day and after a round there we would pedal down to the Quartex, then into Sheepbridge Lane, a hard pedal back with very low spirits after nearly six months of this routine, with applications for other kinds of work in between.

My name was finally called and along with another girl entered the swing door, sadly smiling to my poor unlucky queuing and pedalling comrades.'

AT STATION ROAD SCHOOL

'My first job was at Station Road school at Teversal, starting on 12th October 1936, salary £159 a year.

The domestic science room was across the playground from the main school, adjoining the needlework room. A new range was installed when I arrived and apart from that there was a large gas cooker which was much more reliable than the range.

The children who lived some distance away brought sandwiches for lunch, and some of them brought scrubbed potatoes, carved with their initials, to the cookery room before class to put in the range oven to cook slowly for noon dinner time, a hot and nourishing addition to their sandwiches, especially in winter. No dining room then, lunch being eaten in the school hall.

Another recollection is of a row of deep sinks along one side and the sports outfits, mostly dirty woollen socks from football, which after a match the girls had to wash by hand: and these would be put on an airer near the range to dry. It was very difficult to get them clean as the mud was ingrained.

I don't think somehow the girls would do it today!'

STOCKING FRAMES AND NURSERIES

'At the turn of the century, stocking frame knitting was Woodborough's main industry. There were knitting frames in almost every cottage, all worked by men, but the seaming by hand was done by the women who earned tenpence for 24 seamed stockings, a time limit being given for the work, often causing the women to work late into the night by candlelight or oil lamp. William Lee, the inventor of the stocking frame, we like to think was born in Woodborough; a number of history books claim that to be true.

In the 1920s the knitting industry began to decline and realising that the village had good growing soil, lying as it does in a valley with bunterstone underneath, vegetables and fruit were produced for market and taken at three o'clock in the morning by horse and dray to the wholesale market, held at that time on Bath Street, Sneinton. A poem written in the 1950s said –

"Our heritage was handed down from those
    who've gone before
When they used to turn out stockings on
    their knitting frames galore,
But brussels, peas and strawberries now is
    where our interests lie,
And we hope that market gardening in Woodboro'
    will not die."

At the time that was written there were 20 to 30 market gardeners in the village; now, sadly, there are only four or five.'

WAR & PEACE

Mr Pickering of Worksop, photographed just out of the trenches. Every town and village in Nottinghamshire lost men during that dreadful time.

THE GREAT WAR 1914–1918

The First World War brought Zeppelins over Nottingham-shire, and hardship to many left behind when their men marched off. Villages and towns all over the county lost men, as the war memorials show, and we celebrated with enthusiasm when at last the peace came.

ZEPPELIN!

'I was not born until 1916 so have few memories of the war itself, though I do remember being taken to see the bonfires which were lit around Ruddington after the Armistice. My father related to me how, the night I was born, a Zeppelin came over and he was taken to task for having a chink of light

Arnot Hill Hospital Sports in July 1918, an effort to entertain soldiers recuperating from their wounds.

in the blackout in the front bay window. He was let off without a fine when he explained that his wife was in labour and he was very busy!'

'During the war a Zeppelin flew over Woodborough village, causing great fear and excitement. Fifteen village lads died in that war.'

ON STRIKE

'I was at school during the war when the gypsum miners around Barton in Fabis went on strike. Several brave souls at the school decided to go on strike as well. They went round the village in defiant mood but when they got back to the school, Mr Wood, the headmaster, was waiting for them with a large cane, saying, "Now it's my turn to strike!"
During that war most of the teachers were women because the men were away fighting. Mr Gallagher, the rector, took all the school for singing if teachers couldn't get across Barton Ferry because of fog or other bad weather.'

THE SECOND WORLD WAR
1939–1945

Just two decades later, war touched Nottinghamshire again. Air raids brought terror and tragedy to the county, and we struggled on with everyday life as best we could.

AIR RAID 1940

'I lived in Pym Street, off St Annes Wells Road, Nottingham. One night in 1940 the wail of the air raid siren floated across the city on the night air. The quiet streets were awakened from stillness to panic.

My mother climbed upstairs into the attic of our three storey town house. She aroused me from sleep, my arms were thrust into my dressing gown, then she guided me down two flights of stairs into the living room, which I remember had a black-leaded grate, the fire embers burning low. A clock on the mantle shelf read 2 am. My outdoor coat was wrapped around me for warmth. A small square shoulder bag which contained my gas mask was slung over my shoulder. Gas masks had to remain with us at all times in case the Germans dropped gas on us instead of shells. "Don't forget your gas mask" was a well known slogan posted on walls and notice boards all over Britain. It was a rule we had to live with throughout the war.

The air raid shelter where we were going was very cold, so my mother grabbed blankets which were put aside for the raids and food to sustain us.

My father returned dressed in the navy blue uniform of the ARP (Air Raid Precautions). His job was to patrol the district looking for chinks of light showing through the curtains at windows and doors of the houses. He would bellow "Put that light out" in a loud voice to the offending householder. Another job the ARP did was, if incendiary bombs (fire bombs) were dropped on property, to put the fire out with hosepipes and buckets of water.

My father came in the back door, shutting the blackout curtains which were draped across the inside of the door. The black curtains shut out the glare of electric light from the outside world. (A glow of light from a building would tell enemy planes there was a town below and make a good target for them to bomb.) Father searched the cupboard and drawers for a plaster or bandage. He had cut his hand badly as he dived for cover against a building as incendiary bombs were pelted from the planes.

My mother, myself and dog stepped out into the night air, first shutting the electric light off before we opened the back door. Descending two steps we were to cross the cobbled back-yard to our neighbours. As we crossed over, the sky was alive! One spectacular blaze of light and fire, large searchlights thrust their beams, first left, then right across the heavens, scouring

179

the sky for enemy planes. As one flew into the beam the ack-ack battery stood by, waiting with their giant guns pointed skyward ready to blast it to smithereens before it bombed the city. Incendiary bombs made the sky an inferno, bombs exploding with a fiery blast on the roof tops of the houses.

The beer-off or corner shop was our next door neighbour. It was owned by a friendly couple, Mr and Mrs Richardson (in those days you could pop into the beer-off with a jug for a pint of draught beer to be drunk at home).

Mother knocked on the door. It was opened and we were shown into the living room at the back of the shop. It was a dark room and like all the windows around Britain, the window was criss crossed with brown sticky tape to stop the glass flying if it was shattered by a bomb blast. In the centre of the room stood a large oblong dining table under which had been stood the covered budgie cage.

Quickly Mother tied the dog on a lead to the table leg, so that he wouldn't run amok while we were down in the cellar. Everything was done swiftly, our aim was to get to the safety of the ARP shelter. We didn't realise until later how funny it was, us leaving the dog to keep the budgie company. We entered through the door and walked down the steep stone cellar steps. The coolness greeted us, so did the strong smell of stale beer. It was like going into a tomb, with the hollow sound. Barrels of beer lined the walls. It was very cold and cramped as the barrels took up much of the space. The walls were whitewashed. In the small space people were littered about on chairs and stools, some with blankets wrapped around their bodies to keep out the cold. Finding a seat I squeezed beside Mother, and resting my head on her knee, I tried to sleep. Suddenly we heard a plane above, then a shrill long whistle as the bomb whizzed through the air. The engine cut, we held our breaths and waited for our end. Were we really in a tomb? The air was tense as silently we sat waiting, looking up at the ceiling expecting the bomb to hit us in the next split second. There was a massive explosion, the cellar walls shook, then all was hush. Silence prevailed! As we pulled ourselves out of shock, glancing around the horrified crowd we were all in one piece. The bomb had been very close indeed.

The fear and waiting went on all night long. Four more bombs were dropped on the city that night. After sitting through a long silence the all clear siren wailed. What a relief! Now we could crawl to ground out of the shelter. We dragged ourselves exhaustingly tired up the cellar steps, longing to get into our beds. Hoping Hitler's disciples would not disturb our sleep again that night.

The next day I went to see the bomb damage, which was in the next street. The road looked as if it had been hit by an earthquake. It was blocked with all manner of debris; bricks, mortar, crunched up window frames, smashed door supports, all stuck out of the debris, churned together with household goods and personal effects. The front of two houses had been ripped away by the explosion. The bedroom floorboards were hanging downwards like piano keys. Perched on top was the bed, half hanging as if on a cliff edge. Pink bedding was cascading to the ground, covering the destruction as if curtaining it from view. Luckily no one was hurt, they were safely tucked away in the air raid shelter.'

WE LOST EIGHT LADS

'When war came again to Woodborough we lost eight lads overseas. In the village itself, one night a German plane dropped its load of incendiaries right over us, causing many fires and giving the ARP a great opportunity to use their fire-fighting equipment and show their skills. The only casualty was a farm horse killed in a field by a piece of shrapnel which beheaded it. Over £60 was collected in the village for the replacement of the horse.'

RUNNING THE GAUNTLET

'It was a time when the temporary wards which had been built in the grounds of the Kilton Hill Hospital, Worksop, were occupied at last – by wounded Dunkirk boys. As a Red Cross nurse, I was at last off duty for a day. It was the evening of 8th May 1941, and I was going home to a village three miles outside Nottingham.

The bus neared its destination just as the air raid siren

started its familiar wailing. This meant there would be no transport for the rest of the journey. I started the trek home. At frequent intervals air raid wardens attempted to stop me and get me to go into the shelters but I resolutely refused and marched on, in spite of the bombs dropping all over Nottingham. The throb of the German planes and the thud of the bombs on their targets never ceased. The sky grew red with fire. I finally reached my destination to find the family in their underground room, stocked up with blankets and enough food to last for days. I had run the gauntlet and arrived safely.

I found out that 159 people had been killed that night and many churches, ordinary houses and important buildings had been destroyed.'

YOU GOT HARDENED TO TRAGEDY

'I was married in 1940. My husband had not had a steady job until 1938 so we had to wait but with war breaking out and also both my parents dying quite suddenly (within six weeks of each other), those of us left at home decided we would marry, except the youngest boy who was 15. He went to live with my married sister but joined the air force two years later.

We had evacuees at Ruddington, some of whom did not stay long. I did duty at the receiving station when they came, also switchboard duties at the Home Guard headquarters.

When the sirens went, it was my job to go and help the invalids to get up (if they wanted to), in the street where we lived. My husband was a special constable when at home, but was on loan to the Signals (from the PO); when he was away with them, our only communication was a war field office box number. I eventually worked as a Post Office telephone engineer (before I had to register). I enjoyed every minute of the work, hard though it was.

During the blitz on Nottingham it was pretty horrendous, but somehow in those days you got hardened to tragedy and we managed to survive.

Clothing coupons were a headache, it took ages to gather up enough to have a good "spend up". Even so, life went on, we had dances and whenever possible, played tennis. We kept our courts going for when the lads came home.

During the winter season, we had a goat on loan from a farmer. The goat was kept on the courts, tethered by a rope. We had turned two courts into allotments so we didn't want the goat to stray and eat the vegetables. My mother in law took pity on it and regularly went to feed it with bread. One day, she slightly misjudged the circuit of the rope and the goat couldn't let a chance like that go by. It neatly shoved her from behind and my mother in law landed in the nettles at the side. I wouldn't say she was very pleased about it and said, "That's all the thanks you get for bringing some nice tasty snacks." No hard feelings, she still fed it.

To feed the lads when they came home, a lobster tail purchased from the fish market fed mostly a dozen for supper at my house. Coffee was served in very small cups so that it would go round more than once. Ale was fetched from the beer-off in saucepans.

There was a lot of sorrow for those who did not come back but also thanksgiving for those who did return. Street parties were organized; villagers were always good at these events.

Going off to work was memorable because of the double-decker buses with balloons on trailers at the rear to help out the fuel situation. The journeys were long and tedious but we got to work in the town just the same. Many times we had to get off the bus when going up Station Hill just outside our village, then re-entering on the flat.

During the war, we were allowed an extra two weeks' leave to go to Agriculture Camp due to the call-up of the farm workers. Four of us volunteered and went to a camp in the Broadway area. We worked hard and also had to do chores on the camp (under canvas by the way!).

The first night we were there, our mob said we would do the potatoes and believe me, it turned out to be sacks full. Our plates were washed up in the open and if you delayed your meal too long, I'm afraid you had to wash up in the soup.

Our jobs varied, ie sage bush weeding (acres of it, a back aching job), onion weeding and cherry picking due to the fact that several of us were used to climbing ladders.

We had an American camp next to ours which, of course, was out of bounds but this didn't stop a conversation or two

183

and chocolate and nylons being passed through the wire. We enjoyed our nocturnal amblings!

When we arrived back at Nottingham station, our cherry farmer had sent us a basket of cherries each. A nice kindly thought.'

EVERYTHING CHANGED

'Farming changed when war was declared as grassland had to be ploughed up to provide corn etc for food. I helped on the farm as I had just left school. Neighbours at Bunny helped one another by lending implements or doing various tasks, ploughing, cutting corn with binders etc. I learned to plough with two shire horses, a lovely peaceful life. We had incendiary bombs dropped all over our farm which we helped to put out. On the farm adjacent to us the stacks in the yard went up in flames. One air raid warden cycled down with a bucket of sand after we had put them all out, the other one called next morning! Farmers did a lot for the Red Cross and held auctions at the cattle market where they gave bullocks, sheep, pigs etc to sell.

The Women's Institutes held courses in first aid, knitted for the forces, made felt slippers to send to hospitals etc. Cycling between villages and towns was not easy at night as cycle lamps had to only show a light the size of an old penny or less and all houses were blacked out. Rationing in the country was supplemented by home-produced eggs, milk, and pig killing.

Land Army girls helped on farms, being billeted sometimes in large commandeered houses, or with the farmers and family. German and Italian prisoners of war also helped on the farms. The Germans worked very hard indeed on the threshing machines and stacks at threshing times. The Italians liked their siestas.

Celebrations were held in the villages on VE Day and teas were held in the village hall. The Women's Institute catered for these.

Clothes were in short supply and "make do and mend" was the order of the day. Jumpers and cardigans were pulled down, the wool washed and re-knitted, very often in various coloured stripes.

Farming changed again after the war, tractors taking the

184

place of horses. Even as late as 1946 cattle could be driven on the roads to market or from one village to the other. This had to stop as traffic increased.'

THE MAJOR'S BATH

'During the war the Wiltshire Yeomanry camped in a field on Lowdham Road, Gunthorpe. They were practising putting pontoon bridges over the river Trent. As the field happened to be opposite our house, a batman came and asked if his Major could have a bath. I only had a copper for hot water in those days, so I lit a fire. The Major had to wait, but he had his bath in the end. The batman also asked if he could do the Major's ironing, which he did.'

OKLAHOMA OILERS

'The first find of oil in the UK was in a field at Kelham in 1915 but this was abandoned due to lack of funds. It was not until the 1940s that the war effort required the search for oil to be resumed, and men known as Oklahoma Oilers came over to help and were billeted at Kelham Hall. They developed the oil-fields at Kelham Hills and Duke's Wood at Eakring. The appearance of the men, strutting about in stetsons and cowboy boots, added excitement to village life. The huge lorries carrying drilling equipment were mind-boggling. The men frequented the local 18th century Fox Inn and demanded that the salt cellar was always on the bar to make the local brew more to their taste.'

MAKING DO

'At one time the weekly ration amounts were: 1 lb fresh meat, 4oz butter and ham, 3oz cheese, 2oz tea and cooking fat, 8oz sugar, and 30 eggs a year – though dried eggs were a great help.
Clothing coupons didn't go very far. Underskirts were often made from parachute material and I remember making a pair of PE pants from blackout material for use at school.'

185

YOU HOPED THEY DIDN'T STOP

'I remember when Sheffield was bombed during the Second World War. We lived in Worksop and the pots rattled and all the windows shook; we had part of a German plane in our garden. When the doodlebugs came over you just hoped they didn't stop. We were lucky in Worksop, no serious damage was done.

With clothes rationing and food rationing things were very difficult. I worked at RAF Ranskill during the war as a typist for Dr Groves, who was a scientist. Rockets were made there and these were used in the defence of Malta. Clothes began to be a problem, as we didn't wear overalls, just our ordinary clothes, and as we walked through the factory to the office we came in contact with acid from the chimneys and our stockings and clothes were full of minute holes. Two friends and myself bought some green dusters and made ourselves a short sleeved blouse out of them; they were passable! In the end the powers that be allowed us a few more clothing coupons to recompense us.

The war was now beginning to draw to a close. I was at college when it started and was married just before it ended. When the war ended there were bonfires and street parties all over England. What a joy to welcome loved ones home after so long, but sadness too for sons, husbands and friends who were lost to us. We hope they did not die in vain and pray for peace all over the world.'

MY WAR WOUND

'I'm going to fill in a little of the background before I tell you how I came to have my accident. My friend Joyce always called it my "war wound" although I think that was stretching it a bit.

She was my best friend and we usually went everywhere together. We both loved dancing and fortunately there was no shortage of venues – village halls, church halls, miners welfares, working men's clubs, all had regular dances in order to entertain the large number of troops who were stationed in the area. Not to mention the established dance halls which of

186

course charged a higher entrance fee. The large number of troops also meant that there was no shortage of dancing partners and although Joyce and I would often arrive in a twosome, we very seldom went home unescorted.

As the war progressed we saw men from many different regiments. We even had the air force at one time. There was no airfield but we figured that they had something to do with the hundreds of ammunition dumps on Budby Common. Later on came the Canadians and we learned after they had left they had gone to take part in the D-Day invasion. The only ones we were not allowed to go with were the Americans. Their camp was in Mansfield where the Kings Mill Hospital now stands. The trouble was that my Dad believed what he heard about them – you've all heard it I'm sure! "over paid, over sexed and over here". It was the middle bit that bothered him, hence the ban.

On the night in question, Joyce came round to tell me that her brother had just come home on a 24 hour embarkation leave so she wouldn't be coming to the dance as planned. I decided to go alone which was not one of the most sensible decisions that I've ever made. I hadn't been there long before I knew that I had "got off" with this very nice looking soldier. The main attraction for me was that he was the most beautiful dancer. I knew I was getting envious looks from some of the other girls but I didn't care, he was mine. When he asked if he could walk me home there was only ever going to be one answer.

We had reached the outskirts of the village when he started to get a bit amorous. Gradually the amorous advances became a bit too advanced. I tried being very firm but it became increasingly obvious that he was not going to take no for an answer. It was then that I remembered a trick that one of the girls at work had been demonstrating. The first part involved a violent jerk of the knee aimed at a certain part of his anatomy. I did this with great success although I didn't wait to see what the full effect was as the second part of the trick was to run as fast as you could, which I did.

You have to remember that this happened in the blackout, the rules of which were very strictly adhered to in our village. The ARP warden saw to that. There was not a chink of light

187

from any of the houses, therefore I knew that when I'd gone a few yards it would be very difficult for him to know which way I had gone. I reached a jitty which I knew led to some back gardens, I also knew that if I cut across a couple of these I would come out on the street where I lived – I thought I knew everything. However, what I didn't know was that the lunatic whose garden I was running across had strung barbed wire between two posts and I was heading, hell for leather, straight for it.

I hit it face first. It was just the right height for one of the barbs to pierce my right eye. How I didn't scream I shall never know. I had dropped to all fours when it happened and that is where I stayed.

I don't know how long I stayed there, I daren't stand up as I didn't know whether there were any more booby traps. Eventually I forced myself to crawl in the direction of the next garden and crawled across that one, too, just in case there were any more hidden dangers. I didn't stand up until I reached the road. I made my way home in a haze of pain. My Mum nearly went mad when she saw me. She bathed my eye as much as she could – by this time I couldn't open it so she was unable to see just what damage was done. She took me to the doctor the following day and he sent me straight to the hospital. There was some doubt as to whether I would keep my eye, they weren't very hopeful at first. However, although I lost the sight in it, I didn't lose it.

I wore an eye-patch for ages and had to put up with all the Long John Silver gags and the "You are the one eye care for" jokes. I didn't mind really, I was just thankful to be wearing an eye-patch and not a glass eye.'

HARD YEARS

'The war years were hard, when people worked long hours in factories. I worked 70 hours a week at the rubber works at Clarborough in the winters, which always seemed to be very cold, and then in the summer I worked at Saundby dairy, which was a ten mile cycle ride each day to make cheese.

The day before war was actually declared, evacuees arrived

at Retford station from Leeds. The WVS had a great problem finding places for them all but of course as our boys were called up more and more rooms became available. The second contingent came from Yarmouth and then Birmingham. Some schools had to go on part-time, with the newcomers going in the morning and the locals in the afternoon. The children must have found a great difference coming from the city to Hayton and Clarborough.

The village hall was used by both Hayton and Clarborough for concerts, whist drives and dances. We danced to piano and drums in the early days – waltzes, quicksteps, valeta, palais glide and the Lambeth walk. Then in the 1940s the dances were packed with soldiers and we began to have dance bands. Everyone seemed to go, children too.'

COUNTRY FOLK FARED BETTER

'During the war evacuees came to Laxton and New Ollerton. Children from towns and cities poured into the countryside, some with their mothers and some without. Children were not the only evacuees; military horses from London were also housed and cared for, on the farms and in the vicarage stables. Their regimental masters were serving overseas. Many Land Army girls in their distinctive uniform helped on the farms and even prisoners of war were put to work in the fields.

My Gran took a butter basket to Newark to get rations for the six in the family. On thrashing days extra rations were allowed to feed the men. Country folk fared rather better for food as they could have rabbits, chickens, their own eggs, milk, butter, cheese, fruit and vegetables.

It was a sad day when Miss Willis, a school teacher, was killed in the only air raid over the village. She had just been to ARP lectures, when three bombs were dropped across Laxton. The probable target was the nearby aerodrome at Ossington.

On VE Day there were celebrations in Ollerton and dancing around the bandstand in the Miner's Welfare grounds.'

A Christmas card from a prisoner of war at Langar Camp. Many friendships sprang from unlikely circumstances.

PRISONERS OF WAR

As the war went on German and Italian prisoners of war were often to be found working in the fields alongside local men and women. At first feared and disliked, they often became accepted by local communities, and some friendships were formed which have lasted over 50 years.

THEY CAME EVERY DAY

'I have some very clear memories of the war and its effect on the community, but also of the prisoners of war. My father owned and ran a farm in Widmerpool, and like many other farmers around the county, German prisoners of war were dropped daily and picked up at the end of each day in lorries. They were all held at the POW camp in Langar. Some, after a period of time, were allowed to live in at various farms.

Periodically the prisoners organised entertainment at the camp, which the farmers and their friends were invited to attend. During the evenings, many of the prisoners would carve and craft wooden artefacts, which they would then try and sell to make themselves a little spending money.

After the war ended and repatriation began, many of the prisoners made their way home to Germany but some made their homes here in Nottinghamshire. One who lived in on my father's farm was repatriated in 1948. Since then he has kept in touch. During that period he married, had a family and now has grandchildren. My husband and my family have visited them in Germany and on a couple of occasions they have been back over here to revisit Nottinghamshire in peacetime. On both occasions we have always been shown the greatest hospitality and welcome from their many friends and relations. He has often said that it is because he could never repay the kindness our family showed him during the war.'

THINKING OF HOME

'During the war years my father had a German POW to help with the market garden as the boy we had went into the forces. He worked for us at Gunthorpe for about two years.

Father one day gave him my mother's old bike which had hung on the shed wall for years. This he took for his transport to and from the camp. He repaired it and plaited straw for inside the tyres in place of the tube.

My mother always cooked him dinner with ours but he would never eat with us, he ate his in the shed in the garden. Dad always said he had been crying over his meal. This came to a head when he was invited to spend Christmas Day with us but he would only come if he could work. My mother put him a Christmas dinner with ours – this meal he refused, he just had his normal sandwich.

He told us that when eating our food he thought of his wife and two little girls with one slice of black bread and rice tea which was like brown porridge twice a day in a concentration camp. This was why he could not eat the Christmas meal and yes, he had always cried eating his lunch in the shed.'

THEY WERE HOMESICK

'There was an Italian prisoner of war camp at Bestwood Park during the war. The prisoners provided the manpower in the fields and on making of roads.

An appeal was made for local people to have two prisoners for the day on a Sunday. They had been made to join the army at the age of 16, they had no pictures of their families, and were very homesick.

They had to have an escort to and from the camp, from my parents' house, which I did, although only 14 at the time. It was difficult communicating, but after a while we managed to make ourselves understood.

The prisoners we had were Prospero and Fillipe. Prospero kept in touch with me for two years after they moved to another camp. After they went back to Italy we lost touch, but about eight years ago he managed to trace me through an elderly relative and we corresponded.

Then, 48 years since we had last met, my husband and I went to Italy to celebrate our Ruby Wedding, and we met Prospero for an afternoon; he had travelled from Milan specially to see us.'

AT TOLLERTON HALL

'In the later war years, after the American soldiers had gone home, German and Italian prisoners of war were billeted at Tollerton Hall. The hall itself was the mess and living quarters of our army lads. The prisoners were housed in a high-fenced compound in the grounds. They were guarded by the Polish army. The prisoners were hired out to local farmers for haymaking, potato picking etc. My father had two Germans living in at Grange Farm at Gamston. They were very hard working and trustworthy chaps so were allowed to stay with us until they were repatriated at the end of the war.'

GOOD WITH CHILDREN

'Prisoners of war were billeted at Headon Camp. They were brought by van to work on the farm at East Markham and were able to do most jobs. We provided tea but they did not always sit together to eat their sandwiches. The Italians came after the Germans had moved on. They were friendlier and very good with children. One of them made my daughter a tractor and trailer out of bits of wood and tin. It is now in the Dolls Museum at Cromwell.'

Robert Gorwood in the Home Guard, at Clarborough Tunnel.

DOING OUR BIT

Men and women who did not go into the services still did their bit for the war effort, whether that meant joining the Home Guard or the Women's Land Army, or perhaps taking part in the many schemes for meat pie or jam making, or the regular Savings Weeks.

I JOINED THE HOME GUARD

'At the outbreak of war, I was living in Warsop. My occupation was Resident Gas Fitter employed by the Shirebrook and District Gas Company. I was responsible for the whole of Warsop, Church Warsop and part of Edwinstowe. My transport to cover these districts was an ordinary bicycle, on which I had to carry my tools and piping and fittings. I was on call 24 hours a day and my wage was £2 14s a week. I was also responsible (from late August to early May) for over 206 street lights which I had to go round each evening to see that they were lit and every morning to see that they were out. The lamps were controlled by a clock. I was not allowed to leave the village without the permission of the manager, and then I had to leave word where I could be contacted. I forgot to say that I received gold pence for each journey checking the lamps which made me 14 shillings per week – winter time only. Ninety per cent of the houses had only gas for lighting and cooking.

On Friday 1st September 1939 I received along with my wages a letter from the manager marked "Strictly Confidential". This was at 5 pm. The letter stated that I was to go and shut off all taps to the clocks on the lamps and if anyone asked what I was doing to say that I was to see how quickly in an emergency we could turn off all the lamps. This was three days prior to war being declared. The lamps were never turned on again during the war.

This being a reserved occupation debarred me from the

regular army; I volunteered several times. When the Local Defence Volunteer force was formed I joined them. I was promoted to Section Leader after a few weeks in charge of stores and equipment. When we finally received the title of Home Guard we automatically became spare time soldiers responsible to military law. I was made Quartermaster Sergeant and later promoted to Company Sergeant Major of "D" Company, 8th Clipstone Battalion Notts and Derby Home Guards.

Our duties (along with training every night and weekends) were on air raid alert to patrol the fields and woods surrounding the village. We also mounted guard every night over the headquarters and telephone exchange. The lads I was with were mainly miners. They would do training, mount guard all night, and then go down the pit for a shift of coal getting – they were a grand bunch of men.

My most notable memory was after training one night. I had just set out the guard and issued them with bullets, when the local police sergeant came and wanted a guard mounting on a plane which had landed in a field on Assarts Farm. We mounted a guard from 10 pm until 11.30 am the next morning (without drink or food). When the police arrived at the farmhouse, they found the farmer holding the pilot up against the wall with his shotgun. He thought the pilot was a German but it turned out he was Polish. The pilot was trying to find Hucknall aerodrome and had got lost and ran out of fuel.'

IN THE WOMEN'S LAND ARMY

'These are the reminiscences of two Land Army girls in the Tuxford area. The ladies concerned are both now living in East Markham, having married sons of farmers whom they met during the war years. They came originally from Newton, near Alfreton and from Nottingham, respectively, and joined the Land Army in March 1942 in preference to working in a munitions factory. They were both in their twenties and when interviewed had this to say: "When we arrived initially we had no uniform and were accommodated in a hostel for 40 girls situated on Lincoln Road, Tuxford, within a short distance of the Fountain Hotel. The hostel has now been demolished to make way for housing development. Mrs Poskit, the hostel warden,

196

was regarded as a lady of some standing. She provided food and fair discipline and was well regarded."

Wages were 48 shillings a week and the hours were reasonable except at harvest time when a start at 7 am was followed by work until the job was completed. Bicycles were provided to enable them to get to work at farms in the Boughton, Ossington and Bevercoates areas. Lunch was provided by the warden in the form of sandwiches. The majority of the girls worked on arable farms; only four worked in dairy farming. The work was backbreaking at times, particularly when singling out sugar beet at planting time and when pulling beet out of the ground at harvest time. The farm manager was regarded as a hard taskmaster but the job was well done under his supervision.

But it wasn't all work and bed as the girls were pleased to recount the social events in their busy working lives. An army camp on the site of the present Dosco factory at Tuxford provided an ENSA concert every fortnight to which the Land Army girls were invited. There was also a dance at the camp on Friday evenings. Girls had to be back at the hostel by midnight and 10 pm any other night. Dances also took place at the hostel to which farmers and soldiers were invited. Refreshments were organised by Mrs Poskit, and Mrs Butler's three-piece band provided the music.

A Royal Air Force Injuries Unit at Lound Hall transported airmen to the hostel and although many of them were unable to dance they were able to play games, musical chairs being popular with the girls enjoying sitting on many knees! Other functions took place in a room at the back of the Newcastle Arms Hotel, Tuxford, called The Sink – why we don't know – and at the Fountain Hotel.

Amongst their recollections was one of a bomber manned by a Polish crew crashing at West Markham and of Italian POWs at Headon Camp. The ladies also cycled in to Retford to the now demolished Roxy Cinema in Carolgate and made occasional visits to their own homes after Saturday midday when work was finished. "They were happy days by and large".'

MEAT PIES AND JAM

'Throughout the war, Women's Institutes worked hard for the war effort. Farnsfield WI was only one of many that can look back with pride.

In October 1939, the hall having been blacked out, a letter was received from Lady Sybil Argles, the County Chairman, expressing her wish for institutes to keep together and be satisfied with taking handiwork and having friendly get-togethers when it was difficult to obtain speakers. As the County Library were using the hall on Thursdays from 5.30 to 6.30 members were asked to change their meeting times to follow the library at 6.30 whilst the room was still warm, when they could sit and work and take part in table games. The blackout was also responsible for a drop in attendance at meetings. However, the Christmas party was not to be missed and as in previous years the birthday party was held in March 1940. Mrs Hatcher once again cooked ham and tongue and also baked a birthday cake as she had done for the previous ten years and did until 1961.

In June of that year it was reported that a further allocation of sugar had been granted to WIs but the fruit had to be bought. Mrs Straw's kitchen was to be the jam making centre. Members should take their ration cards to the next meeting to have them stamped for the extra sugar.

It is not usual to meet in August but because a letter had been received from the Ministry of Information offering to send a speaker on "Air Raids, My Neighbour and Myself" it was decided to hold an open meeting. At this time 20 pairs of socks were donated to the searchlight unit and money was in hand for any soldiers who wanted help. Members distributed Salvage Campaign leaflets. By the time of the next Christmas party, which was always given for the invited elderly of the village, food supplies were not readily available so when a large tin of tongue was offered, it was readily accepted.

In 1941 an invitation to make camouflage nets for the army was turned down as jam making was taking up all spare time but there was still time to accept Mrs Sherwin's invitation to have tea in her garden in July. The next birthday party was able to go ahead thanks to a donation of potatoes from Mr and Mrs Reynolds and sausage from Mr Hatcher.

The Preserving Centre was formed which also involved non-members. The WI were also asked to supervise the granting of wool vouchers to relatives of members of HM Forces and several members were involved in street savings collections. A letter from Nottingham asked if Farnsfield WI would teach handicrafts to the searchlight battery at Inkersall Farm but it was thought not possible. A canning machine was demonstrated and even though it was never purchased, a hundredweight of tomatoes were canned and 147 lbs of jam made and sold locally.

Members were asked to collect and dry as many culinary herbs as possible towards the 25 tons target aimed at by the National Federation of WIs. As a result, 8oz of sage, 5oz of mint and 4oz of parsley were dispatched and in due course a postal order to the value of 4s 5d was received in payment.

In 1943 the WI were asked to organise the Meat Pie Scheme in Farnsfield and Edingley but owing to the fact that the Ministry of Supply would not grant Mr Hatcher a licence to buy a pie making machine it was thought best to abandon the scheme. However, in November members were informed a licence had, after all, been granted and the Meat Pie Distribution Scheme would commence on the 17th of that month. Orders were taken for nearly 400 pies costing ninepence each. Any profit made from this scheme was to be divided as follows – a third to the institute, a third to the County federation and the remaining third to go to charity. According to the records, various amounts were sent to the Prisoner of War Relatives Association, YMCA, St Dunstans, Red Cross, Merchant Navy, Comforts for Friendless Soldiers, Sailors and Airmen, Mansfield Hospital and the District Nursing Association. The Pie Scheme was to continue until late 1946.

At the Whit Monday Gala in 1944 the magnificent sum of £25 2s 6½d was made on the Produce stall. Later in the year it was agreed to field a cricket team to play the National Fire Service. The match was played on Mr Johnson's field on Mansfield Road in aid of the "Salute the Soldier" campaign. £14 was raised. Towards the end of 1944, the institute were asked to knit up 3 lbs of wool a month into garments for children in occupied countries. A further 4oz sage, 4oz mint and 2oz of parsley were dispatched.

At the beginning of 1945, members were asked to donate used clothing to the Help Holland Council. At the June 1945 meeting, Mrs Hatcher donated everything for the tea as a Victory celebration.'

A CHILD'S WAR

Children soon came to accept war as part of daily life, getting used to carrying gas masks and nights in the air raid shelter. It was often the arrival of evacuees that made the greatest impact, as village schools were filled to overflowing and strangers came to live in our houses.

SAFE IN NOTTINGHAM

'I had just started my second year at the Manning Girls' Grammar School in Nottingham when war broke out in September 1939. We were evacuated to Mansfield, only 14 miles away, but after sharing the Queen Elizabeth Girls' Grammar School it was decided we were safe in Nottingham. We returned and this time had to share our building with High Pavement Boys' Grammar School as their old Victorian multi-storey building was not considered as safe as our modern single-storey school. We attended on a shift system – girls in the morning and boys in the afternoon. Although we were not supposed to meet all kinds of messages were "posted" in our desks.

The grass banks were dug out and air raid shelters built into them with rockeries over the top – they are still there and used for storage I understand. Whenever the sirens went we had to quickly file out to our allotted shelters and stay there until the all clear sounded. Teachers tried to continue teaching in very difficult conditions in dim light and without books or writing materials. With all these handicaps on our vital teenage years it is amazing that we achieved such good exam results. Out of adversity was born determination to overcome these drawbacks to our education.

Most of my form were called up for National Service in their final year in the sixth form and were not able to sit their Higher School Certificate examination but I was the youngest in the form and the war ended so I was able to go to university where most of my fellow students were returning ex-servicemen.

Apart from bandage rolling and knitting for the troops our war work consisted mainly of working on the land to help produce food for the nation as food could not be imported with the merchant ships being torpedoed by German U-boats. Even as young as 13 or 14 we were released from classes for a week, several times during the summer and autumn to work on local market gardens or farms. I remember beet singling, pea pulling, potato picking, flax pulling and fruit picking during term time. In the August holidays we could go for a fortnight to the School Harvest Camp based at Glenfield in Leicestershire to help the local farmers harvest their crops. Great fun was had "camping" in the village school with our teachers doing the cooking and cleaning. We were stooking, pitching and stacking until dark. We were glad to get to bed on our straw mattresses on the classroom floors.

When we reached the sixth form we were allowed to do fire-watching duties in our school buildings. This involved, by rota, two staff and two senior girls sleeping on camp beds and being on the alert with our stirrup pumps etc, in case incendiary bombs were dropped during raids. I remember many night-time alerts but no bombs dropped on the school. On warm summer nights my friend and I enjoyed sleeping out under the verandah in the quadrangle.

To a teenage girl, clothes rationing was one of the worst things. In order to eke out our precious clothing coupons we used to go to the market to buy flour bags which, when unpicked, washed and cleaned, could be made into peasant-style blouses. Towards the end of the war everyone was trying to get hold of parachute silk remnants to make underwear. I also remember having a coat made out of a blanket and in

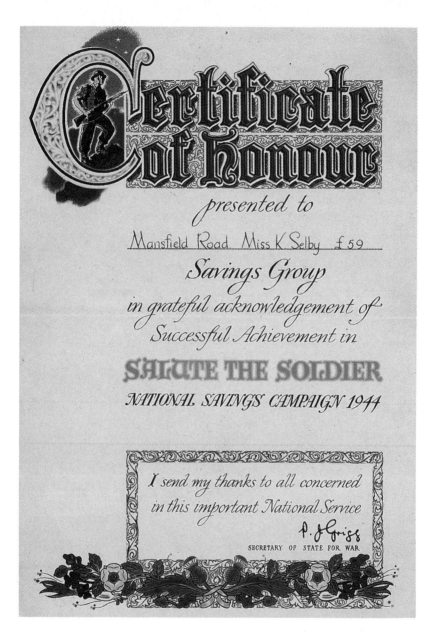

Certificate of Honour

presented to

<u>Mansfield Road, Miss K Selby, £59</u>

Savings Group

in grateful acknowledgement of Successful Achievement in

SALUTE THE SOLDIER

NATIONAL SAVINGS CAMPAIGN 1944

I send my thanks to all concerned in this important National Service

P. J Griss

SECRETARY OF STATE FOR WAR

Collecting for savings campaigns such as Salute the Soldier Week in 1944 was an important part of the war effort.

families clothes had to be handed down. Stockings had to be laboriously mended with a special hook tool and all our jumpers and cardigans seemed to have darned elbows.

We got used to having tiny amounts of meat, bacon, butter, sugar, bread, dried egg, cheese, chocolates, sweets and cakes. My Saturday mornings, as the eldest, were spent queuing for one to two hours at Marsdens of Nottingham to buy a couple of cakes for the family or else waiting for ages at the butcher's for a small Sunday joint – no choice, just what your coupons allowed you. Rabbit was a frequent part of our diet as we had relatives in the country and I soon learned how to skin and prepare them for the pot. Oranges were a rarity and bananas non-existent unless there was a rare distribution for green ration book holders (under fives). As my youngest sister was born during the war we did occasionally get a small taste of a banana.

The prisoners of war we encountered were mainly whilst working on the land. We weren't supposed to speak to them but did occasionally practise our German on them. We didn't see many Italian POWs but there was an Italian camp in huts at the top of Bank Hill in Woodborough.'

MIXED MEMORIES

'War broke out when I was 15 and I did two more years at school. We had to attend school during the summer holiday of 1940, although we didn't have to wear uniform and were allowed to cycle the seven miles in to Newark from Southwell. We later had a girls' school from Worthing billeted on us and each had the use of our school for half a day. This didn't last long and eventually they returned to Worthing.

My memories of the war are very mixed. I hated my brother being in the navy and seeing my mother cry whenever we sang the hymn *For those in peril on the sea*, and it was dreadful hearing of the deaths of the boys I had grown up with, but sometimes there were good things happening and you had to make the most of these.

Clothes, make up and jewellery were scarce and you were fortunate if you could improvise or make your own. I didn't use gravy salt on my legs, as some girls did, but I did use wet sand, which gave your legs a tanned colour. This was great as long as you always got up early enough to wash it off and redo it.'

HELPING OUT

'When the war broke out we had evacuees from St Annes Wells Road in Nottingham – rather a shock for a rural community like Southwell. We had one of the teachers living with us but I didn't like that as she was my class teacher at school. The evacuees soon went back home as we were too near and there was a good train service to Nottingham.

I remember helping the WVS as a runner (on my bike) taking messages around and generally helping out.

The WI started canning fruit and once I remember a lorry from Merryweathers tipping a load of plums into the road and we children helping to load them into hampers and carry them into Burgage House where the sugar syrup was boiling away ready for the canning process.

Each October we were given a week off school to go potato picking – half term today but then we had to help the war effort. A lorry picked us up in the market place and we rode up to Brackenhurst (the best bit). One year it never stopped raining and we were knee deep in mud and wet through. I remember putting on damp clothes the next morning as it was impossible to get them dry and we only had one set. To this day I hate the smell of wet earth and potatoes!

I was fortunate enough to win a scholarship to the Lilley & Stone Foundation School in Newark and felt very proud going to Randalls to buy my uniform. My father's cousin had a shop in Newark and each day I went there for my dinner. One day I was nearly there when I looked up and saw a German aeroplane which had appeared and attacked Ransome and Marles works. I ran like mad, dashed indoors and hid under the table, shaking like a leaf. We didn't have many air raids but it was great when the siren went at school and we all trooped to the shelters with gas masks and rugs. Anything to escape lessons, although we didn't do many as we had Worthing High School for Girls billeted with us and we did half days each.'

BURSTING AT THE SEAMS

'My parents sent me to a school in West Bridgford. I travelled every day on a Bartons bus. The buses to Leicester only went every two hours so if you missed one, you had to get one to Keyworth then walk two miles home.

When Widmerpool started to get evacuees from the Meadows area and Gun Factory my parents thought it unwise for me to travel to Nottingham to school so I was brought back to the little village school. It was one large room with all age groups from five to 14 years, different age groups in each corner of the room. With the influx of extra children from Nottingham, we were taught in the mornings and then went for nature walks in the afternoon.

We then had children from Great Yarmouth arrive. Widmerpool was bursting at the seams. One of the boys who came from Great Yarmouth stayed on my father's farm. When he was 14 years old his father in Yarmouth said it was pointless him returning home as there wouldn't be any work as Yarmouth was badly bombed. He's just retired from Manor Farm, Widmerpool after working there for my father and then my brother for 51 years, a very experienced man in every job on the farm.'

I WAS SEVEN

'I was seven years of age when the war broke out. I well remember when the sirens sounded and my mother and two brothers and myself dived under the table which was surrounded by a chenille table cloth, and we all thought we were safe from any bombing or anything else for that matter; how naive we were.

We never had hot water bottles, but we had the old-fashioned fireplace which needed blackleading every Friday, where you would fill one side of the boiler with water and the other side was an oven, so what else would we have to keep the bed warm but one oven shelf wrapped in an old blanket – nice when it was warm, but it was always me that had to move it or banged my toes on it.

I remember my school at Southwell being used to billet the

soldiers, some injured, and looking very dirty and forlorn, and then being asked if we would have one or two in our homes for teas. During this time we were asked to have evacuees, children from other parts of England; it was either them or letting off part of our house to another couple – this we did to a mother and daughter. They had the front room and front bedroom. This went on whilst the war was on and eventually they were allocated a council house. What bliss, I had a bedroom to myself again, instead of having to sleep on a billiard table balanced on the bath, with a mattress on it, which of course had to be moved when anyone wanted a bath.

We seemed to have much more fun as children then, we were never bored. We skipped, played rounders, marbles, snobs, hoopla and learnt to amuse ourselves even though there was a war.

I didn't see my father for four years, so when he did finally come home, I couldn't really take to him and it took me a long time to come to terms with the fact that he was the "Boss" and not my mother.

Things started to pick up for us – the war ended and out came the old black fireplace and in went a Yorkist range. We still had oven shelves in the winter on the beds, but what lovely smells came from the side oven on a Sunday. The food always tasted much better, and winter days meant toasting bread over an open fire, and crumpets with lashings of butter. It never seems quite the same now, with all the mod cons that we have, but I wouldn't want those days back.'

A CASE OF BAD TIMING

'No one was at all surprised when John announced at breakfast that he couldn't go to school as he "felt poorly".

It was eight months since he'd started school and he'd hated it from the word go. My sister Barbara, brother Ted and I were responsible for getting him there, and could be seen most mornings cajoling, coaxing, bullying and very often carrying him right to the door of the schoolhouse. Fortunately this was not very far away, just across the field from our cottage.

This morning was different, however. He hadn't eaten his breakfast, which was unheard of. Mum said she thought he had a temperature and sent him back to bed. We thought she was being too soft on him but kept quiet as it relieved us of the task of getting him to school.

By the time we arrived home at mid-day the doctor had been sent for, although Mum had already made her own diagnosis. She was convinced that it was scarlet fever, so convinced in fact that Barbara and I were sent to Ollerton to buy two pairs of pyjamas in case he had to go to the "fever hospital". Mum couldn't really afford the pyjamas but there was no way that John was going to hospital in hand-me-down pyjamas that were three sizes too big.

When Barbara and I returned from the shops it was to discover that we need not have gone. The doctor had been and made his pronouncement, it was not scarlet fever, it was German measles. It would be putting it mildly to say that the timing left a lot to be desired.

It was the spring of 1940 and we had been at war with Germany since the previous September. Anti-German feelings were running very high. There was a positive hatred of Germany, the Germans, and anything remotely Germanic – and our John had to go and get German measles.

The doctor had left instructions that none of us were to go to school, it was his opinion that within the next few days we would all be smitten. He was not wrong.

I disliked being away from school; I would not have admitted it to my friends but I liked school. I actually enjoyed most of the lessons, the exceptions being music and needlework. I wasn't very good at either. The rest of the class loved it when Miss Law asked me to find "top doh". It didn't matter how many times she banged the tuning-fork on her desk I never did find it. I'm tone deaf.

At last the enforced holiday was over. I couldn't wait to get to school, but as we entered the playground (dragging John as usual) we were met with a stony silence. Our friends just stood glaring at us, and then the name-calling started. I couldn't believe my ears, these were our friends.

Traitors – Nazis – German spies – Gestapo, they hurled the lot at us. "Why couldn't you have had English measles?" they cried. I've often heard it said that children can be very cruel, well, I can vouch for that.

207

After this no one spoke to us. We didn't dream of snitching to the teachers (well, you just didn't, did you?) but on the third day it was brought to the attention of Miss Law without our help.

Someone had drawn a swastika on the front cover of my nature-study book and Miss Law saw it. She could tell from the look of horror on my face that I had not drawn it. When she demanded to know who was responsible, one of my friends broke down and the whole sorry story came out.

Miss Law was not only the senior teacher, she was also the headmistress. She immediately called the whole school together (there were only three classes, infants, juniors and seniors), and looking at her face I was very pleased that her anger was not directed at me. She certainly had a way with words. I can't remember all of it but I do remember her saying that their actions were the sort of things that we were fighting a war against. I'd been fond of Miss Law ever since she had let me gather her windfall apples, but at that moment I just loved her to death.

Everyone was hanging their heads in shame by the time she had finished. Having just spent the three most miserable days of my life, I have to admit that I revelled in it.

I didn't find it easy to "forgive and forget", despite the effusive apologies. The forgiveness did come eventually, but as you can see I never did forget.'

AT HOME

'Living and going to school in the centre of Nottingham at the beginning of the war, my parents decided that it would be safer for my two brothers and I to be evacuated. With our gas masks round our necks, name tags tied on to our coats, suitcases in hand, we joined our respective buses.

Did we finally end up in some quiet, peaceful, lovely spot? No, not us – my brothers were sent to Mansfield, and I went to Worksop. Eventually, my father rejoined the army and it was decided to bring us home. On going back to school, I discovered that I was the last one to return, and I had been away six whole months.

To celebrate, my brothers and I went roller skating to our favourite rink – Slab Square where we were eventually "moved on" by the local policeman. This was a common occurrence for us; we would go past Griffin and Spaldings where the doorman wore a splendid coat with gold braid trimmings and a top hat; up Market Street and wait at the top until the coast was clear and we could return to our skating.

We had no garden, but spent many happy hours at the arboretum, looking at the birds in the aviary and the ducks on the pond, and playing round the Chinese Bell Garden. Our swimming pool was Carrington Lido or the Trent Embankment and a day out on a Sunday was a bus trip to either Burton Joyce or Gunthorpe where we would try to catch tiddlers and put them in a jam jar, but we were never allowed to take them home. Saturday mornings were spent at the Hippodrome cinema and on a Saturday evening my friend and I would queue for a sixpenny ticket in the "gods" at the Empire where we saw Gracie Fields, Arthur Askey, Vic Oliver, and other well known variety acts of the day.'

LIFE IN BALDERTON

'At the commencement of the war I was a child of seven, living in a terraced house in a street in Balderton. The infants school I was attending was about a half mile walk and deemed within "running back home" distance when the air raid siren blew. This meant a mad dash for me homewards and a frantic dash for my mother to meet and escort me to our nearest thing to an air raid shelter – the food cupboard under the stairs. This was equipped, though not very big, with little stools and a few books and a blanket.

Several mad dashes stick in my mind, when enemy planes were zooming low overhead trying to locate local factories to bomb – and this they did to devastating effect. On one particular occasion when Ransome and Marles ball bearing factory in Newark was directly hit, I stood with my mother in horror and awe and watched from our house doorway the sticks of bombs raining down from the attacking planes. We were joined in the shelter by a neighbour's son whose father was working at the factory whilst my mother sought to comfort his anxious and distraught mother – we found out later her husband was safe. My father worked at Worthington Simpson factory in Balderton at the time and he used to be part of the voluntary fire watch team at nights – looking out for incendiary bombs and any other threats to the factory security. No doubt when he was on duty there or as an air raid warden it was an anxious time for my mother.

At Balderton we were very close to several airfields and we were in the flight path of the nearest and it was a regular thing each night to count the number of planes taking off on bombing raids and how many returned in the early morning. Of course many did not make it back and one in particular stands out in my memory as nearly making it, but not quite, crashing on a house near to ours and inhabited by a couple with six children, many at my own school and in my class. The father was working on nights so was away. His wife dropped the baby out of the bedroom window to helpers and jumped herself – the other children perished. My father was so upset as he tried to rescue them, with others, having seen some of them moving about in their night clothes but unable to get to them because of the fire. They were all buried in one grave in Balderton churchyard.

Newark and Balderton had its share of evacuees – Newark was home to the pupils of a high school and a private school from Worthing as I remember. I think the whole school transferred. I remember them in their distinct uniforms and looking so sophisticated as they went in "team crocodile" formation around the town. Quite different from the Cockney kids in their less salubrious clothes, billeted in Balderton and attending my school.

One memory always etched in my mind is of an audacious pair of twin boys, same age as me, staying with a nearby couple – the wife being a rather rough type with a fearsome voice you could hear from way off. Being birds of a feather, she took to these twins, ever in trouble and mischief, and stuck up for them as if they were her own when accusations flew. One day walking back from school they were teasing me and being a nuisance, and quite against my nature I flared up and gave one of them a push against a few, not reclaimed for war effort, iron railings. To my horror he struck his nose and this

210

made it bleed profusely and all down his jumper. I tried to mop him with my hanky but he fled off home bawling his head off. Mother of course soon spotted my stained hanky and as I was frightened of saying what I had done, I made up a story about the stain. That night when I was in bed I heard the dreaded foghorn voice – going on about what I'd done to her beloved twin and how I had stained a new jumper she'd bought for him, through my actions. I could have died, but I was fortunate that I wasn't brought down until the fearsome "Mag" had gone. I was told off by my mother for telling a lie about my hanky – my Dad gave me a wink and a pat for standing up to the scourge of the district.

We had a bit of garden at the back of the terraced house and before the war my father used it to house aviaries as he bred and showed cage birds – becoming a show judge eventually. This was a popular hobby for men in those days but when the war came it was turned into a hen home and chicken run – to be more productive – but to be out of the ordinary, Dad bought Exchequer Leghorns. The eggs supplemented the rations and Dad had a gun and was allowed to do the shooting on a friendly farmer's land so we did very well with the occasional rabbit and pheasant. As I grew older I was allowed to go with him to do the beating, along with our spaniel dog, Sue. When I was about 15 he let me have a go at shooting crows but the recoil caught me unawares and gashed me under one eye, necessitating it being stitched and leaving me with one very black and closed eye. Dad got into trouble from Mum and I never fancied gun shooting again.

The other thing I remember Mum stretching the rations out with was the occasional sheep's head off ration, which Mum used to make broth and she would scrape all the brains etc to use as an extra meat – it makes my stomach churn now to think of it. Our next door neighbour used his end of garden as a sty to rear a pig and when it came to pig killing time there were mixed emotions. Horror as the actual deed was done – much hiding and covering of ears went on, much awe and revulsion seeing the carcase hung from a home-made frame and much joy among us, especially on Mother's part, as we got a pig's fry for helping to supply scraps to feed the pig.

Our leisure time was spent in seasonal games played in the

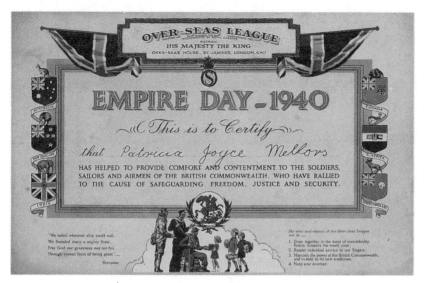

Empire Day provided children with the opportunity to send gifts to servicemen and women overseas. This certificate was presented to a nine year old Nottingham schoolgirl for knitting socks.

street, whips and tops, marbles, ball games against a wall, skipping and hoops and sticks. We played in the street or in the nearby playing field without fear of traffic, abduction or abuse and without much expense – I can't remember going on outings or holidays and all former school trips were stopped because of the war.

When I moved up to the middle school this was over a mile walk each way and deemed too far to go home in an air raid so we were each delegated a nearby house to go to – mine was with a lady named Mrs Snushall whom I only remember meeting once as our air raids were less frequent in the daytime by then. Despite the two and a half mile trip I went home for dinner and back each day which didn't leave much time for dawdling or messing about en route.

Towards the end of the war I went to a school in Newark to which I cycled and I remember when I first went there, it being a technical college, it was full of officer training army cadets – clanking up and down the corridors in hobnailed boots. Towards the end of my time there, the army cadets had left to be replaced by male students from Iraq with whom we teen-agers flirted and played tennis.'

OUR LIVES CHANGED LITTLE

'Just five years old and on holiday with my parents and sisters in a bell tent in Bridlington. One morning great discussion with all the adults, serious faces, and then we were told war had been declared. At that time it meant little to us children who just wanted to be taken to the beach with our buckets and spades, clad in our little woolly bathing suits, which grew to an alarming length when wet. But what happy days.

Back we returned, to school, to again be greeted with serious faces, the issue of our gas masks, the drill for proceeding to the shelters, ration books, evacuees, male teachers who dis-appeared, my friends whose fathers went away, the Home Guard (and it really was like Dad's Army), the arrival of Italian prisoners of war at the farm across the road. But what effect did all this have on children, fortunate enough to live in a small mining village, away from the air raids, the bombs, the destruction and death?

Our day to day lives changed little, we still had loving, stable homes, strict but caring. Season followed season, our games continued uninterrupted.

Spring brought out our whips and tops, skipping ropes (how often I found myself in trouble for "borrowing" my mother's precious clothes line), snobs, bowlers, marbles. Collecting and pressing wild flowers, bringing home our frogspawn and watching our tadpoles turn into frogs to be let loose on Dad's garden. A few newts were added to our collection too.

Into summer and long happy days spent playing in the woods and fields. Collecting wild strawberries and raspberries for jam – how Mum relished these. Hide and seek, our fantasy games in the woods, Robin Hood and his Merry Men (and women), dressing up with a much treasured box of bits, a lace curtain, old shoes, a shawl and old shorts became ballgowns and tunics, wedding veils and trains.

The long days of summer always ended sharply at 6.45 when the roads became deserted – *Dick Barton, Special Agent* and after that bedtime. Out would come the old tin bath – two

213

at a time – one each end in front of a glowing fire (regardless of the heat outside, the only means of heating the water).

Autumn saw us with our conkers, baked in the oven for strength, who had the best? We plagued our Mum and anyone else for a couple of treacle tins – two holes, two lengths of string and we spent days racing on our tins, stilt-like. Hooray, a week off school to pick potatoes, sixpence a day and a bucket of potatoes at the end of the day. Back breaking work but we children enjoyed it. Then great excitement in the village, the threshing machine arrived. We watched the sheaves brought by horse and cart from the fields, through the machines, into the sacks, mice running in all directions so doors had to be kept closed. Many days were spent collecting wood for our bonfire. No need for expensive fireworks – a huge fire, roast potatoes and chestnuts gathered from the woods, what excitement. A huge Guy Fawkes aloft – my Dad often wondered where his gardening clothes disappeared to.

As I only remember sunshine in summer so I only remember the crisp white deep snow of winter. School paths cut off – no hope of getting there but out came our home-made sledges, off into the hills of Annesley. We came home with sore bottoms and wet clothes but sheer joy – who had the fastest sledge, well even an old tin tray could gather speed. On to Christmas. We had no concept of the difficulties our parents faced to fill our stockings and get our gifts but they did – we never went without.

Does it all sound like play? Well we had to work very hard in school, and we took in many evacuees, some arriving in appalling conditions having spent weeks in shelters in Birmingham and London. We all made friends, indeed some never returned but made their homes in our village and became part of its community. We had a recorder band, introduced by a teacher, Miss Wakelin from Birmingham who brought not only the children but the recorders as well.

Strict rules applied regarding our gas masks and if you arrived at school without it then you walked the two miles back home to collect it.

In the shelter we sang songs until we knew them by heart – how shall I ever forget Old McDonald and his farm? Sometimes when returning home serious faces greeted us again,

maybe someone from our village was lost in the war, sometimes it was news of cousins from the North East and London
who had been bombed out of their homes yet again. My most
memorable incident during the war was being woken by my
Dad. The sky was bright red and he explained that Sheffield
had been bombed and we could see quite clearly, some 25
miles away, the glow of the fires.

When one looks back at those years, the lives of children dif-
fered enormously – we now know of the horrors some children
endured, we understand their sheer terror of leaving their
parents to live with total strangers, never to return to their
homes, either because of families dying or sadly, not wanted
by their kith and kin. We were sheltered in our villages, doing
our bit for the war effort with produce, knitting, clothes etc but
still happy, contented, fed (even though the rations were
meagre) and really unaware of the horror all around us. I now
realise what childhood really meant. I wish the children of
today could enjoy the childhood I had – free of pressure, free
of material things, free to roam our beautiful woods and fields,
free to wander to school, free to play the games that cost
nothing, free to enjoy the competitiveness of childhood, free
from the man-made problems of the world – free to be children.'

THEY THOUGHT WE WERE SPIES

'We had problems when we first came to Rainworth in 1940.
My mother had visits from the police who thought we were
aliens because we had a Dutch surname. However, my mother
was very upset when the police came to talk to me at school. I
expect they thought that if we were spies they might get more
from a five year old child who would be more likely to tell the
truth.

We had an air raid shelter which we shared with the next
door neighbours. As a young child I thought this was very
exciting and wanted to sleep on the top bunk. It didn't occur to
me that if a bomb hit us I would be the first it would reach.
We didn't go to the shelter very often however, it was mostly a
blanket under the stairs. If my father was on nights when there
was a raid, he would start cycling home on his push bike, and

very often before he reached home from Eakring, the all clear had gone and he would turn round and cycle back to work.

My father was in the Home Guard, and we have often laughed since, because they were never issued with guns for all the members, and those who did have guns were never given any ammunition. They would not have been able to protect us very well. My father said they used to drill with brush handles as guns.

One day towards the end of the war, as I was walking to school one morning, on the lawn outside the doctor's house I found a strange looking object with lots of string attached to it. I was quite thrilled with my find and carefully carried it to school and hid it under the hedge near the school gate so that I could take it home with me after school to show my mother and father. Imagine how upset I was when I came out of school to find that my "treasure" had gone. That night the family went to the pictures, and there shown on the screen were several different shaped small bombs which the Germans had started dropping on twine so that they did not immediately explode. Guess what, there on the screen was my find of the morning. I guess the police or someone must have found it and taken it away for safety. My parents at any rate were pleased about this, or who knows what might have happened to us!

My sister was born in 1942 and as she was a baby who cried non stop day and night for three years, it fell to me to go to the shops and queue for special things when they came. I remember on one occasion having to queue in Marks and Spencer's, which at that time was only half open because there were not enough goods for them to sell, and I queued in the closed part for what seemed like hours for a few biscuits as a treat for the family.

I also remember having to queue with a lot of women at the Food Office on St John Street for our new rations books. We didn't have a lot to eat during the war, but my mother always managed to make tasty meals for us, although looking back now, it may have been that she did not have much food for herself.

As children, we of course did not fully understand the devastation caused by war, and we had great fun with the games which children used to play, like skipping, and whip and top, where we had our little tin of coloured chalks and used to sit on a doorstep making our patterns, then if we did not like them when the top was spinning, that pattern was wiped off and we started again. The house next door had half a round corrugated shed in their garden, and we used to dress up and put plays on for our parents, hanging curtains on string across the open front of this shed as a stage.

My mother did her shopping at the local Co-op and it was my job to take in the order every week. My mother used to get most upset, because the only cheese which the Co-op stocked was what she called "white mousetrap cheese". This was stocked because it was the best kind for the miners to take for their "snap" but wasn't very much good for anything else.

It was lovely at school during the miners' fortnight's holidays, because there were only a few of the pupils whose fathers did not work at the colliery, so we had a whale of a time, not learning a lot, but training our bodies by playing games.'

POTATO PICKING

'During the later war years, labour was very scarce on farms and children from city schools were asked if they would help with the potato and pea harvests. I was about 13 at the time and, being originally from the country, I jumped at the chance to escape school for a couple of weeks at a time. All in all, I went three times; once pea picking near Radcliffe on Trent and twice potato picking, the first time to Ruddington and then the most memorable – to Clifton Hall Farm.

We were taken by bus early in the morning to the farm and from there we had a very thrilling ride up to the fields by horse-drawn trailer. Each field was marked out with sticks along the rows and it was our job to each clear our own area between them after the spinner had thrown out the potatoes but before it returned to the next row.

At Clifton we were fortunate as the spinner was drawn by a horse, which being slower gave us more time for clearing. At Ruddington there had been a tractor which, besides being very smelly, went along the rows much more quickly meaning we had to work faster. It was hard work, but we enjoyed ourselves being out in the fresh air and we were always ready for our dinner; when we were taken back to the farm and sat on bales of straw in a barn to eat our packed lunches and drink lovely hot cocoa brought from the farm in a milk churn. We were given permission to pick up any fallen fruit in the orchard. Needless to say, the trees were "accidentally" nudged quite a lot and the fruit was great for the afternoons.

Working alongside us in the fields was a German prisoner of war. He couldn't speak any English and though he smiled and helped us we were frightened to death of him, poor man, he was probably very lonely and petrified of us kids en masse.

After work, we walked back to the road a different way to get the bus home, which meant passing a small wood where a gamekeeper had hung a row of dead crows, magpies, jays, squirrels, rats etc to deter vermin and poachers. I was absolutely horrified and dreaded passing there each evening.

We were allowed to take potatoes home, so our lunch bags and pockets were always full of lovely baking size "spuds", and best of all was the pleasure, when we had completely finished, of being able to present Mum with wages – 17 shillings – quite a fortune!'

SCHOOL IN WARTIME

'Going to school in Nottingham during the war years, I remember well. We only attended school in the morning, starting at 8.30 am as a school from Southend was evacuated to the Midlands and used the premises in the afternoon.

I was allowed to be 15 minutes late in the winter months as there was a mile and a half walk to the bus stop, a 40 minute ride and another mile walk. The buses did not always run to time and would sometimes be missing altogether. There was a shortage of drivers because a number of them had been called up into the forces. I was fortunate as my Granny lived close to the bus stop and I could pop in for a warm, and she would put a couple of small potatoes in the oven of the blackleaded range. These were intended to go into my gloves to keep my hands warm whilst waiting for the next bus, but by the time I reached school they had been eaten.

We had to carry our gas masks around with us everywhere,

or we would be sent home for them, and have a detention as well.

Paper was also in short supply and we had to use every inch in our books. Our Domestic Science lessons consisted of learning about food rationing, and on what to spend your points. We were allowed so many for each person and a decision had to be made what to buy, either soap powder, biscuits or tinned goods (if they were available). Sometimes we made bread if we managed to get the yeast and flour, dripping cakes, vegetable soup, or mincemeat and Christmas puddings made from vegetables. The vegetables were a little easier to obtain as my father had an allotment on the local cricket field, which had been dug up as part of the war effort to grow your own vegetables. Sometimes I managed to get a few very small carrots or beetroot by working in the farmer's field for two hours in the evening singling them out (we were paid sixpence a night) or we collected rose hips for fourpence a bucket or vegetables instead of pay.

We were asked to knit a scarf for one of the sailors on the ship that the school had adopted. The wool was provided, but the scarves had to be eight feet long, and I am ashamed to say that the first two feet had faded by the time I reached the end.

There was a lot of homework to do. Some of mine was done at lunch time on the bus on the way home and as soon as I arrived home, unless my mother had left a note saying that there was going to be offal, oranges, bananas etc, at the shops when I would go out and join the queues. If the air raid sirens went we had to go to a shelter under the Labour Exchange and I would take my homework with me. My father was an air raid warden and the way he had to go went by the chip shop so we had chips and we made hot drinks, and the homework was late being finished.

When we left school to go home we sometimes called at the shop that sold Horlicks tablets, this helped the sweet ration along. We had frequent air raid practices, when we had to leave our lessons and go to the shelters.

Cooked lunches were served at school, or sandwiches could be taken, but as butter was rationed we quite often went without butter, particularly if we were saving our rations to make a birthday cake for someone in the family.'

GAS MASKS TO SCHOOL

'Every day during the war years at Gunthorpe, the children took their gas masks to school. One day a large van arrived. In order to test the efficiency of the masks, children wearing them had to stand in the van while tear gas was released.

A school garden was dug behind the maltings (now part of the Unicorn car park) and set with vegetable seeds. It was Gunthorpe school's effort for Dig for Victory. Their efforts did not prove too successful and one year the potatoes turned out very small and riddled with wireworms.'

VACS AND VILLAGERS

Evacuees turned our lives upside down, and when city met country there were often shocks on both sides! We became fond of our little charges and missed them when eventually they returned to their own families.

'During the last few months of 1939, and the entire twelve months of 1940, village life underwent a great change with the invasion of hundreds of evacuees. The children were sent from one area of England at a time, the first arriving from Leeds, Birmingham, Great Yarmouth and London, along with their teachers.

Previously, each household had been visited to ascertain how many "Vacs" could be accommodated, whether it be a whole family, or just a few children. This was compulsory, you were only excused if you were very old, or had ill health. The billeting officer was able to offer extra bedding, and fold-up beds if they were required.

In the cities, parents were warned that their children could be evacuated, although this was not compulsory. Practice runs were often made, with parents having packed just one bag for each child. This contained a change of clothing, a few sandwiches, a favourite toy and their gas mask, complete with name and identification number inside the cardboard box. Each child also had to have a label bearing their name and address, this was attached to a piece of string, and threaded through a buttonhole. They also had an identification card, and a self addressed envelope, which was sent home as soon as they were settled.

Many times, these children walked to their local stations, all ready for their journey, only to be returned home again. Disappointment showed, as they hoped they were going to the seaside, or the country for the day, and would be returning home in the evening.

The trains arrived at the country stations, and coaches had to be organised to take numbers of children to certain areas of the district. Our children were brought to the village school at East Drayton, and we had been given the day off to make room for them all. The able-bodied and fussy women went to the school and chose their children, and sometimes teachers, too. People like my parents, who were unable to do that had to wait at home for the billeting officer to bring some children. All the prettiest and cleanest children had been chosen, and we were given two girls who looked very unkempt. They were Annie, who was about ten, and her younger sister, Eileen, who was about five. They were very pleasant natured girls, but we didn't find that out until later, as they were very withdrawn, and understandably wary of their new home.

Mother saw that they were given a wash, and then we all sat down for tea. There was Mother, Father, my elder sister Doris, my younger brother Billy, and myself, aged ten. Because they had come from Yorkshire, they had very broad accents, and because no one in our family had ever travelled very far, these were the first real strangers we had ever come into contact with, and we had considerable trouble understanding each other.

Our parents had been told to check for head and body lice, and scabies, and after tea out came the newspaper, along with a small-toothed comb. Their heads were very much alive, and

221

they were immediately washed in soap, and when dry they were rubbed all over with paraffin. After that, a bath followed in the front room in the old tin bath in front of the fire. As we had not got any gas or electricity – water had only been laid on a few years earlier – the hot water had to be carried from the copper in the kitchen. The copper had a fire underneath it to boil the water, and the cold water also had to be fetched from a tap in the kitchen.

Next day, the girls sent their envelopes home, and told their parents of their safe arrival and gave them their new address.

When whole families had agreed to be evacuated, they had the awful task of taking their pets to the veterinary surgeon to have them put down.

We village children had only recently been fitted out with gas masks, and smaller children were given a fancier one with Mickey Mouse ears. We had to take them everywhere we went, and if any child had forgotten to take it to school, the teacher made them run home to fetch it.

The village school took pupils from three catchment villages as well as East Drayton, and with there being so many extra children to attend we were told only to go for half days each, which we thought was great, especially when an evacuee teacher taught us.

We all got on and mixed very well, in spite of there being an obvious barrier between "townees" and "country folk". We had been brought up to believe town people were not all that right in the head, so the mixes did people a lot of good.

There was no worry regarding extra food being required, as most people were self-sufficient. Our girls were very perturbed at having to eat vegetables when they had been grown inside the earth – in dirt – and eating greens that had been covered with white butterflies!

My parents kept poultry for our egg supply, and a few cock-erels; the girls loved to collect the warm eggs from the straw nests, and were most delighted when they saw little yellow chicks coming out of the shells. The fun began when they were given boiled eggs to eat, there was a lot of explaining to do! We also had two pigs in a sty, and the girls enjoyed watching them feeding and listening to their squeals and snorting.

Our lavatory was a privy, across a yard between a coalhouse

222

Housewives received many suggestions for making rationed foods go further.

and the sty. It had two wooden seats, and a door which never seemed to fasten properly. They could hear the pigs squealing and moving about, so they didn't sit there long because they were scared the pigs would escape and get them.

The evacuees were all very shy with the village folk, because their parents had told them never to talk to strangers, just in

223

case they were German spies.

We used to go blackberrying, and occasionally we would scare rabbits and hares, I don't know who ran the fastest! All the children were amazed at the quietness of the village, only one or two cars, an occasional bus; and the wide expanses of the fields, the lanes and the tall trees. The fruit trees were climbed very often, and the fruit either eaten, or thrown at each other.

The local children certainly learned a lot of new words, and obscenities were written on every available wall and wooden gate; we were also taught the meanings of these words!

Meal times were a wonderment to our girls. Having neither gas nor electricity, Mother had to use the fire and side oven. The pans and kettle were always blackened, and the oven was only ever used for cooking meats and puddings, etc. The girls didn't think much to not having chips with everything, as they had been used to.

The evacuees would only spend a few months away from their home town, and without reason, their parents would fetch them home. Soon, another coach load would arrive from another city. On one occasion, we had two small girls called Dorothy, who was about five, and her younger sister Freda, who was only about two or three. She was still in nappies, and very immature, but she was extremely pretty.

Their grandmother had been looking after them, with their mother being in the ATS. I remember their mother often used to write, but she was always behind with the payments – ten shillings and sixpence per week. One day, we came home to find their grandmother had arrived to take them home. We had come to love these children very much, all the family were heartbroken; Dorothy used to keep us amused with "Are you my farver?" every time a man came to the door!

A few of the children used to write to their "foster parents" after returning home; they told us their schools had been taken over by the Military, or they had been given "stone food". The elder of these children said they were glad to be home with their mothers, but had been very happy living with us, and missed the countryside and the animals. Some of the children – now adults – still keep in touch with one another, and have even exchanged visits.'

HIGHDAYS & HOLIDAYS

ENTERTAINMENT IN THE VILLAGES

There always seemed to be something to look forward to, from cricket matches to football, amateur dramatics to whist drives. When transport was not easily available we made our entertainment in our home town or village, and many a new village hall was raised between the wars.

LIKE ONE BIG FAMILY

'Village life was like one big family in the past, and the villages of Bunny and Bradmore were no exception. Often there was only one shop, a local inn and a village "bobby" who knew everyone. Fetes were held at the vicarage with fancy dress competitions. There was skittling for pigs when people came from the villages around and tugs of war between neighbouring villages. Villages had football and cricket club matches, dances and whist drives. Harvest Festival suppers were popular, where the local butcher carved large joints of beef and ham. Churches had choirs and at chapel Anniversaries everyone attended dressed in their best clothes and hats. Concerts were held, with local "talent" entertaining the rest of us. A busy social life.'

THE PARISH ROOM

'The parish room was the scene of most social events at Upper Broughton. We had whist drives and dances with the Ruddington Band to provide the music for special occasions and our own village band at other times. Church socials, especially in the time of Rev Pryor in the 1930s, were always popular. The Dramatic Society produced a sketch every month. We had games, singing and dancing – all for ninepence admission.

We had one grass tennis court before the Second World War,

since replaced by two hard ones. Cricket has always been popular, though the field had to be ploughed up during the war to provide land to grow food.'

A NEW HALL

'In 1932 a new village hall was built by Bolsover Colliery Co at Edwinstowe, which was used by Thoresby Colliery Band and many different sectors of the community. During the war dances were held there on a Saturday night, charge one shilling. Troops stationed in the area attended – there were thousands of British, Commonwealth and Allied troops stationed around here training for D-Day.'

'By 1930 it had been decided at Gamston that the village needed a village hall and a committee was formed to raise funds. Mother held weekly whist drives at Grange Farm. People walked or cycled from Tollerton, Radcliffe, Bassingfield and even Nottingham and they were a great success.

We also held a fete and gala rather like our garden parties today only much larger. It lasted all day and took place on a field in Bassingfield Lane. There were lots of stalls, games, fancy dress parades and pony rides, and there was also a greasy pole. Whoever climbed to the top won the prize of a live pig.

Mother also organised a dance at the Palais in Nottingham; 350 people attended from several villages around and it was a huge success.

Now we had enough money to purchase the wooden building. The menfolk collected it with a horse and dray and it was erected on a site in Bassingfield Lane. Everyone was very enthusiastic and we held lots of events there. I held my 21st birthday party there and everyone from the village came, making it a real day to remember. A year or so later the hall was moved to its present site in the centre of the village.'

'The village hall at Ranby was built in 1927 and given to the village by Sir Albert Bingham. The hall's foundations were constructed in such a way that if the hall was not very successful it could be demolished and two dwellings constructed on

227

the site. Previously villagers had had to walk to Scofton to a wooden hut there for dances and whist drives. Now dances could be held in our own village hall, and a billiard table was also available.'

SOMETHING TO LOOK FORWARD TO

'In the winter the old schoolroom was always available for entertainment at Sutton Bonington. There was the annual school play and the village concert party evenings to look forward to, as well as the social evenings, cinematograph shows (forerunners of the cinema), whist drives and dances.

There were no playing fields for us children but the boys had the advantage of the old National school playground in front of St Michael's church where they played cricket and football, using old oil drums as goal posts and wickets. Many an up and coming sportsman acquired his skills there. The village cricket team played in the hallowed square in the Hall Field and the football team were allowed the use of a farmer's field down Pasture Lane. The ladies ran a hockey team for a few years too. Towards the end of the 1920s a bowling green was laid at the top of Marle Pit Hill and a game of tennis could be enjoyed on the rectory lawn. There was also a billiard table in the Temperance Hall and four licensed public houses.'

CRICKET, BOWLS AND BANDS

'Ruddington had several cricket teams; the main team had some very good players, some of whom turned semi-professional. The ground was by the side of the railway and quite often, a lusty six went over the fence into a coal truck, lost ball! I think only six runs were allowed.

There was a wooden pavilion for the teams and scorers and a bit of a kitchen for doing teas. The water for this was carried from the village down the fields and over the railway bridge called the "fifty steps" for obvious reasons. The toilet facilities were a bit poor, but in those days the game was the most important thing. Eventually the team moved to the newly made playing fields and a firm's team played on the original pitch.

Football was popular, they again played on a field down the

end of the village and were jolly good players.

A bowling green was made on Kirk Lane, and in the same area were three tennis courts. A club was run for these sports and they were well supported up until the war years. After that, the playing fields were ready and most of the sports mentioned went to play on the "Rec" as it was called.

'The Boys' Brigade had a band; we had kettle drums, a big drum and bugles in our houses when the boys were at home. Three fellows (brothers) who played the violin and a pianist formed a dance band. They played at all the dances in the village. Mostly there was a whist drive first and a dance later.

Films were shown once a week (mostly Fridays) and what a din went up if the film broke down. A lot of these were serials so nobody wanted to miss going. I think it was twopence to get in.

The church and the Methodist and Wesleyan chapels had choirs. It was a great day when the Sunday school had "the sermons" as they were called, when all the children had new frocks and suits and read poetry. One or two instrumentalists joined in, they were great days.

One of my brothers made a wireless from a blueprint. It was a tedious job but he did it in the end and if the table was nudged on which it stood, it dislodged the "cat's whisker" and it had to be adjusted onto the crystal again to get anything out of it. Earphones had to be used to hear.

The man who lived next door to us who owned the clock shop built a television set. I well remember we all went in to see it work. It was like looking at a shadow picture which was lined; it was quite something and a long time before television came on the market.'

SIMPLE BUT ENJOYABLE

'For entertainment on a Friday night in the church hall at Aslockton we had a travelling film show, often a cowboy film. We sat on hard chairs for about two hours and paid sixpence to go in. Once a year we had a visiting fair set up for a week and we went every night.

We had a Whatton–Aslockton football and cricket club. We

used to go and cheer on the football team and I scored for the cricket team. We had a dance every Saturday night in the Jubilee Hall at Whatton and a whist drive on a Thursday at Aslockton. Our entertainment was simple but enjoyable.'

FOOTBALL AND JAZZ

'In the early days at Meden Vale people entertained themselves by listening to the radio, visiting the village meeting place, seeing the local drama group (our village had a very good one) or walking around the woods in the beautiful area of the Dukeries in which we live. On carnival days floats would be decorated and entered in the parade which was held in Warsop.

We had a ladies' football team in our village about 36 years ago. This was great fun and everyone turned out to see them. The RAF from Cranwell came to the village for a cricket match and a lovely tea was provided. Later on Welbeck cricket team visited Cranwell for a return match. There was a gymnasium which was used by the children and grown ups. The colliery silver prize band in the 1930s wore dark green uniforms trimmed with gold braid. We also had a jazz band formed during the war with navy and red uniforms.

In early summer, a delight to the children was Bell's fair which used to come and set up in what we called the bottomfield. When Mr Bell wasn't running the fair, he would come around collecting rags and bones, in return for which he would give you a glass pen, a balloon or if you were lucky a goldfish!'

A SOCIAL GET-TOGETHER

'In 1918, when I was 15, Mrs Pearson, wife of the major employer in Lowdham village, suggested that I and some of my friends met in the headmaster's room at the village school for a social get-together. We would take our knitting and sewing. We had to go to the Men's Institute to get water for our kettle to make the tea. We paid a penny each for tea and took our own cups. This was the founding of the Lowdham Women's Institute. Most of the women who attended in those days were wives of the men who worked for Pearson's. It costs sixpence for the younger ones to join and a shilling for the

The Nottingham Quincentenary celebrations in July 1949 included a pageant of Robin Hood and King John performed by local schools.

older women. No business was discussed at the meetings (this was all done by the committee) and we just had a social hour or so. There was little else for women to do in those days.'

CHANGING IN THE DITCH

'In the 1930s there were a lot more holiday bungalows on the ferry field between the main village road at Normanton on Soar and the river than there are now. The owners decided a tennis court was needed and, with the help of some of the village farm hands, a court of reasonable condition was made which was well used. The players changed in a nearby ditch.'

SKATING EVENINGS

'By 1946 the Nottingham Ice Stadium was becoming very popular so my friend and I decided to "have a go".

We paid our entrance fee, changed into the skating boots which were supplied by the stadium, then immediately thought we had developed some strange disease of the ankles as they collapsed and our feet and legs tried to go in opposite directions.

A few tottering steps took us to the doors of the rink itself but we were totally unprepared for the blast of cold air which greeted us as we stepped on to the ice. We were soon to discover that the ice was also extremely cold and wet to one's bottom, as on the first evening we spent more time sitting on the ice than standing upright.

However, we persevered and after a few weeks we gathered the appropriate number of clothing coupons and sallied forth in short pleated skirts and our very own new skating boots. They were a great improvement as our ankles were firmly held and we were able to circle the rink several times without coming to an untimely and abrupt stop

We really enjoyed our skating evenings and became fairly proficient although I was never very good at going backwards, but at least we managed to spend more time skating than sitting.'

ENTERTAINMENT FOR ALL

'Over the years entertainment and pastimes at Kinoulton haven't changed much. In the 1940s and 50s the bus ran a two hourly service to Nottingham with a late bus on Wednesdays and Saturdays for the cinema goers.

During the war, dances were held in the new school, the partitions were pushed back and the floor was sprinkled with chalk. The dances were held for the Land Army girls billeted at the manor house and the soldiers from the shooting range at Owthorpe. The music was provided by records on a wind-up gramophone accompanied by Freddie Payne on the drums. After the war these dances became a regular Friday highlight for adults and the older children. I was taught the Palais Glide on the way home from school. There was no bar, just good food and a whist drive was also fitted in – the music by this time had progressed to a live group called the Rhythm Aces. These evenings along with the June Fair boosted the money left over from the VE celebrations to provide the village with a hall. This was built on land next to the school where there had been allotments.

The gentlemen of the village were well catered for – in a building called "The Institute" (now an office) they met for billiards. There was a football team whose home ground was at Mackley's Farm and the changing room was an old bus. The cricket club pavilion was removed to higher ground near the Lime Kiln pub some three miles out of the village to act as HQ for the Home Guard. After the war it was returned and a field was given to the village on condition that only cricket is played there.'

DANCES AND THE BOB HOP

'We used to go dancing at Roscoe's, the Rialto, and in the schools in the 1920s. At Skegby school we had invitation dances; they were very nice, we made and met many friends there. I remember we used to go in parties and a group of us would walk back over Skegby Bottoms ever so late at night. The dance would finish at eleven or twelve o'clock at night and then we'd have an extension for another hour.

When I first went dancing there were many set dances; one was a type of square dance, more sedate than country dancing. I remember the Charleston coming out, I thought it a bit silly really. There were no such things as pop groups but there were jazz bands.

Much lad–lassing was done at the dances but they were quite select, you didn't go with a partner and stay with him all night. The men used to come over and bow to you and say "May I have the pleasure?" and if you thought you would like to dance with him you would accept.'

'Between 13 and 19 years of age in the 1950s we were suddenly "teenagers", not young people or adolescents.

Nearly every night of the week we spent dancing. Monday night was at St Michael's church hall: "The Bob Hop". At six o'clock I would start to get ready. First a bath, then do my hair, into my net underskirt, with layers and layers of net starched with sugar, which pulled threads in your stockings; on with my cardigan, back to front; finally the dirndl skirt. Now was the hard bit. How to put on powder and lipstick without Dad spotting me before I went out. Oh! I nearly forgot, the

233

scent, just a dab, I used White Fire (Evening in Paris did not suit me).

At the Hop I met my pals; we always sat in the same part of the hall. The lads would be looking smart in their Italian style suits and winklepicker shoes, all ready to impress the girls. It was a live band (not a group): records were only played in the interval. In the corner, by the stage, was a "bar" (it was a table really) selling pop and crisps.

I loved dancing and hardly ever sat down all night, jiving with a different lad every dance until it came to the waltz, then I would sit out.'

PERFORMING IN THE PAGEANT

'In July 1949 a pageant was held as part of the Nottingham Quincentenary celebrations of the 500th anniversary of Nottingham's first charter. Robin Hood and the Court of King John was the theme. Two schools were involved – Henry Whipple junior school, newly built on the Bestwood estate after initial plans had been interrupted by the war, and the Trent Bridge junior school. Henry Whipple provided the Court characters, Trent Bridge Robin Hood and his band. The performance took place at the Albert Hall, with "backstage" at the older Albert Hall Institute, and on the final night we were allowed to go home still wearing our greasepaint! The Henry Whipple contingent had their photograph taken on the open fields behind the school, now all gone under the Bestwood Park estate.'

GOING TO THE PICTURES

Regular visits to the cinema were part of our lives and those old "palaces of entertainment" hold a very special place in our affections. Soon they were to be challenged, though, by the pictures beamed directly into our homes.

THE KING'S

'The year was 1930 at Sutton in Ashfield and I was ten years old. My walk home from Hardwick Street school took me past the King's, the shabby little wooden cinema with a corrugated roof. Standing on the corner of Fox Street, it was a place where the ordinary folk of the drab little town could in their imagination be transported to glories beyond the boundaries of their restricted lives. The films were black and white and silent but to an audience knowing nothing of the inventions yet to come, going to the pictures was one of life's greatest pleasures.

The main doors on Forest Street were opened for admittance at somewhere between 5 and 5.30 pm but as I passed by at about 4.30 there would already be in the doorway a small group of people, mostly women, waiting. Even to my young eyes they looked poor, huddled together in the cold of a winter's afternoon. Some had thrown a big dark shawl over their head and around their body. Others wore a man's peaked cloth cap, undoubtedly borrowed by Mam from Dad.

Usually these early arrivals were from the Idlewells area, the town's most run down locality just across the road from the cinema. They had to be quick off the mark to secure a place on one of the hard forms right down at the front. Just two or three pennies would pay for two hours of escape from the hardest of lives imaginable. The waiting itself was part of their night out, a time of uninterrupted chatter and gossip. They didn't mind in the least having to stand out in the cold.

Sometimes as a special treat my mother would take me to the King's, particularly when a Charlie Chaplin film was being shown. I first went home for tea and to make myself tidy and then, in a state of great excitement, set off by Mother's side. We went in the most expensive seats, the ninepennies, where there was sure to be room. Once there, we bought our tickets, then turning, climbed a small staircase to where, on the landing, beneath a potted palm, sat a lady whose name was Miss Charlton. She had neat Marcel-waved hair.

Wearing a black dress, set off with a little white starched apron, she held in one hand a darning needle threaded with strong cotton. I watched as my mother gave her our tickets and with great refinement she tore them in half, giving one part

235

back. She threaded the other with her needle, thus making a little garland to hold with her other hand. Oh, the sheer dignity of it all. It was an act carried out in theatres throughout the land but I only knew or wanted to know about this one. My ambition for when I grew up was firmly fixed. I wanted to follow in the footsteps of the gracious Miss Charlton and like her, seated beneath a potted palm, become a ticket threader. Filled with envy I would turn away and follow my mother into the ninepennies.

Shortly before the film was due to begin the members of the orchestra would wander in to take their places. Excited, I watched and listened as they tuned their instruments. The pianist, Mr Byron, playing a note here and there, inclined his head, listening, then lifting the top of the piano and still playing the notes, he would watch the hammers and strings inside. Meanwhile, the violinist. Mr Goldby would pluck the strings and draw the bow across his instrument.

Now, other interesting happenings were taking place. A young woman was walking round drawing the curtains across each little window, at the same time turning out the gas lights as she went along. As the dilapidated little building became dark, some in the audience would send up a loud cheer and the orchestra would strike up with the real music. The drab curtains on stage were jerkily drawn back. The film began to roll.

Charlie Chaplin, the little man with the funny shuffling gait, would waddle, twirling his walking stick, onto the screen. It was enough, the audience would burst into laughter. The character he portrayed was always that of a loser. Bullied, scorned and knocked down, he would unfailingly pick himself up and doggedly, with little success, try again at the same time remaining anxious and sympathetic to his fellow under-dog.

Sometimes the laughter would subside; the audience for a few moments becoming aware of the tragedy and depth of what the little clown was trying to say. Occasionally someone, briefly carried away by what they were watching would quite spontaneously shout out some comment of their own. This was usually met with a stoic indifference by the audience, but should rain fall during the performance the sound of it bouncing on the corrugated roof would quickly evoke murmurs of impatience.

236

Like all good things, the show would come to an end. The drum in the orchestra would roll and we would rise to our feet for the National Anthem. On the last line many would make for the now wide open doors, but Mother would give me one look. I daren't move, but soon we ourselves were outside in the darkened street, lit only by a few widely spaced gas lamps. Quickly we made our way across the road to the fish and chip shop where I was given a penny and sent inside to join the patient little crowd waiting for the next batch of chips to be taken from the sizzling pans. It was fun to listen to the cheerful banter between Mr Cutts and his adult customers, the smell was mouth-watering, the shop warm and cheerful. For my penny I bought a bag of piping hot chips, crisp, brimming over. I held them so carefully, anxious lest they should spill over into the newspaper which Mr Cutts had wrapped around the bag, I wouldn't have liked that at all. Before leaving the shop, I would reach upward to take the salt shaker and vinegar from the high wooden counter and after liberally sprinkling my chips with the contents, go outside to rejoin my mother. By this time the members of the orchestra could already be seen leaving the little wooden hut across the road.

In 1932 this funny old picture house was demolished, to be replaced by the modern brick-built King's Theatre. Here the films, still black and white, were the talkies, and we could hear as well as see what was happening. Mr Byron and his colleagues, no longer needed to "play" the changing moods in the films, had become redundant. As for Miss Charlton, already a middle-aged lady, she married an Irishman and went with him to live in his native country. There was never again the need of a ticket threader seated beneath a potted palm. Fortunately my childhood ambition was, by then, long forgotten.'

RUN WITH A ROD OF IRON

'A cinema was built in Southwell in about 1931, when I was eight years old, and was very popular. It showed two different films each week. The Saturday matinee was always well attended (seats twopence and threepence). It was built by Tucks, who are still builders in Southwell, and Mrs Tuck ran those matinee shows with a rod of iron and nobody misbehaved. It was a sad day when the cinema closed down.'

'The Ideal cinema – oh, the fun and love on the back row, trying to avoid Mrs Sanderson with her torch or Mr Ellis with his all-seeing eyes. *The Magnificent Seven* was the last film shown there. I was just 15 and cried my eyes out – no more back row cuddles or Eldorado ice cream. Going back a bit, I went to the Saturday matinees, sixpence front row – Hopalong Cassidy, Buster Crabbe, and Kenneth More in *Genevieve* – I watched that film three nights on the trot and washed up for a fortnight to pay for it.'

WE WERE HOOKED

'It was a day in 1950. Dinner was over and Catherine and I had the whole afternoon to ourselves – what were we going to do? Play with our dolls, go down and jump the stream at the bottom of Carsic? No. Play marbles with Catherine's younger brother, Robert? Yes, that was it but where was he? We asked two boys waiting down the lane. "He's in Cheetam's watching the television," they said. Television, we'd heard of it but never seen it.

Catherine decided to knock on Cheetam's door in Packies Puzzle. "Is our Robert here?" she asked Mrs Cheetam when she answered the door. "Yes, he's in here watching television with my son, he won't be long," and she closed the door. There we stood, our curiosity brimming over. Catherine knocked again. "Me Mam wants our Robert," she told Mrs Cheetam when she answered the door again. "You'd better come in," she said, none too pleased. We were ushered into a darkened room. Mr Cheetam sat at the table in his singlet and was eating his dinner and as our eyes became accustomed to the dark we realised the room was full of kids standing watching the box in the corner. We stood transfixed – Andy Pandy and Teddy were just getting into their basket and were saying goodbye. The next moment the test card was on the screen, the curtains were flung open and we were all turned out into the street – our first sight of television but the seed had been sown. We were hooked.'

ROYAL OCCASIONS

Royal jubilees and coronations were celebrated with enthusiasm all over Nottinghamshire, and many of us still treasure those commemorative mugs and medals handed out to us as children.

A GENERAL HOLIDAY

'The Coronation of King George V, on 22nd June 1911, was celebrated by a general holiday in the parishes of Tythby, Wiverton and Cropwell Butler.

A parish meeting was called by the chairman of the Cropwell Butler parish council and a committee was appointed to make suitable arrangements and obtain subscriptions. Over £40 and various donations (presumably in kind) were obtained.

It was decided to have the Arnold Albion Band for the day; a dinner in the new schoolroom (now the village hall) for the adults, estimated number 360, and tea in the old schoolroom for children under 14, estimated number 140. A sum of money was allocated for prizes for various sports and races.

The committee unanimously asked the vicar to hold an open air service but he declined doing so and instead held at 8 am the celebration of Holy Communion in the chapel of ease which was attended by 14 persons, and a service for children at 9.30 am.

The parishioners met at the parish pump and with the band proceeded to the parish church of Tythby for a service at 11.30 am. There was only a moderate attendance. The church was by no means crowded. The service was attended by Mr Chaworth Musters of Wiverton Hall and by Mr Henry Smith JP of Cropwell Grove who was born in the year 1828 and therefore had lived in the reigns of George IV, William IV, Queen Victoria, Edward VII and George V.

There was early morning rain and the day was mostly cloudy but on the whole very pleasant and the celebration went off very successfully.'

CUPS AND SAUCERS

'I still have the cup and saucer (originally my sister's) given to children at Thrumpton when George V and May (Princess Mary of Teck) were married in 1893.'

A MUG AND A MEDAL

'On the Jubilee of George V in 1935 each child at Southwell was presented with a mug and a brand new medal struck for

Above and opposite: Clarborough Hall was the setting for Festival of Britain celebrations in 1951 and for Coronation fancy dress in 1953.

the occasion. There was a carnival and a fancy dress parade, for which the costumes were made with crepe paper. My mother made me a creation in blue and white and I won first prize and a box of six teaspoons! Another competition was for a decorated doll's pram – crepe paper again, and the dancing group I belonged to called "The Nibs" gave a display with, I remember, hoops and flowers made of, yes, crepe paper. It was the most versatile material of that time.'

'Big events were always made a lot of at Trowell, with parties and mementoes. I remember George V's Jubilee with parties and all the children getting hankies and mugs. The men all looked very smart dressed up in their plus fours on the day.'

WE WENT TO LONDON

'My school at Ruddington arranged a train to London to see the decorations for the Silver Jubilee in 1935. It was a memorable journey, without my parents for the first time and arriving back at 11 pm in the dark. The train was, of course, a steam train belching smoke from a huge fire box. I can still remember the decorations on Selfridge's in Oxford Street.'

VILLAGE CELEBRATIONS

'The celebrations for the Jubilee in 1935 and the Coronation in 1937 were held in the village school at South Muskham. A paddock nearby was used for games and races for both grown ups and children. A barrel of beer was put in the farmer's barn and several farm workers kept an eye on it – and had their fair share too! All the trees had red, white and blue streamers hanging from them and everyone's house was decorated with pictures of the new King and Queen and flags flying from the gate posts, porches and washing lines.'

COLD AND WET

'On Coronation Day 1953, 3rd June, a marquee was erected where the village hall in Gunthorpe now stands. The WI drama group performed a play called *Check to the Queen* inside. It was a cold and wet day, I remember, and we sere all shivering.'

THE ONLY TELEVISION IN THE VILLAGE

'There was a party in the village hall at Owthorpe and Mrs Chapman, the farmer's wife, had the only television set in the village. It was a very small eight inch set and I think nearly all the children crammed in to her tiny front room to watch the coronation, then we went to the village hall to have tea, when we were all given a pen and a mug.'

TO LONDON FOR THE FIRST TIME

'The Festival of Britain in 1951 and the Coronation came and went with tea parties and fancy dress events at Clarborough. Clarborough Hall grounds were used for this kind of event. The first time I saw television was at the King's Arms on Coronation Day. The following day a bus trip to London was arranged. It was the first time most of us had ever been and we got back at six o'clock the following morning.'

CELEBRATIONS THROUGH THE YEAR

Wakes and fairs, May Day and Christmas – there were special days to be celebrated each year as welcome breaks in the routine of everyday life. Some have now gone for ever, such as Empire Day, once looked forward to by every child for the half day holiday from school it brought! There are special memories too of the Whit Walk, which once brought the community to a standstill.

ST GEORGE AND PUNCH AND JUDY

'The village children at Ranby were invited to Morton Hall for tea every February. There was Punch and Judy, and the children all went home with a bun and an orange. Lady Bingham gave the children a gift of a jersey every other year, red for the girls and blue for the boys. The jerseys had a collar and as they were made of wool they tended to itch!

There was a school holiday on May Day and Empire Day. On Ascension Day all the children at school would go to church and then have the rest of the day off.

On St George's Day Mr Mason always went to the school and told the story of St George and the Dragon. On Whit Monday there was always a Ranby fair. It was held in the field opposite the Chequer Inn. There was gingerbread and then games to amuse the children, the men played skittles in the yard beside the pub and there was dancing for the ladies.'

MAY DAY

'Attending the village school at Upton from the age of four, I particularly remember the May Day procession through the village. In 1936 it was very peaceful and we had day after day of warm, flower-filled sunshine. I well remember the clanging

243

Sports Day and Red Cross Day at Welbeck in the early 1900s. The whole community took a keen interest in such events.

of the school bell – one of the "big ones" had the privilege of pulling the bell rope and this was a very sought after role. On 1st May our May Queen, resplendent in her beautiful white crepe paper gown and crown headed the procession up the village street, attended by four small girls following closely behind – in my case too closely, as I trod on her train and tore it, much to my embarrassment. We carried a garden cane in our right hand with a bunch of garden flowers tied to the top with a wide ribbon bow, and we all felt very proud of our important role.'

OTHER MAY DAYS

'Empire Day on 24th May (Queen Victoria's birthday) was always celebrated at school, and on Oak Apple Day (29th May) children at Thrumpton had to wear an oak leaf or risk being stung with nettles by their friends, but only until noon.'

'On 29th May if we didn't wear a piece of oak we were stung with a nettle. We used to sing:

> Royal Oak Day, 29th of May,
> If you don't give us a holiday
> We will run away.

THE WHIT WALK

'When I was small the big day in the Sutton calendar was the Whit Walk. Everyone had new clothes and went round to relatives, friends and neighbours to show off their clothes and receive a penny. Everyone turned out either to walk or watch.

Sutton walked on Whit Sunday, Huthwaite on the Monday, Skegby and Stanton Hill the week before.

Crowds gathered hours before the parade just to get a good spot. They were ten deep around Portland Square and up Low Street. To be a flower carrier was the ultimate – that's walking round with a basket full of flowers or carrying one of the ropes to a banner. I went to St Mary's church which is the main church in the town and always had a large turn out. When you got up to the market place where the service was held it was

245

packed. It always seemed to be hot with the St John's man doing a roaring trade in drinks of water from his hip flask.

There were lots of bands from the smart and tuneful colliery bands to the noisy not always in tune Boys' Brigade. The service was taken by a different vicar or minister each year and we always seemed to be singing the Doxology. There was strict protocol as to which church or chapel led on to the market and which led off. You'd spend your time looking for relatives so you could wave and they would take your picture. When the walk finished we from St Mary's would go into the parish rooms and receive a buttered currant bun.

Relatives came from far and near for the big day and I remember we seemed to have dozens back for tea in our small bungalow.

In the evening you'd walk down to the lawn along with everyone else and the band would be playing in the bandstand.

The photo shop's window on Portland Square would be full from top to bottom of pictures of the walk so if you happened to be on one you could go in and order.'

'The most important period of the year at Sutton in Ashfield was Whitsuntide. It came as something of a shock to my mother to discover that at Whitsuntide every child (and most grown ups too) had to have a new outfit. These Whitsuntide clothes were sacrosanct. Regardless of the size of the family, their social standing or their income, come Whit Sunday morning all the children of the town donned their new finery and went from relation to relation: from friend to friend: from neighbour to neighbour, and on being visited by these children the householder would give them a coin, maybe only a ha'penny but as the morning progressed each child's pocket got heavier and heavier! A lot of the families saved up all year in clothing clubs in order to buy these clothes, and if they fell short, as many did, there was always the pawn shop, where, incidentally, many of the clothes ended up once Whitsun was over. But rich or poor, new clothes were there for the children so that no family need feel ashamed when their little ones "walked".

"Walking round" was the coloquial term for the procession

246

of witness which originally took place on the Tuesday after Whit Sunday. On that day the entire town turned out, either to take part or to watch. The chapels walked in the morning and the churches walked in the afternoon.

The entire town centre was cleared of what little traffic was about in those days, and from quite early in the morning the crowds would start to gather. At the bottom of the Market Place was positioned a dray, a flat horse-drawn waggon with the horse removed and the shafts down. The dray was decorated and steps put to it to enable it to be used as a platform.

At the same time as the townspeople were filling the streets, those who were taking part in "the walk" would be gathering at their place of worship, dressed, of course, in their fine new "Whit clothes". The processions were formed up in exactly the same way at each church or chapel. First the banner; huge banners needing strong men to hold the main poles and several young people to hold the strings and ribbons which held it in place. This was followed by a specially constructed banner made rather like a ladder, which was carried horizontally by five or six young girls dressed in their frilly pretty dresses with white shoes and socks, and all wearing flower trimmed bonnets. The rest followed. Girls with baskets of flowers, boys in their grey shorts and knee-length socks (no jeans and trainers here!). The very young ones were "shepherded" by older ladies using coloured silk ropes to form a passageway for them. Finally, the older members of the congregation, the elders and the clergy and choir.

At the given time each procession, preceded by a brass or silver prize band, would set off by a designated route from their church or chapel – in some cases, quite a lengthy walk – and make their way to the Market Place. It was wondrously well organised by the local police and I can never recall any trouble, despite the fact that there were three pubs on the Market Place and many others close by which were open all the time this was taking place.

Once assembled, the Market Place was full to bursting point. The clergy took up position, with the choirs, on the platform and one of the many bands taking part in the walk was selected to play for the hymns. There followed a service of prayers and hymns which lasted about 40 minutes, and everyone,

247

walker, watcher, police and ambulance service, joined in.

At the end of the service the whole thing began again in reverse. All the walkers processed back to their church or chapel and each child was presented with "a bun", a teacake which they took home for their mother. These buns were purchased from a fund set up for this purpose from money raised by the charges made for the services of "the parish bull" – honestly!

In the years that followed, first the war, then dwindling congregations and increased traffic making it difficult to close down the entire town, caused the event to be changed to Whit Sunday itself and for both church and chapel to walk together. It was like that when my children "walked" in the 1950s, but the passing of time and changes in lifestyle have taken their toll, until now when Whitsuntide is almost forgotten and is no longer, even, a public holiday.'

DUCK AND GREEN PEAS

'The feast of St Swithun was always celebrated at Woodborough, on the first Sunday after 2nd July. Duck and green peas was always served on that day.'

OLLERTON FAIR

'Ollerton Fair was held on 1st May. The fair was pitched in front of the Hop Pole Hotel. Pretty lights were supplied by Harry Hall's steam engine, the "dragons" sailed around and music was played by the fair organ. Who could forget the coconut shies, and the water pistols in front of the White Hart!'

CROPWELL BISHOP FEAST

'Cropwell Bishop Feast was observed each year, the first Sunday after 12th September, when roundabouts and stalls came to the village prior to the Goose Fair. There was great hospitality and everyone joined in, really better than Christmas. The roundabout people gave two or three hours' takings to a local charity.'

A rare holiday treat for the Blythe family at Skegness in the 1920s. Many Nottingham families went to 'Skeggy' on the train.

EDWINSTOWE FEAST SUNDAY

'At the end of the last century a fair was held on the Sunday nearest 26th October, Edwinstowe Feast Sunday, when shooting galleries, roundabouts and all the fun of the fair arrived. It was the most exciting time of the year, watching the man on stilts.

In the 1960s "Gala Days" were held in the sports field off Fourth Avenue, and there were parades down High Street with floats decorated from different organisations taking part.'

THE WAKES

'A big event in Ruddington village was "The Wakes", the nearest weekend to St Peter's tide. Show men came and set up on the village green. Roundabouts, cake walk, horses, swingboats, coconut stalls, roll-a-penny stall, hoop-la, in fact, all the fun of the fair with wonderful music played on the old organs with the puppet players on the front. Later the dodgems were brought there.

The week before, when they started to arrive, the cry always went up: "Wheel off on Bunny Hill." This meant a wheel of the steam engine that pulled the heavy stuff for the fair. Of course, all the lads with bikes raced off in that direction to see this spectacle, but I can never remember them coming back and telling us it had actually happened!

The caravans the fair people lived in always attracted great attention. It was a sad day when trailers came instead of the lovely old painted vans, spotlessly cleaned with brass highly polished. The same families came, one generation after another and still come to this day.'

TWO FAIRS

'Two fairs came to Lowdham village, one set up by the Ship and one by the Magna Charta. War broke out during the visit of one of the fairs in 1939 so it had to stay in the field throughout the next six years.

Cot Fund Day was always a great occasion. This was a sort of fete, with floats, one of which always had people dressed in nurses' uniforms on it. The occasion was to raise money for a bed in the hospital.'

A SPECIAL TIME

'Easter was always a special time, when each child received just one egg. If you were lucky it had your name on it as Woolworth's stores would do this service.

Christmas was also very special. For the children at Laxton and New Ollerton there would be a party at school and each received an apple and an orange from Father Christmas. In their stocking on Christmas morning would be a sugar mouse and often an annual to read. It was a very busy time in every farm kitchen where turkeys and geese were killed. The birds had to be scalded in the copper and gutted and plucked. Everything had to be scrubbed and cleaned on Christmas Eve, and it was very late before any decorations could be hung but somehow it all got done.'

SUCH A FEAST!

'Christmas time was exciting. Mother made the cake and puddings. I rubbed currants and raisins in a tea towel with flour to rub off the stalks. She bought preserved fruits and I had the sugar out of the middle of them, and we all stirred the pudding mixture and wished! A week before Christmas we bought a small tree.

We had a large chicken on Christmas Day (the only time we had chicken the whole year) and we had a huge ham Mother had boiled for tea and supper. There were mince pies, Christmas cake and Stilton cheese. Such a feast!'

Index

⬭

252

254

List of Contributing WIs

Entries were received from the following Nottinghamshire WIs:

Abbey Gates, Annesley & District, Attenborough, Beckingham, Bircotes, Blyth, Bottesford, Bunny & Bradmore, Burton Joyce & Bulcote Evening, Calverton, Carlton in Lindrick, Caunton, Clarborough, Cropwell Bishop, Cropwell Butler & Tythby, Dorewood, Dunham & District, East Leake, East Markham, Edwalton, Edwinstowe, Farnsfield, Flintham & Syerston, Forest Town, Gamston & District, Gedling, Gotham, Gunthorpe, Kilvington, Kinoulton, Lady Bay, Lambley, Laxton, Lowdham, Meden Vale, Normanton on Soar, Nth & Sth Clifton, Oldcotes, Ollerton, Parkdale (Carlton), Ranby, Ruddington, Selston, Shireoaks, South Muskham & Little Carlton, Southwell, Southwell Morning, Sutton Bonington, Sutton in Ashfield, Teversal, Thrumpton & Barton, Thurgarton, Treswell, Trowell, Upton, Watnall, Wilford, Willoughby on the Wolds, Woodborough.